Missions Beyond the Wall

Factors in the Rise of Missionary Sending Movements in East-Central Europe

edition afem
mission academics 34

Scott Klingsmith

This book is part of the series "edition afem",
ed. by Prof. Dr. Thomas Schirrmacher, Dr. Bernd Brandl,
Friedemann Knödler M.A., and Thomas Mayer M.A.
http://www.missiologie.org

Bibliographic information published by the Deutsche Nationalbibliothek
The Deutsche Nationalbibliothek lists this publication in the Deutsche Nationalbibliografie; detailed bibliographic data are available in the Internet at http://dnb.d-nb.de.

ISBN 978-3-941750-55-5 (VTR)
VTR Publications
Gogolstr. 33, 90475 Nürnberg, Germany, http://www.vtr-online.com

ISBN 978-3-86269-037-4 (VKW)
VKW (Culture and Science Publ.)
Friedrichstr. 38, 53111 Bonn, Germany, http://www.vkwonline.de

ISSN 0944-1077 (edition afem – mission academics)

© 2012 by Scott Klingsmith

Layout: VTR

Printed by Lightning Source

*To Carol, my wife and best friend, for her encouragement
to start and complete this project,
and to my children, Kali, Toby, and Kerri,
for locking me in my office until I finished,
and for willingly sacrificing security and comfort
during the upheavals.
I love you with all my heart*

Contents

Acknowledgments 10

1. The Research Concern 11
    Historical Background 11
    Contemporary Third-World Missions 12
    Missions from East-Central Europe 13
    Problem Statement 15
    General Research Questions 15
    Definitions 15
    Delimitation of the Investigation 17
    Generalizability and Limitations 19
    Researcher Bias and Presuppositions 19
    Overview of the Inquiry Procedures 19

2. Precedent Literature 21
    System of Systems Model 21
        Parsons 21
        Bertalanffy 25
        Hiebert 29
        Summary 30
    Movement Theory and Diffusion Studies 31
    Eastern European Issues 32
        Social System 33
        Cultural System 35

3. Research Procedure 38
    Theoretical Framework 38
    Problem Statement 39
    Research Questions 39

Contextual Questions 41
Description of Cases 41
Selection of Cases 41
Methodological Issues 43
    Case Study Research 43
    Interviewing Procedures 43
Instruments 44
Issues of Access 45
Procedure 45
Data Analysis 47

4. Background and Context 48

Background and Context – Country by Country 48
    Albania 49
    Bulgaria 50
    Czech Republic and Slovakia 51
    Hungary 52
    Poland 52
    Romania and Moldova 53
    Ukraine 54
    Former Yugoslavia 54

Individual Cases 55

5. Hungarian Reformed and Lutheran 56

Description of the Case 56
    General Missions Interest 57
    Lutheran Missions Context 57
    Reformed Missions Context 58
    Summary of Historical Situation 58
    The Story 59

Themes and Factors 61
    Spiritual Factors 61
    Social factors 65
    Cultural Factors 76

Contents

Interaction between Factors 85
Conclusions... 86

6. Aletheia Church, Timişoara, Romania 88

Background and Historical Development 89

Themes and Factors 90

    Spiritual Factors 90
    Social Factors 91
    Cultural Factors 100

Interaction between Factors 105

Conclusions... 107

7. Biblical Mission Association, Poland 108

Background and Historical Development 109

Themes and Factors 110

    Spiritual Factors 110
    Social Factors 113
    Cultural Factors 125

Interaction between Factors 135

Conclusion 136

8. Romanian International Mission, Romania 138

Selection of the Case 138

Description of the Case 139

Major Impetus 142

Key People 143

    Western Missionaries 143
    Romanians 144

Current Situation 145

    Current Involvement 145
    Advantages Romanians Bring to Missions 146
    Missions Motivations 147

Themes and Factors 148
    Spiritual Factors 148
    Social Factors 149
    Cultural Factors 154

Interaction between Factors 162
    Personal Experience Leading to New Understanding 162
    Role of Western Missionaries 162
    Work of God's Spirit 162
    Effects of Other Systems on Economics 163
    Role of Theological Education in Changing Attitudes and Structures .. 163
    Development of Structures 164

Conclusion 164

9. A Thematic Comparison of the Cases 166

Spiritual Factors 167

Social Factors 168
    Key People 168
    Economic Factors 169
    Political and Legal Factors 170
    Ecclesiastical Factors 171
    Approach to Organization 172

Cultural factors 172
    Biblical and Theological Understanding of Missions 173
    Interest before Revolution 175
    Educational Factors 175
    Role of Western Missionaries 176
    Ethnocentrism and View of Self 177

Interaction between Factors 179
    Spiritual Factors Influencing Social and Culture Systems 179
    Personal Experience Influencing Cultural System 179
    Spiritual and Culture Factors Influencing Economic System 179
    Western Missionaries Influencing Culture and Social Systems 180

Why Have New Missionary Sending Movements Begun in ECE? 180
    Key Factors in Each Case 180
    Factors Common to All The Cases 181

Implications for Theory 186

10. Conclusions 189
To What Extent Are These Cases Movements? 189
Projections 190
Practical Applications 191
Recommendations 192
ECE Church 192
Social Level 193
Missionary Training 194
Western Church 195
Areas for Further Research 195
Evaluation of the Research 196
Conclusion 197
Reference List 198

Acknowledgments

I would like to thank Dave Wedin and the leadership of WorldVenture for their permission and encouragement to pursue this study. Tom Keppeler offered helpful comments on parts of the early draft. My wife Carol endured every word with a proofreader's critical eye. Paul Hiebert went beyond the call of duty with many editorial suggestions. I am very grateful to each of you. Finally, I would like to thank those brothers and sisters in East-Central Europe who cheerfully shared their knowledge and visions with me. May God bless their efforts to expand his kingdom through the ministry of hundreds of new cross-cultural missionaries in the years to come.

1. The Research Concern

In the Fall of 1989, Communist governments across Eastern Europe fell in rapid succession. Evangelical churches in those countries suddenly experienced never-dreamed-of freedom to engage in ministry opportunities of many kinds. Large-scale evangelistic rallies, church planting in villages where no evangelical churches existed, orphanage and street children ministries, and theological education programs all exploded. Gradually the vision increased for church planting in parts of the countries where evangelicals were weak or absent. More recently, some groups of evangelicals have begun to develop a vision for sending missionaries to other countries or to other people groups where the gospel has not been proclaimed. This vision is increasing, but so far, it is occurring in only a few situations. The question which gives rise to this study is why missionary sending movements are arising now, and why they are arising in only some places. Why are these movements beginning in some areas, among some groups? Do certain historical, political, social, spiritual or theological factors coincide with the development of a new vision for sending missionaries, or do these different movements begin spontaneously, with no correlation to other factors? How does the fall of Communism relate to the recent rise of these movements? Is the timing simply coincidental, or is there a relationship? Do the factors which seem to have led to mission movements in the past have a bearing on contemporary developments?

Historical Background

Missionary sending movements have arisen periodically throughout the history of the church. The church in Antioch, as reported in Acts 13, was the first church to call and send missionaries to other parts of the world. The Irish church in the eighth and ninth centuries, the Jesuits in the sixteenth century, the Moravians in the eighteenth and the modern Protestant missionary movement beginning at the end of the eighteenth century are all examples of broad-based mission movements. The best known is the latter, which continues to the present.

Pierson (1992) identifies four factors for the rise of the modern missions movement. He sees the influence of the Pietists on the English speaking churches, a succession of revivals, the rise of Colonial commerce and the influence of one man, William Carey. Carey was the main catalyst for this movement. He showed that the Great Commission was binding on the church of all ages, outlined how Protestants had been involved in missions throughout their history, recognized how the changing historical context in which he lived made a missionary movement possible, and called for a plan of action. Carrying this one step further, Schattschneider (1998) shows how the Moravians and Carey were part of an informal network of evangelicals, combining the threads of German Pietism with those of the English Evangelical Revival.

A more recent missions motivation arose among Roman Catholics in the United States and Ireland in the early years of the twentieth century (Dries 1991; Hogan 1979). The contributing factors seem to be the influence of missionaries from other countries, an increase in spiritual awareness, political changes in the world scene, the development of bureaucratic structures, and reforming movements within the Church.

Contemporary Third-World Missions

The growth in the number of third-world missionaries sent by third-world and Western mission agencies has been dramatic in the past twenty years. Pate and Keyes (Pate 1991; Keyes 1982; Keyes 1983; Keyes and Pate 1993; Nelson 1976) describe some of this growth. They describe the new sending movements, identifying where they are, where they are sending missionaries, what their partnerships are and what the major issues are that they will be facing in the coming years. The tone is one of celebration and excitement. However, very little has been written attempting to understand *why* this world-wide movement is occurring. Researchers have done little analysis of causes or factors in its rise. Nelson (1976), for example, in a collection of early writings on the subject, includes lots of description and prescription, but almost no analysis. Little has changed in the twenty years since he gathered his material. Some work in this area is appearing in dissertations by Korean students.

Keyes (1983, 91) lists four ways which third-world missionary initiatives began. These include foreign influence, indigenous influence, cooperative agreements, and individual service. While his specific concern is the development of indigenous mission agencies, these four factors are instructive of the ways in which missions vision in general can begin. Further, he finds a strong correlation between the number of foreign missionaries in a country and the number of indigenous mission agencies in that country (Keyes 1983, 61).

Keyes' figures have been strongly criticized by Fiedler (1989, 1994), whose research shows the number of indigenous African missionaries to be highly inflated because many of the participants of the survey did not understand the survey instrument. He nonetheless agrees with Keyes' conclusions that third-world missionaries are an important new force for world evangelization. Fiedler filled his helpful study with detailed descriptions of African missions but included little analysis of reasons for these new movements. Most of his reasons involve individuals who get a missions vision somehow and who then convince their church to get involved. He notes that the countries which send missionaries are those who are relatively better off economically. Asking whether only the wealthy nations can afford to send missionaries, he suggests the need for international financial partnering.

Although the growth in Korean missionary activity began more slowly than that of some other third-world countries, in the past ten years it has skyrocketed. Park (1994) sees several reasons for the dramatic growth in the missions vision and involvement since the middle 1980s. They include several factors internal to the church, such as the rapid growth of the Korean church, mission work as a means of self-identification for the Korean Church, the birth of mission theology in Korean churches, and the decline of Western missions (although he does not specify how this contributed to Korean missions growth). Other factors are independent of the church. These include the stimulation from globalization and open door trends inspired by the 1988 Olympics, and the somewhat related new economic prosperity of Korean society. He perceives part of the increase coming from a sense of what he calls "constructive competition" between different mission agencies and missionaries. Finally, some negative motivations have contributed. Some people see missions as a way to get ahead or to get to America. Missionary status is high and it is easier to become a missionary than to become a pastor.

Missions from East-Central Europe

The third-world missions movement is the larger context for the emerging movements in East-Central Europe. Although the countries of East-Central Europe are not third-world countries, the emerging movements share some common features with those movements.

Keyes and Pate (1993) were among the first to draw attention to the potential for the formerly Communist countries of East-Central Europe (ECE) to give rise to missionary sending churches. They point out that these missions share four characteristics with third-world missions. They are emerging late in the history of global missionary activity. They are sent from developing countries. The indigenous models of missionary sending structures will be unique to their own historical and cultural situations. In addition, they will be sent from countries which are not usually considered Western. All four of these factors are true to a certain extent, and all four can be partially disputed.

Protestant missions are new in this part of the world, but these countries have been involved in missions for up to 1300 years. They include a mix of developing and developed countries, all of which desire to be seen as Western. The structures they develop are broadly influenced by the contact they have had with Western missions for the past 150 years. Fiedler (1994) also mentions the possibility of Eastern European churches as missionary senders, giving examples from Hungary. He remarks that some kinds of financial innovations may be necessary before Eastern European churches will send Eastern European missionaries.

Information on current missions efforts from East-Central Europe and the former Soviet Union is difficult to find and difficult to evaluate. The Christian Resource Center in Moscow published a list of indigenous missions in the former Soviet Union. They list 12,355 staff members and 16,231 volunteers working with more than sixteen denominations and admit that Orthodox and Catholic parachurch groups are underrepresented (Linzey 1994). No definition of mission is given, but clearly these are not cross-cultural missionaries in the sense defined below. From this list no determination of cross-cultural missionaries is possible.

Until now, almost nothing has been written on the new missions movements beginning in East-Central Europe today. This can be illustrated by an almost complete absence of articles on missions in the *East-West Church & Ministry Report*, a newsletter reporting on the activity of churches, missionaries, interchurch and church-mission relations in ECE and the former Soviet Union. Articles about missions refer inevitably to Western missionaries working in the East. Missionary movements originating in these countries have apparently not yet reached the level of visibility which would warrant inclusion in this source.

Examination of other journals reveals a similar state of affairs. Journals such as *Religion in Eastern Europe*, *Religion, State and Society*, and *Journal of Ecumenical Studies* contain many articles discussing the effects of Western missionary involvement in the region, but nothing on missionaries from the region. Articles on the Czech Republic and Slovakia, Hungary, Poland and Ukraine in the *Evangelical Dictionary of World Missions* (Moreau 2000) contain very brief mention of new missionary initiatives.

Some churches and organizations are beginning to publish missions magazines. The Biblical Missions Association (BSM) in Poland and the Lutheran Mission Center in Hungary, both have regular periodicals. Two organizations in Romania either have published, or plan to publish, missions magazines in Romanian. In addition, a small number of the new missions groups have developed Web sites, where regular reports about their ministries are published. BSM in Poland is again an example.

Despite the lack of current materials, ECE is a region which has a historical tradition of missions. The Moravians are the best known of the movements to originate there, coming from what is now the Czech Republic and settling in the southeastern corner of what was East Germany. Their impact on the modern missions movement is well known, affecting as they did such pioneers as Bartholomaeus Ziegenbalg, William Carey and John Wesley (Schattschneider 1998, Latourette 1970).

1. The Research Concern

Many of the churches which are now considering sending missionaries are the fruit of a missions movement themselves. The Baptists in East-Central Europe, in particular, are largely the result of the missions visions of the German Baptist leader Johann Gerhard Oncken (1800-1884). His motto, "Every Baptist a Missionary", encouraged Baptist believers to share the gospel wherever they went. Their primary target audience was the German-speaking diaspora of Eastern Europe, but they eventually established churches among their non-German speaking neighbors in Hungary, Romania, Poland, Yugoslavia, Russia and the Ukraine. In the 1870s the German Baptists made foreign missions an official part of their strategy, although this was opposed by Oncken at first (Balders 1978, Klammt 1994, Luckey 1958).

Most Eastern European churches have followed a similar course in their own countries. First they have sent missionaries (not defined as cross-cultural workers) to unreached parts of their own countries, and only later developing a missions vision for unreached peoples. Periodically, various Eastern Europeans have served as missionaries. For a time between the two world wars, the Romanian Baptists had their own missions agency, and Hungarians served as missionaries with the American Southern Baptist Convention as well as with the interdenominational German Liebenzeller Mission (Fiedler 1994).

Problem Statement

This research examines the social, cultural and spiritual factors which are influential in the rise of four missionary sending movements in East-Central Europe. These movements are located in Hungary, Poland, and Romania.

General Research Questions

What do the participants of new missionary sending movements see as the factors which led to the rise those movements?

How do the participants of those movements view the relationships among these factors?

What is the relationship between spiritual and social factors in the rise of missionary sending movements? More specifically, what is the relationship between economic capability, theological reflection, political freedom, and openness to others?

Definitions

East-Central Europe (ECE) – Those countries which until 1989 were ruled by Communist governments. These include Poland, the Czech Republic, Slovakia, Hungary, Romania, Bulgaria, and, by extension, the Ukraine. No consensus exists as to the exact makeup of East-Central Europe. Luthans (Luthans, Patrick et al. 1995) includes the Commonwealth of Independent States (CIS)[1] in Central and Eastern Europe (CEE) while Bookman (1995) includes neither the CIS nor former East Germany. The somewhat arbitrary definition adopted here includes the Ukraine but excludes the rest of the CIS. Austria should be included geographically but not politically, because it is not a formerly Communist country.

Missionary sending movements – Indigenous movements, not begun by Western agencies, supported by local constituencies. They may have some kind of partnership agreement with a Western agency, but the leadership and main support are local. They are not necessarily mission agencies. They could be a local church or group of churches, a denomination, either national or regional, or a more diffuse group of individuals, churches, or parachurch organizations.

This use of missionary sending movement can be contrasted with other uses of the term. The World Evangelical Fellowship Missions Commission has recently published a book, *Starting and Strengthening National Mission Movements* (2001), where "mission movements" is

> an inclusive term that refers to various missions structures, programs, or initiatives in a particular country. Some people use the term 'missions committee' or 'missions commission.' Others prefer to use 'missions association' or 'missions alliance'. A few others call their missions organization a 'missions fellowship'. (3)

These "national missions movements" are organizations which pull together the resources of a variety of missions agencies, training institutions, and denominational programs from an entire country, with the intention of helping each organization fulfill its function better. This is not what is meant here. None of the countries of ECE have national missions movements in this sense.

The groups studied are not national cooperative efforts. They are, rather, individual missions initiatives, encompassing a local church or a cooperative effort between churches, a missions agency, or a cooperative venture of several agencies. One of the groups studied here may, in time, become a national missions movement in the WEF sense, but it is not there yet. The word "movement" may itself be a bit overstated. In some cases these are organizations, others are less structured, more ad hoc efforts.

Missions leaders – Key individuals who are instrumental in the rise, growth, instigation, and direction of missionary sending efforts. They may be those in

---

[1] The Commonwealth of Independent States (CIS) is an alliance of 12 of the 15 former Republics of the Soviet Union (Armenia, Azerbaijan, Belarus, Georgia, Kazakhstan, Kyrgyzstan, Moldova, Russia, Tajikistan, Turkmenistan, Ukraine, and Uzbekistan). The headquarters of the organization is in Minsk, Belarus. The three non-members are Estonia, Latvia, and Lithuania.

the home country who are leading the church or agency, or they may be the initial missionaries sent by the various movements. This definition includes expatriate missionaries who have had a significant role in the development of missions interest and activity in ECE.

Missionary – For the purposes of this study, a missionary will be defined as someone who crosses a cultural and linguistic border to either evangelize and plant churches or to assist existing churches in education and development. This distinction is important because in much of Eastern Europe "missionary" means something more like "evangelist", without a cross-cultural dimension. This "missionary" is often a theologically untrained lay person sent to another village to try to start a church. A church which sends their youth group or choir to another town to sing in a sister church is sending them to do "mission". The "missionary" status is considerably lower than a pastor.

Missions and mission – "Missions" may occasionally be used interchangeably with "mission". No missiological distinction is made here between the two terms. This definition will be discussed further when we look at the individual cases. The ambiguity in the use of mission or missions reflects inconsistent usage in the literature and in conversations with the people involved in missions movements. Further, this distinction between missions and mission cannot be made in several of the languages of East-Central Europe.

Delimitation of the Investigation

In the past fifteen years, many churches in traditionally missionary receiving countries around the world have become missionary sending churches. Throughout the third-world, missionary sending movements are proliferating. More research needs to be done to understand why this rapid increase in missions interest is happening in so many places at the same time. In this study one particular piece of that worldwide phenomenon is explored, the specific geographic focus of East-Central Europe. The research is informed by what is happening in other places in the world, but not guided by those events.

Even within this particular geographical area, certain missions related issues are excluded. The study does not look explicitly at what might be called "accidental" missions or missions "on the way". Migration, trade, business, and persecution might all be causes for the spread of the gospel throughout the history of the church, but in most cases these have been a natural part of the life of those affected.

The focus here is more on the Acts 13 phenomena rather than that of Acts 11: on missionaries who are called and sent rather than those who simply go. In this regard, also not examined are the missions motivations of individuals apart from indigenous movements, for instance, those Eastern Europeans serving with international mission agencies. The research examines four new missionary sending movements in East-Central Europe.

The following theoretical taxonomy of missions involvement in East-Central Europe (Table 1) can help to clarify the scope of the proposed research. It shows the range of levels of indigenization of missionary sending movements, from fully indigenous to fully foreign. The two primary factors considered are sources of financial support (from within or from outside the country), and the nature of the agency (source of leadership, initiative, vision).[2] Between the two extremes of fully indigenous and fully foreign are various levels of cooperation, or joint venture. These joint ventures include various degrees of cooperation at the level of financial support and of agency leadership. The center box (JAJS) could mean that both nationals and foreigners would serve on the board and that financial support would come from both within and outside the country. Given the current level of economic development in the ECE churches, it might be asserted that indigeneity is more fully indicated through national leadership than it is through fully internal sources of funding. However, it must also be recognized that money always has a power aspect, and that donors can influence policy to a significant degree, even if leadership is national.

		Agency		
		Indigenous	Joint	Foreign
Support	Indigenous	IA IS	JA IS	FA IS
	Joint	IA JS	JA JS	FA JS
	Foreign	IA FS	JA FS	FA FS
Code: IA = indigenous agency IS = indigenous support JA = Joint venture at level of agency JS = support from internal and external sources FA = foreign or international missions agency FS = financial support from foreign sources.				

Table 1. Taxonomy of missions movements

The research focuses on those cases towards the upper left of the table.

---

[2] Agency is probably not the best term to use here, as it implies a degree of organizational development which is higher than most movements possess. What is in view here is the source of the impetus and leadership which is given to the movement.

1. The Research Concern

Generalizability and Limitations

The collapse of the Communist governments in these countries in 1989 provides the major historical and political context for the groups studied. The findings may be generalizable to other missions movements within political situations where this change has occurred. This would include Russia and the rest of the former Soviet Union. Even more broadly is the possibility of application to countries where some of the other factors may apply, i.e. new political freedom or new economic stability. Various authors have made fruitful comparisons with similar transitions in Latin America during the 1980s (Rosenberg 1995; Centeno and Rands 1996).

The experience of Communism was not uniform in all the countries of Eastern Europe and the former Soviet Union. Each country has a particular cultural, historical and social identity, as do the churches within each country. In fact, not all factors are in place in all situations, and the experience of Communist oppression is not a sufficiently shaping factor to explain all common developments.

Researcher Bias and Presuppositions

I admit to looking at new missionary sending movements as a positive development on the part of the churches of East-Central Europe. Having been involved for fourteen years in leadership and pastoral training in these countries, I am excited to see churches taking the next step of development, from internal concerns to external. I recognize the possibility of viewing the movements I research in too optimistic a light, and have therefore tried to maintain a balanced perspective during the data gathering and interviewing. At the same time, I am not so idealistic as to suppose that all developments are unambiguously positive, or that some issues may need to be evaluated negatively. One of my ministry goals is to encourage the further development of missions vision and action, and trust that the findings from this research will allow me to do that more effectively. My approach to missionary movement leaders is as friend, advocate and encourager.

Overview of the Inquiry Procedures

The answers to the research questions were sought through a three-step procedure. First, interviews were conducted with fifty of the key participants in four of the new missionary sending movements. Their answers were analyzed to discover themes, or factors, which they perceived to be present in the rise and development of new movements. The relative importance of the factors was determined by the informants responses.

Second, the small number of available documents were analyzed for further insight into the generating factors.

Third, the responses of the participants were evaluated through a historical and socio-cultural theoretical grid to determine whether factors not mentioned by the participants are relevant to understanding the subject.

2. Precedent Literature

Three bodies of literature will be examined as background for the study. A theoretical model will be discussed as a grid through which the study can be organized, and through this grid issues affecting East-Central Europe as it makes the transition from Communism to democracy will be explored.

System of Systems Model

A systems approach to social analysis based on Talcott Parsons (1951, 1968, 1971), balanced by Ludwig Bertalanffy (1968), and modified by Paul Hiebert (1998; Hiebert, Shaw et al. 1999) has been chosen as a theoretical framework for this study.

Systems language is ubiquitous in today's world. We regularly speak of computer systems, weapons systems, political systems, belief systems. What is meant by system? System in popular language often means a particular kind of structure or organization. Thus, a computer system has a CPU, a keyboard, monitor, printer, and so on. A stereo system has a receiver, CD player, and speakers. However, what distinguishes a system from a collection is the nature of the interactions between the components. A system involves reciprocal interaction, whereby a change in one component or element brings about changes in the whole. The difference between a belief system, for instance, and a collection of beliefs is the degree to which they are integrated. New components can be added to collections *ad infinitem*, without changing the nature or relationships between them. A system implies that changes in one aspect of belief will have implications for all other aspects.

Systems theory was developed as a reaction against a mechanistic view of reality developed in modern science. The object of inquiry was thought to be reducible to ever-smaller units for purposes of analysis, and discreet chains of unilinear causality could be determined. Causes and effects could be clearly identified. Further, the investigator was seen as an objective observer who had no effect on the process or the results. It was thought that if we could develop precise enough instruments and were able to break things down into small enough pieces, eventually we would be able to perfectly understand and control the universe.

A systems approach takes a more holistic view of reality. It highlights the relationships between various aspects of life, rather than considering them in isolation.

Parsons

Talcott Parsons developed his theory of action systems in a number of works. This study will focus particularly on his theory as outlined in *The System of*

Modern Societies (1971). Parsons worked at the level of pure theory and at the level of an entire society. What he developed may not fit any one society. In *The Social System* (Parsons 1951) he writes "at this point a pause will be taken in the high level of sustained abstract analysis, to illustrate what has gone before in terms of a kind of case study" – after 420 pages! He practices what I call taxonomic terrorism in his attempt to define everything and put everything in neat little boxes.

Parsons defines system as

> the concept that refers both to a complex of interdependencies between parts, components, and processes that involves discernible regularities of relationship, and to a similar type of interdependency between such a complex and its surrounding environment. (Parsons 1968, 458).

He explores the boundaries where sociology touches anthropology, political science, economics and psychology. Because these different disciplines each have their own research traditions, they rarely talk to one another. Parsons attempts to cross those disciplinary borders. What will be attempted here is a partial description of what is a very complicated and intricate analysis of Parsons' theory of social systems.

Parsons begins with a general theory of action systems, consisting of four subsystems: behavioral organism, personality, social system, and culture system (see figure 1).

The organism is the first subsystem. It is "the locus of the primary human facilities which underlie the other systems" (Parsons 1971, 5). Its primary function is adaptation as it interacts with the physical environment. The personality, or psychological system, is the individual as a person, interacting with society through various roles, and with culture as one shaped by various norms and values.

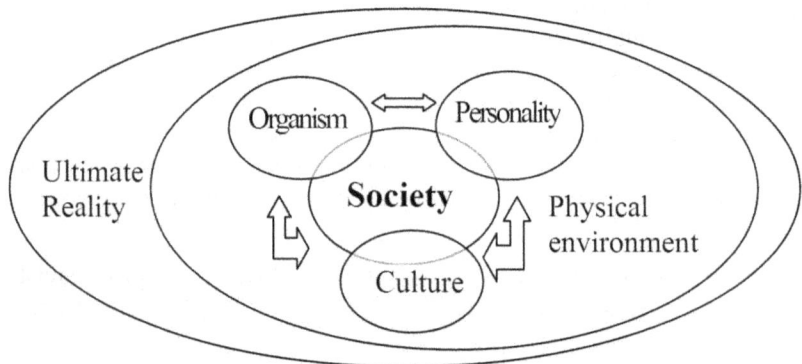

Figure 1. Parsons' model with society in center

2. Precedent Literature

The social system involves the interaction of groups of individuals concerned with solving collective problems. It consists of four subsystems: the societal community, legal, economic and political (Parsons 1971). The culture system deals with "complexes of symbolic meaning" (Parsons 1971, 5), and involves the subsystems of ideas or beliefs, expressive symbols, and value-orientation (Parsons and Shils 1952).

Parsons distinguishes the social and cultural systems.

> Whereas social systems are organized with primary reference to the articulation of social relationships, cultural systems are organized around the characteristics of complexes of symbolic meaning – the codes in terms of which they are structured, the particular clusters of symbols they employ, and the conditions of their utilization, maintenance, and change as parts of actions systems. (Parsons 1971, 4).

Specifically excluded from his understanding of action systems are the physical environment and "ultimate reality". These together form the environment in which action systems play themselves out. However, this exclusion seems to betray Parsons' idealist mindset, because it ignores the extent to which both material and spiritual realities affect human systems. Rather than being the inert playing field, these are rather active participants in the functioning of the systems. Hiebert (1998; Hiebert, Shaw et al. 1999) is therefore correct in including both of these as separate systems, as well as showing the larger reality of God as creator and revealer.

In Parsons' view, each of these four systems has both a controlling and a conditioning effect on the others. The organism sets conditions on the personality, which in turn conditions the social and the cultural systems. Inversely, the cultural system provides organization and control to the social system, which controls the personality and the organism. In addition, each system interacts with the others. The organism supplies inputs of motivational energy to the personality, which in turn provides the organism with controls which increase performance potential. For example, in a dangerous situation, the organism supplies adrenaline, which allows the person to flee. At the same time, the personality can articulate performance goals which push the organism to perform at a higher level than would occur naturally without some external threat. Likewise, the culture system provides norms which become part of the internal regulatory mechanism of the individual, while the personality provides the "motivational commitment" which allows him or her to internalize the norms of the society. The other systems interrelate in various ways. These relationships are not simply bipolar, however. They are tripartite as well. The systems are not discrete entities, clearly distinguishable by clear boundaries and characteristics. To illustrate, here again is Parsons.

> The integration of members into a society involves the zone of interpenetration between the social and personality systems. The relation is basically tripartite, however, because parts of the cultural system as well as parts of the social structure are internalized in personalities, and because parts of the cultural system are institutionalized in the society. (1971, 9).

It is very difficult at times to determine conceptually which aspects of life belong to culture and which to society. Parsons tells us further that

> The boundary between any pair of action systems involves a 'zone' of structured components or patterns which must be treated theoretically as common to both systems, not simply allocated to one system or the other. For example, it is untenable to say that norms of conduct derived from social experience ... must be either that [parts of the personality of the individual], or part of the social system. (1971, 6).

Because the primary difficulty in any action system is the integration of its constituent parts, either individuals or groups, Parsons, following Durkheim, feels that the social system is primary. "There is a sense in which the social system is the core of human action systems, being the primary link between the culture and the individual both as personality and as organism" (Parsons 1968, 459). The other systems make up the larger environment of the social subsystem. Just as the function of the social system is integration of the parts, so the function of the organism is adaptivity to the environment, that of personality is goal-orientation, and that of culture is pattern maintenance and preservation (Parsons 1971).

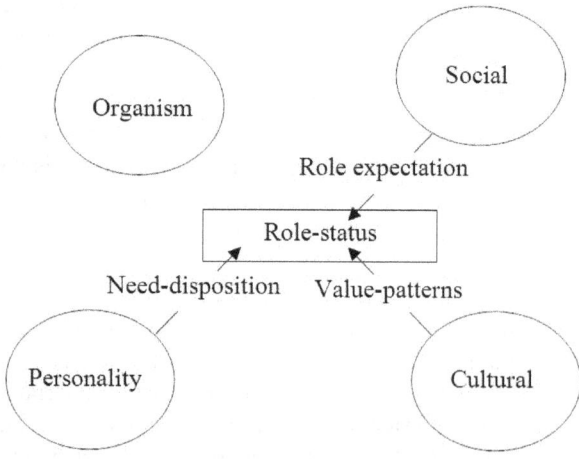

Figure 2. Parsons' model with role in center

The point at which the personality, cultural and social systems most clearly relate is in the role/status position a person occupies (Parsons 1971)(see figure 2). The personality brings a certain need-disposition, the social system defines the expectations of that role, and the culture places value-patterns on it. So, through some kind of drive or desire, an individual seeks a particular role or status provided by that role. The society determines how a person in that role should behave, and the cultural system provides the standards by which it can be decided whether the person fulfills that role appropriately.

To illustrate: suppose a person decides, through a combination of personal motivations such as drive for power, prestige and/or approval, and the desire to accomplish great things for the good of the people, to become President. The political system, as part of the social system, stipulates the contents of the role of President, including his relationship with Congress, with foreign countries, and with the people who elected him. It determines functions such as leadership, diplomacy, image setting and protocol, initiating legislation, and waging war. The cultural system provides ways to evaluate how well he fulfills each of those roles; whether he upholds the honor of the office, keeps the country at peace with other nations, and generates pride on the part of the people. In the same way, we could look at the role-status of a pastor in a local church, analyzing the interaction between the individual and the church, both in terms of the degree to which he fulfills the expectations of the role, and of how well he does what he does.

Bertalanffy

Parson's emphasis on the primacy of the social system can be balanced by another, alternative approach to systems. This theory, originally developed by the biologist Ludwig von Bertalanffy, maintains an equilibrium between the different systems, rather than assigning priority to any one system. He developed his systems theory from a different starting point than did Parsons. As a biologist, he recognized that an organic system better described an organism than did a summation of the individual parts. This led him to what he called General Systems Theory, an attempt to discover the characteristics of systems in general, not in any particular branch of science. It was a response to limitations he had found in scientific method to that point.

> We may state as characteristic of modern science that this scheme of isolable units acting in one-way causality has proved to be insufficient. Hence the appearance, in all fields of science, of notions like wholeness, holistic, organismic, gestalt, etc., which all signify that, in the last resort, we must think in terms of systems of elements in mutual interaction. (Bertalanffy 1968, 45).

Bertalanffy defined systems as "a set of elements standing in interrelation among themselves and with environment" (1968, 252). General systems theory was intentionally interdisciplinary, and sought to bring together scholars from many different disciplines. In this respect, Bertalanffy was similar to Parsons in trying to explore the boundaries of disciplines. General systems theory has been influential in a number of areas. From its origins in theoretical biology, it has since spread to encompass a variety of academic disciplines. A *Festschrift* to Bertalanffy (Laszlo 1972) included articles demonstrating its impact on such diverse fields as biology, economics, communications, psychology, psychiatry, and education. For some of its adherents, General Systems Theory has become a life philosophy and a cogent proof of evolution (Laszlo 1996).

Reacting to the notion in modern science of "isolable units acting in one-way causality" (Bertalanffy 1968, 45), which did not allow for purpose or direction, Bertalanffy came to see the need for systems of elements in mutual interaction.

> The Greek conception of the world was static, things being considered to be mirroring of eternal archetypes or ideas. Therefore classification was the central problem in science. ... In modern science, dynamic interaction appears to be the central problem in all fields of reality. (Bertalanffy 1968, 88).

Complex systems can not be understood as a sum of the parts, each disassembled and analyzed separately. Systems work as integrated wholes. He writes:

> You cannot sum up the behavior of the whole from the isolated parts, and you have to take into account the relations between the various subordinated systems and the systems which are super-ordinated to them in order to understand the behavior of the parts. (Bertalanffy 1968, 68, cf. Laszlo 1996).

Bertalanffy finds common features in systems of all kinds. These include "wholeness and sum, mechanization, centralization, hierarchical order, stationary and steady states, equifinality, etc." (Bertalanffy 1968, 86). Like Parsons, Bertalanffy recognizes hierarchy as a feature of systems. Each system can be seen as a subsystem of a larger system.

> Systems are frequently structured in a way so that their individual members again are systems of the next lower level. ... Such hierarchical structure and combination into systems of ever higher order, is characteristic of reality as a whole and of fundamental importance especially in biology, psychology and sociology. (Bertalanffy 1968, 74).

Parsons and Bertalanffy have much in common. However, Parsons' functionalism can be balanced by Bertalanffy in two particular areas: the idea of open systems and the role of the individual. Neither of these emphases is unique to Bertalanffy, but he gives greater weight to them.

Open Systems

Both Parsons and Bertalanffy characterize their systems as "open systems". Parsons speaks of the social system as an open system. "A social system, like

2. Precedent Literature

all living systems, is inherently an open system engaged in processes of interchange (or "input-output relations") with its environment, as well as consisting of interchanges among its internal units" (Parsons 1968, 460). In this sense, the social system is a subsystem of even larger systems. However, Parsons understands the openness to refer primarily to other subsystems within the system.

Piaget speaks of Parsons' "definition of structure as a stable disposition of the elements of a social system impervious to externally imposed disturbances" (Piaget 1970, 102). Lash criticizes Parsons on this point, charging that he ignores the possibility of change within and between systems.

> In the first modernity, the modernity of structure, society is conceived as a linear system. Talcott Parsons' social system is such a linear system. Linear systems have single points of equilibria, and only external forces can disturb this equilibrium and lead to systems change. The reflexive individualization of the second modernity presumes the existence of non-linear systems. Here system dis-equilibrium and change is produced internally to the system through feedback loops. These are open systems.... Complex systems do not simply reproduce. They change. The individual is the point of passage for the unintended consequences that lead to system dis-equilibrium. (Lash 2002, viii).

Bertalanffy specifically contrasts open and closed systems. Physics typically deals with closed systems. The second law of thermodynamics, for example, is true only in a closed system. In a closed system, the outcome is determined by the starting point. Equilibrium is the natural state towards which all closed systems tend. Characteristic of open systems, however, is that "the final state may be reached from different initial conditions and in different ways" (Bertalanffy 1968, 40). Not only the social system, but all living systems are open, in that they exchange inputs and outputs with their environment. Closed systems tend toward equilibrium, but open systems allow for change, progress and direction.

Bertalanffy criticizes Parsons' functionalist approach to systems theory, which tends to be static and ignore issues of social change. He calls for an emphasis on progress and movement in our account of reality.

> The main critique of functionalism, particularly in Parsons' version, is that it overemphasizes maintenance, equilibrium, adjustment, homeostasis, stable institutional structures, and so, with the result that history, process, sociocultural change, inner-directed development, etc., are underplayed and, at most appear as "deviants" with a negative value connotation.... Obviously, general system theory in the form here presented is free of the objection as it incorporates equally maintenance and change, preservation of system and internal conflict; it may therefore be apt to

serve as logical skeleton for improved sociological theory. (Bertalanffy 1968, 196, cf. Clark 1972).

Parsons calls his a theory of action systems. His systems are active, like a clock, but they are not going anywhere. Growth and change are not desired products of the system. All the functions of the system are described, but progress does not occur.

We can see the outworking of the contrast between open and closed systems in Marxism as it developed in ECE. Marxism promised growth and development towards a specific utopian social goal. In practice, Communist governments tried to isolate their people from the outside world, in effect creating a closed system. Instead of movement towards a goal, entropy set in, leading society increasingly towards disorder and randomness. Where the system was somewhat open, for instance, where Western media was heard or where people were listening for God's voice, positive change could occur.

Role of the Individual

For Parsons, individuals were important primarily for their function in the system. They play roles and inhabit status within the social system. Bertalanffy recognizes, with Parsons, that persons do function according to roles, and that these roles have a place in systems theory.

> That here and there the statistical law is broken by "rugged individualists" is in its character. Nor does the role played in history by "great men" contradict the system concept in history; they can be conceived as acting like "leading parts," "triggers" or catalyzers" in the historical process – a phenomenon well accounted for in the general theory of systems. (Bertalanffy 1968, 116).

One of the strengths of Bertalanffy's systems theory, however, is that it recognizes the value of individuals in the system as individuals. They are not interchangeable parts, replaceable elements, or holders of role or status within the system. They have personality and purpose. Individuals have a value and function within the system, not simply in their role but as personalities. This personality was previously seen as beyond the scope of science, relegated to philosophy or religion. He sees the individual differently.

> What should be stressed, however, is the fact that teleological behavior directed towards a characteristic final state or goal is not something off limits for natural science and an anthropomorphic misconception of processes which, in themselves, are undirected and accidental. Rather it is a form of behavior which can well be defined in scientific terms and for which the necessary conditions and possible mechanisms can be indicated. (Bertalanffy 1968, 46).

2. Precedent Literature

Bertalanffy called his view "humanistic" because he placed value on people and not just cogs in a system. Systems are highly complex and the analysis of systems complex. Nevertheless, there is always the role for people.

Gray discussed what he calls the five "Bertalanffian principles" (1972), highlighting the unique contribution of Bertalanffy to systems theory. Each of these five points, framed both positively and negatively, describe how systems theory departs from much of modern science. Bertalanffy's approach is "antireductionistic", with a concern for the organism as a whole, "antirobotic", insisting that organisms do not just react to stimuli but are purposefully active, "antizoomorphic", concentrating on those areas of life, such as symbolism, where humankind is distinguishable from animals, "antivitalist", recognizing that systems are open and hierarchically organized, and "antimechanistic", claiming that a place must be found for values, ethics, and morals, which are essential for human systems to function properly (Gray 1972, 127-133).

Hiebert

Hiebert takes systems theory and modifies it. He calls his model a "system of systems". (see figure 3.) In some ways, saying "system of systems" is redundant. Bertalanffy and Parsons both assume that any given system, whether biological, social, technological, cultural, or any other kind, interacts not only within the system, but with other systems as well. However, "system of systems" makes this complexity explicit.

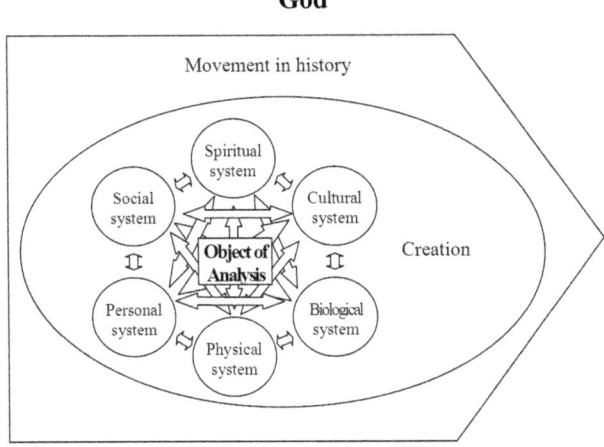

Figure 3. Hiebert's system of systems model

In addition, Hiebert introduces an element ignored in the systems literature. He adds a spiritual system, which includes God, Satan, angels, and other unseen beings. He takes seriously the perspective that this present material world does not exist in isolation from a spiritual reality. We may not be able to study this spiritual system empirically, but it exists nevertheless. Religion exists as a subsystem of the culture system. It can account for people's understanding and perceptions of the unseen world, but does not explain the objective reality of that world. Secular social scientists deny spiritual reality, assuming it exists only as a human construction. At most they may admit its existence, but exclude it by definition from exploration. Hiebert, however, gives it equal weight, as a system, with the others.

Summary

Parsons is helpful in that he thinks carefully about the elements of the different systems and their functions and interactions. We will follow his delineation of the various subsystems. Bertalanffy is a helpful balance in his emphasis on open systems and on the features that systems of all kinds have in common. His approach is non-linear, which recognizes that different casual starting points may lead to different conclusions, and that similar conclusions can be reached from different starting points. Hiebert's contribution is that he reminds us that the physical universe is not a closed system. God and the spiritual world are as real as the material world and must be taken into account for any explanation of events.

By identifying cultural, social, psychological, biological, spiritual and personal factors, we can gain a more in-depth understanding of how each system works. However, it is equally important to look at places where systems overlap. It is in the interplay between systems that we can find the new insights. Perhaps this would be graphically more helpful if we could show (in three dimension or as Venn diagrams), not only the ways in which the various systems interact, but also the ways they overlap. Often certain things do not clearly lie in one system or another, but are part of both.

What then do the overlaps tell us, as well as the interactions? What can we learn from the interaction between culture and society or between society and the individual personality? Can we predict changes in one system based on changes in another? A systems approach can be a somewhat static model, but the examination of the interactions can help to give it movement and allow us to understand change.

A systems approach further helps to separate issues of structure, functions, and roles from personalities. System implies interchangeability. Things should work the same no matter who is in what position. In the church, for examples, we can look at the roles of leadership, or ministry, or giving, or evangelism, and see how they function. We can then look further at the people who are filling those roles, to evaluate whether they are being effective. Individuals certainly do make a difference, but in interaction with and within the boundaries established by the cultural and social systems.

In its focus on structure and function, a system implies stability and integration. Stability and integration are, however, increasingly not characteristic of today's world. Perhaps in cities more than anywhere else, cultures and societies are fragmenting rather than integrating. Globalization, immigration, war, refugees, and dislocations due to poverty are all shattering the fragile unity of cultures. Schreiter (1997) reminds us that boundaries are increasingly not of territory but of difference. Members of various cultures live alongside one another, groups live alongside other groups, and the members of these groups share multiple identities. Therefore, when we attempt systems analysis we do so attempting to capture in a moment something which is in flux. We take a snapshot, recognizing that the reality is shifting even as the photograph is developing. A theory and analysis of social and culture change are also needed to complete the picture.

Not only do the various systems interact at a variety of levels, they also allow for multiple avenues of cause and effect in different directions. This balances, for example, the view that human persons are more or less passive recipients of social forces which control and shape them. While they are shaped by social and cultural contexts, they are also active agents who can, in turn, shape the cultural and social systems of which they are a part.

No attempt will be made here to develop a detailed explanation of each of the separate sub-systems. If one follows Parsons' and Bertalanffy's examples, each sub-system can be subdivided indefinitely. As a general guideline, the social system can be said to include the political, legal, and economic systems, while the cultural system includes behavior, beliefs, rituals and symbols, and worldview (Hiebert 1998). To understand the spiritual system it will be necessary to have some awareness of spiritual, unseen realities of angels and demons as well as a recognition of spiritual warfare.

Movement Theory and Diffusion Studies

While a system of systems approach allows for process and change, it does not explicitly attempt to understand them. Social movement theory and diffusion studies seek to understand the processes and stages through which a movement travels. Stewart, Smith, Denton (Stewart, Smith et al. 1994) describe five stages in the life cycle of movement: genesis, social unrest, enthusiastic mobilization, maintenance, and termination. Parker Palmer (1998) lists four stages: Isolated individuals who decide to live integrated lives, like-minded individuals who find each other and form communities of convergence, these communities start going public, and a system of alternate awards emerges. Missions movements in ECE are too young to have gone through Steward, Smith, and Denton's five stages, and are somewhere in the middle of Palmer's process.

The processes that bring about change have been carefully studied by diffusion scholars over the past sixty years. The specifics of innovation and change are described by Rogers in the classic work, *Diffusion of Innovations* (1995). "Diffusion is essentially a social process occurring through interpersonal networks" (Rogers 1995, 82). He discusses the creation of innovations, the innovation-diffusion process, the attributes of innovations and their rate of adoption, innovativeness and adopter categories, the change agent, and the consequences of innovations. Critical here are the kinds of people involved in bringing about change and the aspects of the innovation itself which make it more likely to be adopted. Compatibility with existing values, past experiences, and the needs of potential adopters, trialabilty of the innovation, and observability of the results are all factors which will ease the process of adoption.

Gladwell (2000) likens the process of social change to that of an epidemic. Epidemics are a function of the people who transmit infectious agents, the infectious agent itself, and the environment in which the infectious agent is operating. The role of key people, the "stickiness" of the message, and the social context are crucial elements in determining whether a new idea will become widely accepted or not. He analyses religious movements, particularly Wesley's revival in the eighteenth century, and attributes it to the skillful use of group power. Wesley

> wasn't one person with ties to many other people. He was one person with ties to many groups. ... [He] realized that if you wanted to bring about a fundamental change in people's belief and behavior, a change that would persist and serve as an example to others, you needed to create a community around them, where those new beliefs could be practiced and expresses and nurtured. (Gladwell 2000, 173)

Epidemics start very small, but through their interactions and interrelationships with their context, they can grow and spread very rapidly. An appropriate social structure will allow them to become embedded in a group.

Eastern European Issues

The transition from Communism to democracy has been traumatic for most Central and Eastern European countries. While the process seems irreversible for the western-most countries, for others the transition is very much in doubt. The current economic crisis in Russia threatens to pull neighboring countries down. Romania and Bulgaria, as well as the former Soviet Union countries, are facing severe economic shocks. This transition is complicated by the fact that two concurrent processes of transition are occurring simultaneously: a political transition from Communism to democracy, and an economic transition from a state planned and controlled economy to a capitalist, market economy (Bookman 1995).

The literature on these transitions is very large. A new scholarly occupation has come into existence, that of "transitologist", those scholars who specialize on the economic, political, cultural, or social aspects of the transition (Siklova 1997). Bookman speaks of

> the plethora of academic books and articles on that region [East-Central Europe]. Five years after the onset of the transformations, the pace of publication remains frenzied, and the literature is saturated with information. Not all of it, alas, is analytically useful or even sound. (1995, 604)

Since 1995 the pace of publication has continued unabated, in every discipline. Her review article of several important books dealing with these transitions is very helpful. The development of new degrees of freedom and the loosening of economic straitjackets have allowed entrepreneurs, both in the business and the religious realms, to initiate new programs and products (Luthans, Patrick et al. 1995). Businessmen are facing the same contextual factors as mission leaders. They have to understand how economic and political changes affect their ability to carry out their vision for the future.

It is not necessary to review all the literature dealing with these transitions in order to have some concepts which can help guide the specific focus of research envisioned here. The intention is to highlight those aspects of the transition which may play a part in the transition from missionary receiving (and non-missionary oriented) to missionary sending. A brief overview as relates to the social and cultural systems will be given.

Social System

Centeno and Rands (1996) attempt an assessment of the political, economic and cultural changes which have occurred since 1989. They note that political reform is the most common change throughout the region, that economic reforms have been uneven, but have resulted in increased social inequality in all countries, and that enthusiasm and optimism for democratic change have decreased.

Political System

Three criteria for the establishment of democracy have been determined (Centeno and Rands 1996): the possibility of government turnover, existence of a free press, and respect for human rights. In their evaluation, the first two are clearly in place, but gains in minority rights are less clear.

Plesu (1996), speaking for Romania, declares that things in general have not gone as badly as opposition has asserted and not as well as the government claims. His opinion as to the current situation could be stated for the other countries as well.

> The truth is that the events of December 1989 found us unprepared. We were more adapted than we thought to life under a dictatorship; we did not have illusions about an eventual change, and we had never seriously reflected on a normal political alternative. Under these circumstances, the reformulation of mentalities, the recovery of "democratic" instincts asphyxiated by forty-five years of totalitarianism, the rehabilitation of pluralistic political action (after the paranoid monotony of the unique party), require time and imply long episodes of confusion and contortion. (Plesu 1996).

Many new leaders have emerged, who, while enjoying popular support in the early days of the revolution, have proven themselves too inexperienced in politics to successfully lead a country. Consequently, in many countries former Communists have regained power, at least temporarily. One reason for this is a lack of cooperation on the part of new leaders. A plethora of political parties have been formed, which have led to unstable coalition governments (Bookman 1995).

Economic System

The various countries of East-Central Europe have experienced very different paths toward a market economy. In general, the countries closer to Western Europe have made the transition easier than those further east. Hungary, Poland and the Czech Republic have withstood the transition rather well, though certainly not without difficulties. Romania, Bulgaria and the Ukraine are still struggling, due to a weaker tradition in capitalism, more serious damage done by Communist regimes and by a lesser political desire for rapid change. The fact that former Communists remained in power for longer in these countries certainly contributes to their relative backwardness. In general, it can be said that those countries which undertook more radical reforms have recovered more quickly than those which chose a gradualist track (Healey 1996; Aslund, Boone et al. 1996). Despite the fact that more reforms are needed and the road which could lead to a Western European standard of living is long, most economists are optimistic that the East-Central European countries are on the right track.

Nevertheless, many people are still suffering economically. In many cases, income policies which were developed under the Communists have not yet been replaced with adequate social security mechanisms (Standing 1997; Tomes 1997). One of the urgent needs seems to be to find ways to ease unemployment and to provide a social security net for those who are not yet able to support themselves (Trojan 1994).

Cultural System

An important cultural factor for the success of the transitions would need to be the perception on the part of the people that life is better now than it was under the Communists. Despite the fact that by many objective measures life has gotten better, many people's perceptions is that things are more difficult now than before. Intellectuals have found themselves increasingly marginalized, with the result that many look nostalgically back on the Communist past when they had a clear status to play – that of dangerous opposition (Plesu 1996). Now no longer seen as dangerous or even important, they are ignored and replaced by politicians, journalists, and entrepreneurs as public stars. Plesu speaks of a friend who confesses that he was happier before. Siklova (1996) also asks whether people are happier now. Again speaking for intellectuals, she claims that in the revolutions they lost a number of things that they did not realize were valuable. They lost their "self-definition, ideology, eschatology, or something that goes beyond us" (535). They lost the glory that came from being admired around the world for their courage in the face of persecution and their qualification for political struggle. She writes that

> everything we gained in the real world we lost in the sphere of wishes. We lost our childish innocence, illusions about our own potential and ability that could not be proven, and lack of responsibility for ourselves and the world around us. To our amazement, we found that compared to many other countries, we were quite rich, and we were not longer the ones who needed help. (Siklova 1996, 540).

Disillusionment has set in on the part of common people as well. Support for both democracy and market economies seems to be dropping, political will for economic reforms is declining, as is interest in politics and participation in public life (Bookman 1995; Centeno and Rands 1996; Nelson 1996). People seem to profess an understandable set of apparent contradictions in response to the changes brought about by the revolutions of 1989. For example, "Russians appear to want a market without risk, capitalism without rich people, equality with quality, and a democracy with strong and disciplinary leadership" (Centeno and Rands 1996). While these contradictions seem irreconcilable, they may simply be part of the process of moving from one type of society to another, aspects which need to be held in tension as different perspectives on the same reality (Isaac 1996).

Religious System

The religious sub-system is one that illustrates clearly the interaction between systems. Religion is inherently an overlap between culture, society, personality, and spiritual reality. In its beliefs, it is culture; in its structure, it is social; in its affects, it is both spiritual and personal. Here we will examine the religious situation in East-Central Europe without differentiating between the various systems.

Pre-Revolution

The evangelical churches have been the subject of little systematic study. Most of the extensive study of religion in East-Central Europe deals with the state churches – Lutheran, Calvinist, Roman Catholic and Orthodox. Evangelical churches are often considered in the literature, as they are by the general population, as sects or new religious movements. Before the revolution, the evangelical churches were not ignored, but they were primarily treated in the context of persecution. Keston College was the most notable institution focusing on persecution of the church, whether evangelical or state. Beeson (1982) is the standard work on general religious conditions before the revolution. However, little work has been done on specific beliefs or social structures of these churches. Even denominational statistics were notoriously inaccurate, and even today are difficult to find.

Revolution

Volumes have been written describing the church's role in bringing about the downfall of the Communists in the fall of 1989 (Swoboda 1990; Bultman 1991; Bourdeaux 1992; Swoboda and Pierard 1996). In the euphoria immediately following the revolution, the churches and church leaders were celebrated as a significant force for democratic change. However, soon evidence began to emerge of collaboration between church leaders and the Communist authorities, particularly the *Stasi* in East Germany and the *Securitate* in Romania (Conway 1994, 1995; Monshipouri and Arnold 1996). A balanced perspective would show that the church (usually State churches, seldom evangelical) played a substantial, but not unambiguous, part in the revolutions. Probably the impact of the churches was less in Hungary and Czechoslovakia than in East Germany, Poland or Romania.

Post-Revolution

With the sudden outbreak of religious freedom following the revolution, churches have had to learn to operate in a totally new environment. Able to practice and worship in public for the first time in forty-five years, they have not always known how to proceed. Intense periods of open evangelism in the early months of 1990 led fairly quickly to new inertia. Evangelical churches quickly experienced a new form of opposition, not from the governments but from the majority churches, who were fighting for renewed official status as state churches (Elliot 1996; Barker 1997; Borowik 1997; Richardson 1997; Tomka 1997). Church leaders as well as ordinary Christians had to adjust to new realities. They had been used to being small, persecuted minorities,

2. Precedent Literature

whose status was always questionable. Formerly marginalized, now they were able to enter the mainstream of society. But how to adjust?

> Father Vaclav Maly of Czechoslovakia, jailed by the Communists in 1979 for his dissident activities, said in 1990 that "psychologically, Christians have been in exile". When a people, or a group, returns from a long exile, it is unrealistic to expect it to shed all at once the psychological effects and habits of mind developed under those conditions. The reintegration of believers on a normal basis, like the rebuilding and reintegration of these societies as a whole, will be a lengthy process. (Ramet 1994, 2).

It seems possible that religious leaders faced some of the same issues as intellectuals. They lost some of the focus and attention from the West they had enjoyed as persecuted heroes. Now they had to work to fulfill the new expectations of their congregations.

Years of Communist attempts to exterminate religion were quickly shown to be in vain. Two distinct trends can be identified. De-Christianization and secularization as a result of atheistic propaganda were most successful in East Germany and to a somewhat lesser extent in Hungary and Czechoslovakia (Gautier 1997). The opposite trend is toward renewed religiosity. Beginning with a revival starting in 1978 (Tomka 1991; Borowik 1997), and continuing to the present, people in the former Soviet Union, Hungary, Czechoslovakia, and Romania declare themselves to be more religious than ten or fifteen years previously. A survey commissioned by a group of evangelical organizations revealed that in Poland, Slovakia and Hungary, over half of the population hold to a Christian worldview, while a third of those from the Czech Republic do so (Religious Attitudes in East Central Europe. 1993). Gautier concludes that

> these findings demonstrate that religious belief remains alive and well in these posttransition societies. Although the effects of repression of the churches will continue to be felt, probably for several generations, there is a vitality to religious belief in these countries that reflects well when compared to that of religious believers in western Germany. (Gautier 1997, 29).

In contrast with the collapse of the political and economic systems following the revolution, churches and religion have maintained their social organization well (Tomka 1995). They are filling a stabilizing role as the countries make the transition from Communism to whatever form of society they will eventually assume.

3. Research Procedure

This chapter outlines the theoretical framework which gives direction to the study, clarifies the research problems, and develops some of the more important research questions necessary to answer the problem statement. It describes population, selection of the cases, instruments, and operational procedures. In addition, specific methodological issues are discussed.

Theoretical Framework

This research is designed to elicit and explore the views of participants in new missionary sending movements in East-Central Europe. It is not intended to test hypotheses or to prove questions of causality. No theoretical grid is imposed on the responses of the participants. However, to ensure that significant questions were asked, and to give me a grid to evaluate their responses, a theoretical framework, or what Stake calls "abstract dimensions" or "foreshadowed problems" (Stake 1994), is introduced. Stake, following Malinowski says, "we can distinguish between arriving with closed minds and arriving with an idea of what to look for" (1994, 245). The theory used here gives guidance in this sense (Silverman 1993; Yin 1994). Malinowski says "Preconceived ideas are pernicious in any scientific work, but *foreshadowed problems* are the main endowment of a scientific thinker, and these problems are first revealed to the observer by his theoretical studies" (Stake 1994, 245).

It is possible to proceed without a theory base, and to seek only to understand the perspectives of the participants. However, the scope of this research is broader than a purely emic understanding; it includes the attempt to evaluate that understanding from an etic perspective. Undoubtedly some interviewees may respond in ways which do not fall neatly into the theoretical grid. The theory is not intended to encompass all possible answers, but to provide a scaffolding for the answers. If unanticipated responses come, the theory will be adjusted to accommodate the new insights.

Based on a review of the literature and on personal experience, several factors which might be instrumental in the rise of new missions movements can be anticipated and explored. A system of systems approach, as developed by Parsons, given balancing features by Bertalanffy, and modified by Hiebert, were used to structure the discussions. The basic assumption here is that changes in the social, cultural, personal, and spiritual systems unleashed by the fall of Communism have all contributed to the emergence of new missionary movements. Further, the assumption is that the various systems interact in different

3. Research Procedure

ways in each case, contributing to each one's uniqueness. The major question explored was the nature of these contributions and interactions.

While not ignoring the personal, physical or biological systems, the focus of the analysis is on the cultural, social and spiritual systems. Individuals are seen primarily in the context of their social roles rather than studied as a separate system. It is recognized that history affects each system and the interaction between systems. In particular, the specific historical situation of years of Communist domination and the transition to democracy set the context in which the movements to be studied occur. For this reason, history is not be treated as a separate factor.

One of the unique values of this research, and the theoretical approach employed here, is that it allows us to ask the question not only why missions interest or vision emerged, but also what turned this vision into action. Individual actions are set into the larger social and cultural context in which individuals act. Another value is the qualitative investigation of specific movements. Most studies of current movements are primarily based on survey data, with the resultant difficulties caused by unfamiliarity and misunderstanding of survey instruments (Fiedler 1994).

Based on this theoretical model, the following problem statement can be articulated.

Problem Statement

This research examines the social, cultural and spiritual factors which are influential in the rise of four missionary sending movements in East-Central Europe.

Research Questions

The research was guided by the following three research questions.

- ❑ RQ1. What do the participants of four new missionary sending movements see as the spiritual factors which led to the rise of those movements? Some of the issues explored were the extent to which one could speak of a specific work of God in the rise of the new movements, the existence or not of a revival in the church, and the question and nature of a missionary call.
- ❑ RQ2. What do the participants of new missionary sending movements see as the social factors which led to the rise of those movements? Several operational questions were used to answer this question:
    - OQ1: To what extent has the shift from Communism to democracy influenced the rise of missionary sending movements?

OQ2: In what way, if any, did economic factors play a part?

OQ3: In what way, if any, did political or legal factors play a part? For instance, freedom to travel?

OQ4: In what way, if any, did ecclesiastical factors play a part?

OQ5: Did certain individuals play a key role? In what way?

OQ6: In what ways does extensive contact with foreign missionaries relate to the likelihood that churches in East-Central Europe will send missionaries?

❏ RQ3. What do the participants of new missionary sending movements see as the cultural factors which led to the rise of those movements?

OQ1: In what way, if any, did theological factors play a part? In particular, how did mission leaders understand their church's missions responsibility before 1989 and how has it changed since then?

OQ2: To what extent did missions leaders in East-Central Europe have an interest in missionary sending before the fall of Communism, and to what extent has this interest developed since the revolution?

OQ3: In what way, if any, did educational factors (particularly theological education) play a part?

OQ4: In what way, if any, did openness to and contact with outside (Western) influences play a part?

OQ5: To what extent, if any, did issues of ethnocentrism and openness to others have to be handled?

A fourth research question was part of the original protocol, "What do the participants of new missionary sending movements see as the relationship between the various factors in the rise of missionary sending movements? More specifically, what is the relationship between economic capability, theological reflection, political freedom, and openness to others?" However, it was quickly seen that the question was too complicated for participants, and did not necessarily correspond to the kinds of answers they were giving. In order not to prejudice the conclusions drawn by the participants, this question was dropped from the interviews. It remains an important question, but will be necessary for me to determine the answer.

A further research question was proposed but then abandoned. Originally, the plan was to compare the responses of mission leaders who stayed at home with missionaries on the field. However, the number of missionaries is very limited compared to those at home, and their responses were not significantly different to warrant this extra question.

Contextual Questions

A narrative approach was used in the interviews. Respondents were asked to tell the story of the movement in which they were involved. The kinds of questions which invited the narrative were the following.

- ❑ What is the movement like? How many missionaries have been sent? Where have they come from and where do they serve? How are they supported?
- ❑ Describe the movement: its history, growth and development.
- ❑ How did the movement come into being? How did it come to send missionaries? Why did it develop? What was the major impetus? What were the important incidents? Who were the key people?
- ❑ To what do you attribute the development of new missionary sending movements?

Further, some concluding questions were asked, which required the respondents to reflect on the interview and the process of development they had observed. These questions included some of the following.

- ❑ What contributes to the change from same culture mission to cross-cultural (or from same country to another country) missions?
- ❑ What recommendations would you give to someone who is trying to start a missions movement? What lessons have you learned which would might be helpful to others in a similar situation?
- ❑ Reflecting on the preceding conversation, what would you say are the most important factors in the development of the movement you are a part of?

Description of Cases

No one knows how many newly developing missionary sending movements have begun in East-Central Europe in the past ten years. These are emerging movements and the number is changing constantly. The population for this study consists of the participants in missionary sending movements in East-Central Europe which have started in the past ten years. These participants include those who give direction from the home country and those who are serving as missionaries in other countries.

Selection of Cases

Four movements were selected for study. Two are in Romania, and one each is in Poland and Hungary. They were chosen because they demonstrate a variety of different forms that movements can take. They represent different denominations, agencies and churches from three different countries. Although they are not intended as any kind of proportional sample, they do seem to represent the variety in missionary sending movements in the area. In addition, they were selected because I was familiar with them and because of the relative ease of access which they afforded.

Patton (1990) speaks of purposeful sampling, and lists the following options in selecting cases: typical case, extreme or deviant case, critical case, sensitive case, convenience case, and maximum variation. Stake (1994) distinguishes between intrinsic, instrumental and collective case studies. The cases selected here fall into several of Patton's categories. The study as a whole can be seen as one of Stake's collective case studies. "They are chosen because it is believed that understanding them will lead to better understanding, perhaps better theorizing, about a still larger collection of cases" (Stake 1994, 237).

The first case is a joint project between the Reformed and Lutheran churches in Hungary, who have sent a young couple as missionary schoolteachers in India. The second case involves the Aletheia church in Timişoara, Romania. This small independent charismatic church has sent two missionary families to Albania. The church leaders have taken a very active role in supporting these couples, including regular visits to the field. The third case is a Polish missionary agency, Biblical Mission Association (BMS), with branches in Wrocław and Ustron, Poland, which has sent missionaries primarily to Central Asia, but also to a variety of other countries. The fourth case is a Romanian cooperative effort, Romanian International Mission (MIR), which is a network of missions agencies, denominations, training institutions and churches who are sending missionaries to a variety of countries.

From each of these four movements certain individuals were selected to interview. The founder or main leader and one or two other key leaders, and one or two missionaries were interviewed. If it was determined that one individual had a decisive influence on the initiation of a movement, a more in-depth interview was conducted to uncover the formative influences on his or her missions vision.

During the course of investigation, changes were made in the selection. Originally, two other movements were proposed. One of them had disappeared since the proposal, primarily due to the death of the pastor who was the driving force behind it. Another was seen to be too complex for the purposes of this study.

In addition to the four cases selected, other cases were considered for study in less depth. Those included the Ukrainian mission agencies Light of the Gospel, Gospel to the Nations, and Bread from Ukraine, among others. Missions movements in both former East Germany and the Ukraine were also considered for this study, but were rejected for different reasons: East Germany, because of the difficulty of separating East and West Germany, and Ukraine, primarily for reasons of access and geographical and cultural distance from me.

Methodological Issues

In this research, four cases are studied. Case study research has a couple of unique features which distinguishes it from other types of qualitative research. These will be briefly outlined, as well as some underlying issues of interviewing.

Case Study Research

One question which arises with case study research is the extent to which results can be generalized. Stake (1994) prefers to emphasize the individual case, asserting that seeking generalizations weakens the impact of the particularities of the case. He acknowledges, however, that the extent to which generalizations are made is a choice which must be made by the researcher. Yin (1994) claims that generalization is important, but its nature must be properly understood. He urges not statistical generalization but analytical generalization. Previous theory should be used as a template with which to compare empirical results. The researcher generalizes to theory, not to other cases.

Yin's approach is similar when it comes to selecting cases in a multiple case design. What is important is not sampling logic, as would be required for a quantitative study, but what he calls replication logic. This is the selection of cases which open the door to similar kinds of results, which can then be compared more easily. The selection of participants within each case followed this logic. It was not so important, for instance, to find an equal number of mission leaders, missionaries, pastors, and so on, to have proper representation. More important was finding people with the greatest experience and expertise. The number of interviews was not determined in advance by any kind of sampling procedure. Each case was different in both size and scope, so the number of interviews necessarily varied. The actual termination point was determined when the same information began to be repeated regularly. At that point it was determined that saturation had been reached.

Interviewing Procedures

Little agreement exists regarding interviewing procedures. Some authors suggest interview protocols; others do not. Some recommend tape-recording interviews; others do not. Some affirm the need for an extensive literature review and a clearly defined theory base before beginning to interview (Yin 1994; Rubin and Rubin 1995). Others view both of these things as biasing the hearing and the perspective of the respondent. What is clearly agreed upon is the need to allow the interviewees to speak for themselves and to understand their perspectives in an emic way. In this project, a clearly defined theoretical framework for analysis was used, but little literature was available which related directly to the topic of study and no theory base to confirm or disconfirm was developed in advance.

As noted above, a narrative approach was taken at the start of the interview. Following the telling of the story, specific questions relating to the research questions were asked, filling in gaps in the narrative.

The consequence of this approach was that the interviews often wandered. Careful listening was necessary to determine which questions had been answered through the narrative and which still needed to be asked. Further, the analysis of the data was not always straightforward. At times it was difficult getting to the actual research questions. The narrative nature of things, just trying to hear the story, made things more circular.

Instruments

The primary method of data collection was through interviews with key participants in the selected movements. These were primarily topical interviews (Rubin and Rubin 1995) rather than cultural interviews, ethnographic interviews (Spradley 1979), or in-depth, phenomenological interviews (Seidman 1998), although the techniques applicable to each of these approaches were used where appropriate. The intention of the interview was to identify all the relevant factors which play a part in the new missionary impulse. The protocol included questions which compare the current situation with that before the demise of Communism, as well as questions which deal with contemporary issues.

The protocol covered the following themes: spiritual issues, cultural issues (including theological questions), social issues (including economic and political issues), and individual issues.

Care was taken not to predetermine answers by leading questions. Questions were used to open the door for the respondent to think carefully in new ways, but did not suggest answers which did not apply to the informant's situation.

In addition to interviews with key persons involved with each case, documents were collected wherever possible. These documents were of several types: charters, letters, reports, promotional materials and magazine articles. In fact, very few documents were available. Several things account for this. The missionary movements are still in their initial stages, and much of the data is oral. With the exception of Romania, where much has been written, the others functioned more as an oral culture. One missions leader in Poland showed me a stack of half a dozen pieces of paper, and said that was all his agency had.

Issues of Access

Preliminary research identified the key players in the cases studied. In many instances, I already knew the key people. Where I did not know them, access to them was facilitated by friends and colleagues. As expected, key leaders were able to open the door to other people in the movement. The reputation of the leader was a large factor in the positive reception I received. Fluency in the language, previous ministry in the country, and association with a ministry with a wide and positive reputation also contributed to a warm welcome.

Collecting documents related to the various movements was more sensitive and difficult than making contacts for interviews. Many of the groups are spontaneous movements, rather than planned organizations, and therefore have little documentation, and loose organization. Moreover, gaining permission to copy documents required a higher level of trust than did simply interviewing people. Consequently, the collection and analysis of documents took second place to interviewing. They were useful when obtained, but were not critical to the analysis. Significant documentary evidence was only available from the last of the four cases.

Procedure

I contacted the leaders of each movement selected for study. In some cases, they suggested and arranged interviews with others in their organization. In other cases, it was necessary to make such contacts personally, and arrange the interviews. Only in one case were all the interviews conducted on a single trip. The other cases required multiple trips to talk with everyone. Ten of the missionaries were interviewed in their home countries. Nine others were interviewed in their fields of ministry. The selection process was through snowball or chain sampling (Gall, Borg et al. 1996), that is, people not originally scheduled were added if participants suggested that they should be interviewed.

Visits to each site were arranged, and interviews scheduled in advance. When it was not possible to arrange meetings, attempts were made to assure that the participants were in town during a visit.

Four countries were visited and forty-four interviews with fifty respondents were conducted. Several days were spent at each site. Interviews lasted between one and two hours, with the average around one and a half hours. Interviews were held in English, German and Romanian, as well as through translation from Polish and Hungarian. Formal and informal interviews were conducted in offices and living rooms, but also on buses and trams traveling across Wrocław, Poland, in a car traveling through Ukraine, Slovakia and Poland, in a car traveling from Timişoara to Oradea, Romania, and in meetings where multiple other conversations were going on.

Many times things did not take place as expected. It was not unusual to have uninvited participants present, or others I did not know who were invited by the conversation partner. Some of these people had agendas which were different from the intended topic of conversation, but which sometimes led to fresh information and new insight. Three of the interviews turned into focus group discussions. Finally, four interviews were conducted by telephone because of difficulty of access. There were both advantages and disadvantages to these interviews. An advantage was the ability to enter notes directly into the computer. The natural disadvantage was the lack of face-to-face contact, with the resulting loss of non-verbal communication.

Eighteen of the interviews were recorded, but many times the setting or atmosphere made the use of a cassette unwise. When the interview was not recorded, all attempts were made to record field notes into a cassette or on paper immediately. On at least one occasion, out of my control, two interviews and one group meeting were held in succession, without a break between the events. In this situation, I attempted to reconstruct the conversations as well as possible. Recording did play a certain role in the interview process. Nobody objected to recording the conversation, but it seemed to affect some people more than others. More than one participant made specific references to it and looked at the tape recorder. They also gave references and background information which was unnecessary given their relationships with me. Another did not say anything about the tape, but looked at it several times. He even made some comment about the tape not understanding him. His whole style was more stilted and academic than it probably would have been otherwise.

At other times, respondents made comments like, "I wouldn't want others to know", "this isn't really public", or so on, but when I moved to stop the tape they said not to bother. Other times they really did want the tape stopped.

In summary, the tape recorder did seem to have some effect, but it does not seem to have hindered the gathering of needed information and its value as a memory aid overcame the difficulty. I feel that maybe I forgot something important when interviews were not taped, especially when interviews came without breaks and there was no time to dump field notes. On only one occasion, however, was the interview not taped when it would have been particularly useful. I had received the message that the person to be interviewed had information about someone else or another group, with whom it would then be necessary to schedule an interview. However, it turned out that he himself was the one involved in doing something new. Keeping up with taking notes of his comments was a challenge, compounded by the fact that he spoke quickly.

The tapes and field notes were transcribed and entered into the computer. They were then printed out, read and reread to determine themes, coded and organized by theme, and analyzed.

After each set of interviews, the protocol was evaluated and revised as necessary for the next set. Preliminary analysis was begun with a view to improving the instrument. An example of the revision of the protocol was to drop research question four. It seemed too confusing a question to ask. Often times the question was asked instead, "what recommendations would you give to another group who was just in the process to trying to develop a missions vision?"

On four occasions, follow-up interviews were conducted with key participants. In addition, further contact through correspondence brought new information and updates.

Data Analysis

Since the primary data were field notes based on the interviews with the participants, verbal analysis was the primary method of data analysis. The field notes were entered into Microsoft Word, read repeatedly, then coded and analyzed for themes, patterns and similarities and dissimilarities. If certain themes showed up consistently, a correlation between those themes or factors and missionary sending movements could be demonstrated. Causal factors are not being sought here. Rather, the findings show which factors tend to be present whenever new missionary sending movements arise. The themes were analyzed to determine whether the factors could be weighted in order of importance. Where possible, the initial findings were shared with the primary informants, which allowed for feedback, confirmation, corroboration or clarification. In case of contradictory or unclear findings, follow-up interviews with the same participants were arranged, or if further generalizability was found necessary, participants in other movements were contacted and interviewed.

Documents were available in two of the cases. These included a policy manual and missions statutes and the minutes of meetings. These documents were similarly analyzed to determine if they added to, confirmed, or disconfirmed themes uncovered through the interviews.

The primary unit of analysis is the case rather than the individual (Yin 1994). Therefore, analysis was done first within cases and only then between or across cases. The cases should be understood primarily as illustrative of the range of mission-related activities. The boundaries between these cases and the larger context of missions in a particular country can be very fuzzy.

Following final data entry, the data were analyzed and an initial draft of the findings of each case was written. Themes in each system were noted, followed by an examination of the interaction between systems. After all four cases had been written, themes were analyzed between cases, first, system by system, followed by the interactions between systems. The cases were then compared and contrasted.

4. Background and Context

The history of missions in East Central Europe is, in most cases, still to be written. The Hungarian historic churches involvement in missions has been fully described by Kool (1993). Brachmann (1991) describes some aspects of missions interest in the former East Germany. A University of Utrecht student is researching the ecumenical missions history of Poland, and aspects of Polish Catholic missions have been described (Conner 1980). Beyond this, one searches in vain for snippets of written modern missions history. Although this might indicate that not much has been done, and therefore, not much written, Kool's experience might indicate that more has been done than has been researched.

Background and Context – Country by Country

To understand the results of the study of the selected cases better, it is helpful to understand the general situation regarding cross-cultural missions in ECE. This larger context includes neighboring countries from which no cases were selected, and international missions agencies excluded from the scope of this study.

Campus Crusade for Christ (CCC), Operation Mobilization (OM) and Youth with a Mission (YWAM) are active in most, if not all, of the ECE countries. In some cases, most particularly with CCC, workers from the region have been sent to work longer term in other countries. Hundreds of young people have participated in some kind of short term cross-cultural experience with OM or YWAM. Pioneers-Europe has recently been incorporated in Slovakia, with headquarters in Budapest. It currently has somewhere around twenty-three missionaries, many from Eastern Europe.

A short analysis and comparison of the figures presented by Patrick Johnson (Johnstone 1993; Johnstone and Mandryk 2001) help give an impression of the growth of missions activity in ECE in the past eight years. In some countries, the number of missionaries active in 2001 was slightly higher than in 1993, notably Slovakia and former Yugoslavia. In others, the rise has been dramatic, for example, Albania, Romania and Ukraine. The others have seen a steady rise in missionary activity.

What follows is a brief country by country survey of missions activity, including a table using Johnstone's figures, followed by a description of some of the new missions initiatives. The information was gathered primarily through interviews with people involved with the missions movement in a particular country, or those who have a region-wide interest and expertise in particular aspects of mission outreach.

4. Background and Context

In tables 2-9 below, the growth in missionary activity is made graphic. We compare the figures from the 1993 and 2001 editions of *Operation World*, even when the categories are not identical. The first column lists the number of missionaries and the second the number of agencies (without saying whether they are indigenous or international). The third column lists the number of countries in which missionaries from that country are deployed, and in a few cases where they are concentrated. In this column are also the 1993 figures attempting to determine how many of the missionaries were working cross-culturally or in other countries. The last three columns give information about missionaries working outside their home country, the percentage of the missions force serving cross-culturally, and the number of churches needed to support one missionary.

We need to say something about the definition of missionary. Johnstone has attempted to walk a tightrope between various definitions of missionary. The definitions of who is a missionary differ somewhat by geographic region. The North American usage is the most restricted, that used in Latin American and Europe a bit broader, and the African and Asian usage the broadest. Johnstone and Mandryk discuss their choices in appendix six. "In this book we have sought to synthesize differing perspectives in dividing all missionaries of each country and region into the three categories of foreign, cross-cultural and home/domestic" (Johnstone and Mandryk 2001, 757).[3] The definition of missionary adopted by Johnstone and Mandryk is obviously different from that used in this study, which focuses on the cross-cultural aspect of missionary sending. As will quickly become apparent, the large majority of missionaries listed below work in their own countries, and most of these have no cross-cultural dimension. The column in the tables below showing the percentage of missionaries working cross-culturally bears this out. A single example can demonstrate this. Poland shows 117 missionaries, of which 105 are in Poland. However, Poland is a very homogeneous country with very few cross-cultural opportunities and no significant church planting movement. By this definition, these 105 "missionaries" are working in their home country, but apparently "away from their home area" (Johnstone and Mandryk 2001, 757). These presumably include pastors or student workers working outside their home towns. This tells us very little about interest in missions as defined here.

Albania

Although the first missionaries from the West entered Albania in 1990 when there were only a handful of believers in the entire country, Albanian churches

---

[3] This definition (or lack thereof) is actually a carry over without change from the 1993 edition. It is confusing because the 2001 edition does not use those three categories, but rather, "other country" and "cross-cultural." One gains the impression that the authors themselves struggle to be clear on this point.

have already begun to catch a vision for missions outside the country. (Table 2 shows the growth in missionary activity in the past several years.) They have sent people primarily to Kosovo to work with ethnic Albanians there, but have encountered unexpected cultural differences, making ministry in Kosovo significantly cross-cultural. Difficulties of culture and dialect, clan, economics, and church history all make ministry there a challenge for Albanian Christians.

OM in particular has an ongoing ministry in Kosovo, which includes church planting and running a Bible school for new church leaders. Some Albanians have worked with ethnic Albanians in Macedonia. Others are reported to be interested in ministry to other Islamic countries, including Turkey. Several Albanians have spent time serving on OM ships.

	[a]Missionaries	Agencies	Where	[b]o.c.	[c]% x-c	[d]C:M
[e]OW93	0					
[fg]OW2001 text	50	6				
OW2001 app	66	8		0	4.5	2.4

Table 2. Albanian missionary activity

[a] See (Johnstone and Mandryk 2001, 757) for a discussion of the definition of missionary. Their definition seems to me to not reflect accurately the nature of cross-cultural missions activity in East Central Europe. The figures generated by this definition give a grossly over-exaggerated picture of the true level of attention given to cross-cultural missions.

[b] Refers to the number of missionaries working in other countries

[c] Refers to the percentage of missionaries working cross-culturally

[d] Refers to the ratio of Churches for each Missionary, showing how many churches are needed, in general, to support one missionary.

[e] OW93 refers to Johnstone (1993)

[f] OW2001 refers to Johnstone and Mandryk (2001)

[g] As will become apparent through a comparison of this row with the next row, Johnstone (2001) gives two different sets of numbers. "OW20001 text" refers to the numbers given under the article for the country. "OW2001 app" refers to the numbers given in appendix 4, p.750. No reason is given for the discrepancy of figures.

Bulgaria

Missions is a new idea in Bulgaria. In 1993 there were no known missionaries. Now missions interest is spreading, although still in the early phases (see Ta-

4. Background and Context

ble 3). Missionaries are or have served in Turkey, Macedonia, Ukraine, former USSR, and India. Non-resident evangelists travel to Turkey and Central Asia. People have expressed an interest in China and Muslim areas of India and are preparing to go there. Cross-cultural ministries are active among Turkic peoples in eastern Bulgaria. Most missionaries have been sent by local churches rather than by mission agencies. A few churches have begun to support missionaries in small ways, but most funding comes from outside the country.

	Missionaries	Agencies	Where	o.c.	% x-c	C:M
OW93	0					
OW2001 text	89	6	Bulgaria 77, Turkey 12			
OW2001 app	92	8		13	26.1	19.3

Table 3. Bulgarian missionary activity

One new missions agency has been started to work with Turkish peoples across the Caucasus along the Silk Road, especially Kazakhstan among the Uigars. Currently most ministry is through short term trips of two weeks. About fifteen people were involved between 1996 and 2000. Others in the team came from Turkey, Uzbekistan, and other countries in the region. The board of this agency is composed completely of Bulgarians, half Bulgar, and half Turkic. Most of them are Pentecostal, but others are involved.

Czech Republic and Slovakia

During the darkest days of Communist oppression, a group of pastors and lay people were active in traveling to the Soviet Union to help the wives and families of pastors imprisoned in the Gulag. One man reported that, if he had been caught, he could have been sentenced to death five times because of the amount of money he was carrying, and could have been thrown in prison many other times. Since 1995 a number of missionaries have been involved in either long- or short-term missions (see Table 4). Most have gone through international agencies, some of which have developed Czech branches; OM, Wycliffe Bible Translators, and YWAM are examples. Some of the missionaries have been sent through local churches, and a few small agencies have begun. Missionaries serve or have served in Ukraine, Russia, Central African Republic, Croatia, Mongolia, Tanzania, Morocco, Turkey, SE Asia and Albania. Most missionaries have had major funding from outside the country, but some churches are involved in financial support in small ways.

CR/Slovakia	Missionaries	Agencies	Where	o.c.	% x-c	C:M
OW93	3/0					
OW2001 text	24/7	6/3	10/ Slovakia 6			
OW2001 app	23/16	7/6		9/4	39.1/ 80	56.4/ 57.4

Table 4. Czech and Slovak missionary activity

Hungary

Interest in missions is growing in both historic and evangelical churches in Hungary. Table 5 shows some of this growth. Missionaries have been sent to India, Pakistan, Lebanon, Italy, France, Britain, the Ukraine, Russia, and Croatia. Wycliffe, OM, and Liebenzell have Hungarian branches. The historic churches and other international agencies have also sent Hungarian missionaries.

	Missionaries	Agencies	Where	o.c.	% x-c	C:M
OW93	46	10	[a]7 o.c., 9 x-c, 37 [b]dom			
OW2001 text	122	13	16 (Hungary 99)			
OW2001 app	127	14		25	29.9	24.5

Table 5. Hungarian missionary activity

[a] Johnstone uses different terminology and different categories in the fifth (Johnstone 1993) and sixth (Johnstone and Mandryk 2001) editions. For ease of comparison here, the 1993 categories will be adjusted to match those of 2001.
[b] "dom" (domestic) refers to the number of missionaries working in their home country.

Poland

The Polish Catholic Church has a tradition of sending missionaries. It is estimated that one-third of all Catholic priests in Austria are Polish. Over one thousand Polish Catholics are involved in missions worldwide (Davies 2000). Even during Communist times many Poles served outside the country. Missions is a much newer idea for Protestants. CCC has sent student workers to Russia and Ukraine, and Biblical Missions Association has sent missionaries

4. Background and Context

to a variety of countries. Some local churches have sent a few missionaries, but it is difficult to gather information about them. Table 6 shows how Poles are active in missions.

	Missionaries	Agencies	Where	o.c.	% x-c	C:M
OW93	67	5	6 o.c., 6 x-c, 61 dom. Catholic 1,028 (73 figure)			
OW2001 text	117	11	7 (Poland 105)			
OW2001 app	126	15		14	16.7	9.7

Table 6. Polish missionary activity

Romania and Moldova

Estimates of Romanian missionaries serving cross-culturally vary widely. Guesses range from 12 (DP) to 30 (RT) to 50 (MC, SD). Each person interviewed had his or her own sources of information. Moreover, it is not possible to determine whether some missionaries are counted twice. Definitions come into play here as elsewhere. Regardless, the numbers in Table 7 are significantly lower than those reported by people involved in sending missionaries in Romania. A variety of indigenous agencies have been started, as well as new denominational missions initiatives. Two of these will be considered in detail below. Both Baptists and Pentecostals have missions organizations.

From Moldova come reports of dozens of missionaries who have been sent out, many with little more than a blessing from the church. One church has reportedly sent out twenty-four couples, who are serving across the former Soviet Union. The pastor of a large Baptist church in Chisinau does not know how many have been sent, but says, "Lots". Another respondent says that Moldova seems to be more of a spontaneous missions movement than does Romania.

Rom / Mol	Missionaries	Agencies	Where	o.c.	% x-c	C:M
OW93	9 / na	4	2 o.c., 2 x-c, 7dom			
OW2001 text	115 / 23	15 / 3	6 (Romania 107) / 2 (Russia 12)			

Rom / Mol	Missionaries	Agencies	Where	o.c.	% x-c	C:M
OW2001 app	123 / 25	14 / 4		12 / 12	9.8 / 52	62.8 / 26

Table 7. Romanian and Moldovan missionary activity

Ukraine

Ukraine has by far the largest and most active missionary force. Already by 1993, Ukrainian churches had sent more cross-cultural missionaries than the rest of the ECE countries. They have sent missionaries to Turkey, the former Yugoslavia, Germany, and China, as well as to the former USSR. Many students from different parts of Russia and Central Asia have come to Ukraine to study at theological institutions and have returned to their home areas as church planters and evangelists. It is unknown how many of these are listed in the figures for missionaries in Table 8. Several very large missions agencies have been active. At least one, Light of the Gospel, was founded in 1988, well before the revolutions. Protestant denominations have also sent out a significant number of workers.

	Missionaries	Agencies	Where	o.c.	% x-c	C:M
OW93	330		30 o.c., 34 x-c, 296 dom			
OW2001 text	960	16	10 (Ukraine 530, Russia 359)			
OW2001 app	934	14		377	82	6.4

Table 8. Ukrainian missionary activity

Former Yugoslavia

Very few missionaries have been sent by churches from the former Yugoslavia. For the most part the churches are very small and struggling. The wars of the past ten years have been crippling to the region as a whole, and missionaries from the outside have been sporadic. One new missions agency, Antioch, was founded by the Slovakian Baptist Union in Serbia in February 2001, with the purpose of sending missionaries throughout the region of the former Yugoslavia. Table 9 gives a picture of missionary activity from Yugoslavia.

	Missionaries	Agencies	Where	o.c.	% x-c	C:M
[a]OW93	0					
OW2001 text						
Bosnia/Herz.						
Croatia	20	6	19 in Croatia			
Macedonia	18	1				
Slovenia	3		all in Slovenia			
Yugoslavia	29	8	5			
OW2001 app						
Bosnia/Herz.	1	1		0	0	60
Croatia	19	7		6	41.4	9.3
Macedonia	19	2		6	94.7	3.3
Slovenia	3	1		0	0	23.7
[b]Yugoslavia	31	10		6	38.7	32.6

Table 9. Yugoslavian missionary activity

[a] Only former Yugoslavia is listed.
[b] Yugoslavia consists of Serbia (including Kosovo) and Montenegro

Individual Cases

In the next four chapters we will look at the findings from the individual cases. These will include narrative descriptions of the case, showing origins, historical development and the current situation, as well as an analysis of the themes which arise in each case. The cases are handled more or less in isolation from the others. Despite attempts to keep them separate, however, each case is informed by the preceding cases, making efforts to keep them apart analytically difficult. Following the finding from the four cases, we will offer an analysis of the various factors across the cases.

5. Hungarian Reformed and Lutheran

The first case is a very limited one, but it offers a view into the wider Hungarian missions scene, especially in the historic churches. In 1999 a young couple, Andras and Angelika Jo, was sent by both the Hungarian Reformed and Hungarian Lutheran churches to serve as schoolteachers in an International school in Kodaikanal, India, where they teach religious education, world religions and values.

The Hungarian Lutheran and Reformed churches are "historic" or "mainline" churches, in contrast to the "evangelical" or "free" churches, with which they sometimes have a tense relationship. The Reformed Church of Hungary has around two million members, or about twenty percent of the population of Hungary. Twelve or thirteen percent attend church occasionally. Perhaps half of these are active participants (Kool 2001a).[4] The Lutheran Church is about one-fourth the size of the Reformed Church, and has about 400,000 adherents. (This compares with somewhere less than 100,000 members of free churches.)

Eight interviews were conducted with twelve people. These included members of the Lutheran Missionary Society (LMS), the director of the Lutheran Mission Center (LMC), staff members of the Protestant Institute for Missions Studies (PIMS), a Hungarian Reformed bishop, the missionary couple themselves, other Hungarians within the historic churches who have had missionary experience, and foreign missionaries who live and work in Hungary. In addition, I participated in conferences where a key person in the movement gave reports, which allowed me to gather further information. Few documents specifically relating to the sending of this couple are available, but the Lutheran missions magazine *Misszioi*, reports prepared for conferences, and missionary newsletters were consulted.

Description of the Case

Before we come to the details of the case, we will outline the missions context in Hungary. This includes a brief description of the interest in missions in general, followed by Lutheran and Reformed missions contexts.

---

[4] Cf. *Operation World*, which lists 1.6 million affiliates (Johnstone and Mandryk 2001) and Kool (2002), who quotes a 2001 census which lists 14% Reformed, 3% Lutheran, 52% Roman Catholic and 4% other Christian denominations. Of these, around 200,000 of the 1.2 million Reformed people attend church each week.

5. Hungarian Reformed and Lutheran 57

General Missions Interest

Missions interest in the historic churches is growing. A missions orientation course is offered at the English Department of Gaspar Karoli Reformed University. In the year 2000, a record number of twenty-eight students applied. A number of training events are offered for missions consultants within the Reformed Church. The five theological seminaries and universities in the Hungarian speaking world offered missiological courses with around one hundred students (Kool n.d.). Missionaries with mainline church roots serve or have served with Wycliffe Bible Translators (WBT), Operation Mobilization (OM), Liebenzell, and Neuendettelsau missions in Central Asia, Ecuador, Peru, Spain, Ukraine China, and on the OM ship Doulos (Kool 2001a). A missions day among the Lutherans of western Hungary drew over 400 participants (Kool 2001b). In 2001, thirty-five Reformed seminary students participated in short-term mission projects in Romania and Ukraine, and twenty-four students in the English Department of the Reformed University expressed interest in participating in a short term missions project sometime. A Missions Expo in February 2001 drew 5,000 visitors. This included 2,000 young people who attended a concluding evangelistic concert (Meroff 2001). Thirty-five Hungarian young people (including a 70 year old pastor) traveled by bus to the 2002 TEMA missions conference in Holland, including six students from the Reformed Seminary in Papa. These final two events also included people from free churches.

Lutheran Missions Context

Two missions structures exist in the Lutheran church. Those involved in these two groups have different philosophical positions regarding cross-cultural, especially foreign, missions. They are also divided on generational grounds. These will be described in more depth in the section on ecclesiastical factors below.

The Lutheran Mission Society existed between 1909-1952. Kool has dealt exhaustively with the missions situation up until 1952 (1993). During Communist times, although greatly hampered by the government and the church hierarchy, missions activity did not totally cease to exist. Those who had been trained in the missions school kept their interest in missions, even though they could not personally go as missionaries. Several young women became pastor's wives. These kept in contact with a Swiss missionary in Japan until 1959, when the government broke off the contact. They raised money through embroidery. Because of currency restrictions, they sent the handcrafts to a friend in Switzerland who sold them. After the revolution in 1956, matters became much worse for the church. The word "mission" was not allowed to be used. Any relationships with those outside the country were severely restricted.

However, some people managed to continue to receive news from former Hungarian missionaries and Hungarian mission fields. One of the men received information, translated it, typed ten copies, and passed them in *Samizdat* to another ten people who also made ten copies, and so on. In the 1970s and 1980s things got easier, especially in Budapest. Missions conferences were organized and small groups met regularly to talk about and pray for missions.

In the middle 1980s, after government restrictions began to be eased, a family, the Balints, went for six years to Zimbabwe as technical experts, through the Lutheran World Federation. Their work in Zimbabwe was not necessarily related directly to missions (AMK). It was more of a tent-making ministry, although members of LMS say they were sent as "real missionaries". "So, at that time this couple was not sent officially by the church, but people knew they were committed Christians, and people kept in touch with them" (AMK). After the revolution, their mission agency sent them to serve in Papua New Guinea, helping in infrastructure development, and planning roads and bridges. They were sent by a three way partnership between the Bavarian Lutheran church, the Lutheran church of Papua New Guinea, and the Hungarian Lutheran Church. Although they are Hungarian, they are largely supported from Germany.

Reformed Missions Context

The Reformed church also has a well-developed missions history. The best known Hungarian missionary was Maria Molnar, who was killed by the Japanese in the Admiral Islands in 1943. Many other Reformed missionaries served with other missions organizations. (See Kool 1993 for much more complete information.)

Under the Communists, two couples were sent to Kenya in 1974 with an official agreement between the Reformed Church of Kenya and the Reformed Church in Hungary. One was a theologian and professor in a theological faculty. The other worked as an engineer. Some people looked on them with suspicion, wondering how it was possible in 1974 for someone from Hungary to be officially sent as a missionary. Nevertheless, their sending was an important fact, showing the Hungarian church that they could play a part on the world stage.

Summary of Historical Situation

In spite of what most Hungarian Christians believed at the end of the 1980s, Hungary had a rich tradition of missionary sending prior to Communist times. To some extent this had been forgotten over the decades, and to some extent it had been hidden. Because many of the Hungarian missionaries served with German and other non-Hungarian mission agencies, they were not as visible as they might have been. Revival had played a major role in the growth of missions activity before the Second World War. Kool summarizes:

> Both in the Reformed and Lutheran Churches the revivals of the 1920s, late 1930s and late 1940s were preceded by endeavours (literature, tours,

5. Hungarian Reformed and Lutheran

conferences) to promote the cause of foreign missions. Only in second instance the revivals in their turn contributed to a growth of interest in foreign missions. The sequence was thus: foreign mission interest – revival – more foreign mission interest, etc. This reciprocity of (foreign) mission and revival influenced the Hungarian Protestant churches mainly at grassroots level and could therefore continue even after it was officially banned. (Kool 1993, 891f).

This grassroots level interest continued throughout Communist times as small groups of people met to pray and share missions information with each other.

Immediately after the revolution in 1989 the Reformed Mission Society and the Reformed related missions such as Liebenzell and the Bible League quickly restarted, as did the Lutheran Mission Society.

The Story

Andras and Angelika Jo are a young married couple who teach at an international school in Kodaikanal, India. The husband, Andras, comes from the Hungarian Reformed church, and the wife, Angelika, is a member of the Hungarian Lutheran church. They both studied theology – he at a Reformed seminary and she in a Lutheran seminary. In addition, they studied English at the Reformed University in Budapest. In October 1998, they met an American missionary, David Zomer, who was teaching in the English department of the university. Around the same time they met the Dutch missionary, Anne-Marie Kool, who also taught there. Starting in January 1999, during their final year of university, they participated in a six month long program of missions studies at the Protestant Institute for Missions Studies (PIMS) in Budapest, where both Kool and Zomer taught. There they attended courses and guest lectures and met a wider range of perspectives than they had encountered during their theological studies. Andras says of that experience,

> In the final year we came for half year course at the Institute [PIMS] with other people who didn't go that far right now, who are also preparing for some kind of mission. The Mission Institute is a very good thing. Without it I doubt if anything could have happened from the church itself. The idea is basically coming from the West. (AJ).

The two come from different church traditions. Their personal relationship indicates a wider perspective than many of their friends, because often those from different churches do not have much to do with each other. Before coming to PIMS, both had had various overseas experiences already. Andras said, "At PIMS we met people from States, England, Scotland. We both spent time in Scotland, she spent time in the States. We have a more international perspective than most of the other people have here" (AJ).

The Jos observed the personal examples of Kool and Zomer and saw them as positive models and as people who served the Hungarian church. These Westerners opened their eyes to broader possibilities, and encouraged them to consider missions involvement for themselves. Angelika noted, "We didn't have information about missionaries, we didn't read novels about missionaries, we didn't hear about missionaries, they were the first examples we encountered" (AJ).

Their decision to become missionaries was part of a process. He says,

> The whole idea of mission, how we came to this, is very interesting. Through a series of preplanned events from above, education, marriage, both of us became interested. None of us were the type who wants to be missionary from childhood. Anne-Marie [Kool] remembers how I said, 'I never want go abroad, my place is here, I want to teach here'.

Angelika agrees. "My best friend wanted to be a missionary, and I always just looked at her. She's just dreaming; he wanted to be stewardess, she a missionary." Andras continues,

> We never had a romantic idea. We had this type of teachers, right time, these two majors, the two of us, we met, we worked in the church. We met other people. Our vision was formed quickly, in one to two years. Very suddenly. We were open.

Once they made a decision to pursue missions, their attention turned to India. They considered further missions studies in a school there, but then they were challenged to begin working, not just studying. Zomer made the contact with the school in Kodaikanal and with sponsors from the United States. In the summer of 1999 they flew to India to begin their service there.

Although they are married, their respective churches treat them as individuals, not as a couple. In essence, they are two missionaries, sent by two different church bodies, who only coincidentally are married. The situation is unique because these two historic churches, which typically have very little to do with each other, agreed to cooperate in sending the couple to India. The Lutheran missions pastor says, "It's good that Reformed and Lutheran work together. This is not self-evident. We live separated from each other, that's a historical issue. Especially in mission is it good that we cooperate" (PG). Two other partners were also involved. The Reformed Church of America paid for plane tickets. The Church of South India was the sponsoring partner in India. After the first year, the school in India took full responsibility for their salary. The Jos initially went for a one year term. This was then extended by at least two more years.

5. Hungarian Reformed and Lutheran

Themes and Factors

The Jo family was sent out within a specific social, cultural and spiritual context. These three aspects will be examined to see what the most important factors and themes were which gave rise to this specific case.

Spiritual Factors

The question here is to what extent this missionary activity is due to a special work of God. Is it the result of revival or spiritual life in the churches or is the spiritual condition of the church unimportant? In particular, how do respondents understand God to be working? This question takes seriously both the reality of the spiritual world, and the perceptions of the participants themselves.

The responses fell into three main areas: 1) Hungary experienced a revival fifty years ago and the results can still be seen in some ways, 2) the spiritual life of the historic churches is minimal, and revival must come before anything significant will happen in relation to missions, and 3) the general condition of the churches is rather lifeless, but there are encouraging signs to be seen, indications that God is beginning to work in people's lives. Finally, the question of call to missions will be discussed.

Revival of Pre- and Post-War Years

A great revival took place in Hungary in the early part of the 1940s and the years following WWII. In the 1930s, a small group of people began to pray for revival. Kool describes the Lutheran situation before the war.

> Despite that need [for a full time worker] and despite the presence of a nationalistic spirit within the Lutheran Church, especially among the church authorities, the upcoming revival caused a significant increase in foreign mission interest in the late 1930s and early 1940s, especially at the grassroots level. It was not anymore a cause of the German speaking Hungarian Lutheran Churches only, but had also gained the interest of the Hungarian speaking ones. (Kool 1993, 659).

The revival came before and during the war, in a very difficult situation. Some of the older respondents see the revival as a preparation for the war, and maybe for Communist times as well. "The religious awakening in Hungary in Reformed and Lutheran church before the war might have been preparation for the war. God prepared people for the wartime" (IR). This revival led to a large interest in missions, including the founding of a Lutheran mission school in 1948. Between 1948 and 1952 the missions school trained several people who desired to be sent into foreign missions. Kool observes:

Now, with 'grateful wonder' could be observed, that what is shown in the history of revivals is also becoming true in Hungary. The Hungarian revival was in growing measure accompanied by an interest for foreign mission ... the significant number of missionary candidates, the growing number of participants in foreign mission conferences (in 1950 more than a hundred!) as well as the increase in offering for mission purposes show, that the observation that the revival 'as if revival just began to produce its fruit in this respect' was very true! (Kool 1993, 879f).

Similar interest occurred in the Reformed church. The Dutch missiologist Hoekenkijk visited Hungary and "sensed a great upcoming revival in the Hungarian Reformed congregations for the foreign mission cause." He said, "One of my most surprising experiences during my visits to Hungary was that I found a warm interest toward mission everywhere" (Kool 1993, 778).

One Lutheran pastor interviewed says he can still see evidence of revival in his church among older people. He said:

As far as I understand the Hungarian revival history, in the 30s a small group had for years prayed for revival. Then the revival came unexpectedly, in a difficult situation, the second world war. In my old church we can still feel the traces of the revival among the older people. But it can't be simply passed on. (PG).

Those who had experienced this revival first hand as young people were the ones who restarted the missions societies immediately after the revolution.

Current Status of Churches

Despite the residual effects of the revival among the old people in the churches, most respondents felt the church situation now is very different from that of the days following the war. To the question of what it would take for a missions movement to emerge, one respondent answered laughingly, "A miracle" (DZ). The respondents are generally pessimistic because the churches show few signs of spiritual vitality.

One Reformed Bishop reports, "90% of Hungarian society say church members do not have a living faith" (BB). When asked about revival he replies, "Revival? Very difficult to say. In the last ten years, more than one hundred new church buildings have been built, but only five or six new congregations. We have survival strategies" (BB). He feels there is no revival, but there is a good atmosphere. "People have a feeling of trust in the church. People have a very strong relation to the church" (BB).

Tomka (1997) agrees that people did have a positive view of the church after the revolution. The historic churches were "models of social reconstruction and representatives of cultural heritage (Tomka 1997, 214). However, he feels the churches squandered their moral capital by focusing on their own needs.

> They put great emphasis on their own institutions and requested financial support from the state for this. The restitution of church property, nationalised at the beginnings of Communism had been decided in one of the last acts of the Communist parliament. Each building became, however, a source of conflict with the present users. In the resulting quarrels, churches lost much of the credit they had won in previous years. (Tomka 1997, 216).

This view is confirmed by a Lutheran pastor who sees a great need for revival. "Our pastors and churches are sleeping churches" (PG). A few small missions circles exist in churches, but probably in not more than ten churches in the whole country. The biggest problem is a "financial weakness, tied to an overall weakness. If our churches would experience revival, then would come a financial responsibility" (PG). The problem is that with the political freedom no revival has come. People had a false expectation that when the Russians marched out and the churches became free, people would come back to the church and the churches would be full.

> People are secularized, indifferent, want to reach a western standard of living. Earlier it was an ideological atheism; now it's a practical atheism. Lots of people are chasing money. In the churches are a lot of active people, but many feel that if they attend church an hour a week they've fulfilled their obligation to God. (PG)

Signs of Life

While the churches are often seen as sleeping, nevertheless they exist, and in some places spiritual vitality is evident. A pastor comments:

> You can't force revival. We were too naïve at the beginning. We thought we could do everything. Sometimes we were too active instead of first praying. In these ten years we've had to learn that we have to trust God, we can't cause revival ourselves. We have to wait on a gift from God. (PG)

Anne-Marie Kool's regular newsletter is called *Signs of Life in Hungary*. It is a conscious attempt to look for positive aspects of the life of the historic churches. Kool acknowledges that many people feel the churches are dead and people are fighting, but recognizes another, more positive, development.

> I do see among young pastors a genuine desire for renewal. We have been organizing conferences for theological students for ten years now, at sixty, seventy students per year were participating. And among these students, now young pastors, I see a genuine sense of renewal going on. It's

not really coordinated. But I am quite often traveling through the countryside, and I am surprised all the time by discovering signs of life, about which I'm trying to report in my prayer letters. (AMK)

A Reformed pastor compares the situation in Hungary with that in the Czech Republic. He says, "Seventy-five percent of Czechs are either neutral or agnostic,[5] but in Hungary only 886 Hungarians declare themselves atheist. Eighty-three percent are religious of some kind. What is needed is not revival but renewal" (DS).

The Jos describe what they see as a positive movement of God among their generation, or at least within certain sectors of it. The missions prayer group at seminary flourished, even when general prayer groups struggled. They speak of personal revival and revival in their church youth group, although they acknowledge that "revival" is perhaps too strong a word. It is not something widespread, but rather occurring in a few churches in big cities where one or two people each year go to seminary or into mission work. Andras Jo says:

> In our churches there's still strong youth program. Good congregation, good local church. Priority, youth pastor talking about mission, not foreign mission, mission in general, you are salt of earth. That was every Monday the message. Always something to think about. Interesting. Never thought about it as revival. As you say, can be considered revival for us and friends. (AJ).

This spiritual life still does not generate an interest in foreign missions, but rather a general desire to serve.

Call to Missions

A question related to spiritual life is that of calling. Does God call through specific actions in a person's life or through a combination of circumstances? One member of the LMS called foreign missions the "product of a vacant soul. Not a matter of rationalistic decision, whether to serve in the country or outside." Quoting a verse from the Bible, she said, "I sent you towards pagans" (IB).

Because the numbers of missionaries involved here is so small, it is impossible to draw general conclusions as to whether this understanding of call is widespread, or whether "call" is a useful concept. The Jos speak of a gradual recognition that God could use them overseas. Andras Jo recalls never wanting to be a missionary, feeling that his place was in Hungary as a teacher or minister. They now see their time in India as a use of talents. Angelika Jo says, "We got an opportunity, wanted to use it, but it's not the only opportunity, and the only

---

[5] (Cf. Barnes (1998), which says 80%).

thing we should do with lives." Her husband responds, "It's not like committed missionaries, whose only calling is to stay there for life." On the other hand, Anne-Marie Kool, talking about them, says that they "really had a sense of clear calling when they went there" (AMK). The Lord had changed Andras' mind from only wanting to work in Hungary to being willing to go to India. "It's quite a miracle" (AMK).

In another case, a Reformed pastor who spent a couple of years in missions in South America with another missions agency and now works in Spain, spoke of her "call" to missions. "I really liked the work (of being a pastor), but I always knew that I would go into missions one day. I don't understand it myself, but God planted it in me and I simply couldn't get away from it" (IrBu).

In general, the extent to which we see evidence of spiritual life depends at least in part on our attitude. Two people can look at the same situation: one sees nothing to celebrate (dead churches); the other sees reasons to be optimistic (signs of life). Perhaps this is also related to expectations. If one expects vitality or revival and does not find it much, disappointment is the result. If one expects to find nothing and nevertheless sees even small movements of the Spirit, then one can be hopeful.

Summary

Revival had a major influence on the rise of missions interest following WWII. However, little evidence exists that revival influences interest in missions today. Rather, a lack of true spiritual life and interest seems to characterize the historic churches, with exceptions. The lament is heard regularly that the churches are spiritually dead, and filled, or rather, not filled, with people who are basically Sunday Christians. The churches are more concerned with repairing their dilapidated buildings than they are with ministry in the world, whether at home or abroad. Where there is interest in serving God, that interest can be channeled towards cross-cultural efforts. The people who are concerned about mission are rather hopeful that mission will instead influence spiritual life at home.

Social Factors

Social factors include the sub-systems of economics, politics, ecclesiastical structures, and networks. Included here as well is the impact of key individuals acting within the social system.

Key People

Five people can be singled out as being influential in developing missions interest. Three are expatriates, one is a Hungarian emigrant, and one a Reformed pastor.

Without question, the most influential person in promoting cross-cultural mission awareness and involvement in Hungary, at least in historic church circles, has been the Dutch Reformed missionary Anne-Marie Kool. Kool first came to Hungary in the 1980s as a staff member with the International Fellowship of Evangelical Students (IFES) to work with the Hungarian Student Movement. To get a visa, she came as a student herself, to do doctoral research on Hungarian Reformed missions history. People she talked to told her there was not enough material to write a dissertation, and that, to find enough information, she should study both Reformed and Lutheran missions history. Her research uncovered far more than anyone expected, resulting in a dissertation of over a thousand pages (Kool 1993). Respondents, almost without exception, referred to her book as the thing that got them thinking about missions. Her research showed that Hungarians had been much more active in missions than anyone knew, having been involved in missions sending at one level or another for two hundred years until the Communists ended significant missions activity. This discovery has encouraged Hungarians to see that what they once did, they could do again.

A second area where Anne-Marie Kool has been influential has been through the establishment of the Protestant Institute for Missions Studies (PIMS). This Institute, an official program of the churches, offers a variety of courses related to missions. It also sponsors various consultations dealing with topics such as urban ministries and ministry among Gypsies. Formed at the suggestion of a Reformed seminary professor, and in consultations between Hungarian church and mission leaders, and leaders of the Reformed Missions League from Holland, PIMS has become recognized as *the* center of missions life among the mainline churches in Hungary, and, to a certain extent, among free churches as well. Kool has also become a professor in some of the Hungarian state universities, where she has been able to bring an evangelical perspective into institutions which are theologically more liberal.

The third area of Kool's influence has been through her ability to network people. For example, when Wycliffe Bible Translators (WBT) wanted to start work in Hungary, Dutch Wycliffe workers came to Kool for help. She put them in touch with many of the most important people in the churches, including missions professors, key pastors and sympathetic bishops.

Janos Bütösi is credited as being one of the most influential people in reviving missions vision in Hungary. As a young pastor and "a great evangelist" (BB), he was active in the revival during and following the Second World War. In 1948, he was sent to Western Europe to study revivals, in order to help keep the Hungarian revival on track, but he was not allowed to return to Hungary, so he moved to the United States. He finished his doctorate and became a Hungarian Reformed bishop. In 1990, one of the bishops invited him back to Hungary to teach missions in the Reformed Seminary in Debrecen. There he reestablished the chair for mission and ecumenical studies. According to

5. Hungarian Reformed and Lutheran   67

Bishop Bölsckei, "his main task and main point was mission, mission, mission." He served as one of Kool's mentors on her doctoral thesis, and was the founding board chair of PIMS.

Bütösi energized and encouraged young people both to study missions and to consider missions for themselves. He promoted missions study and research, but always emphasized that missions was the task of the church. He was a "good theologian" (BB), who was influenced by the missiology of David Bosch's book, *Transforming Missions* (Bosch 1991). He could communicate at a high academic level with church and theological leaders. As a teacher in Debrecen, he had the opportunity to touch a whole generation of young Reformed pastors. Further, since he was the board chair of PIMS, church leaders had to take the Institute seriously.

At the same time, Bütösi was able to communicate well with the members of the older generation, because he had been involved with them during the revival. He was a bridge builder–between old and young, and between the official church leadership and the members of the old and newly restarted mission agencies. Kool says, "The future will prove how big his influence has been in Hungary, in preparing Hungarian missionaries, and Hungarian churches, to take up their responsibility as a sending agency or a sending church" (AMK). Another calls him a "very important key person" (BB).

A missionary with the Reformed Church of America, and an English teacher at the Reformed University in Budapest, David Zomer taught the Jos and was a networker between American and Hungarian churches. When the Jos were considering further missions study in India, he urged practical work instead of more study, and arranged the connections between them, the RCA and the school in India. He has led several short-term experiences for students from the university and seminaries, primarily to Romania.

In 1990 a couple with Wycliffe Bible Translators from Holland began traveling into Hungary, returning every year, before moving there for a year in 1996. They met with Kool, who introduced them to many church leaders and professors. They met Janos Bütösi and Daniel Szabo (see below), among others, and moved them in the direction of missions. By their own account, they were very influential. The wife says, "We were the ones who got people interested in missions. We met Bütösi. He said 'Oh, we can't miss out on this. We can't!' We got the groups talking together and they said, 'We need to do missions ourselves!'" Kool also mentioned this couple, but a bit less enthusiastically. Her comment was, "but I observed that they have not really yet been able to make inroads into the churches. I mean, they have been visiting church leaders, they have some church leaders on their board, but they do not have a kind of historical background which we sense here [in the mission institute]."

Of the Reformed pastor Daniel Szabo, Kool said, "If there is something good going on within the Reformed church, then Szabo Daniel is probably involved in it" (AMK). He serves as board chair of Wycliffe, is on the board of PIMS, and is President of the Hungarian Evangelical Alliance. He is an influential pastor at many levels. He was also a member of a delegation sent by the Hungarian government to Moscow to negotiate the return of treasures taken from Hungary to the USSR. While not directly involved with the Jos, he is important in promoting missions interest in a wide circle.

The data suggest that without extensive agitation on the part of either foreign missionaries working in Hungary, or Hungarians who had lived for long periods of time outside the country, little would have happened regarding crosscultural missions in the historic churches of Hungary. Of the key individuals identified, only one is a Hungarian who remained in Hungary for the entire Communist era. Even he traveled extensively outside of Hungary, and had contact with outside people within Hungary. The influence of key people is a strong factor in the rising interest and development of missions vision and involvement, and in this case, the key people come from outside the normal church authority structure.

Economics

Everyone interviewed says economics is a big problem, maybe the biggest hindrance to Hungarian churches sending more missionaries. Many people say it will be impossible for Hungarians to be sent out by Hungarian churches alone. They are able to contribute in a small way, but for the near future will not be able to support missionaries without Western partnerships. Most churches are worried about meeting their own financial needs. It is difficult to pay pastors, and many church buildings need to be renovated. Church members have not developed a habit of regular giving. However, when an immediate need is presented, they often give.

To the question of whether lack of financial giving is a true economic problem or a lack of vision, the typical answer was "Both".

Most people acknowledge a true financial difficulty. This is shown by the fact that the Jos needed outside partners to go to India. The Reformed and Lutheran churches supported the Jos with the equivalent of one teacher's salary each, plus health insurance and pensions. "This showed that the two biggest Hungarian Protestant churches weren't able to send missionaries without American help. Financial difficulty is true difficulty" (PG). Hungarian salaries are twenty to thirty percent of an Austrian's,[6] for example, so people do not

---

[6] A respondent used this comparison, knowing I lived in Austria. This would correspond roughly to 15-20% of a typical American income.

have much of discretionary money. Although inflation is no longer a big issue, living expenses consume most of income.

At the same time, a lack of vision is commonly cited as a cause for the economic weakness of the Hungarian churches, particularly regarding missions. Hungarians are not used to giving regularly. Although the economy is growing and many people are better off than they were under Communism, life is still not easy. In addition, materialism has become a major factor. Many people are now building their own homes, which demand financial resources larger than most Hungarians possess.

A Lutheran pastor says one of the biggest problems is that the Church is ninety percent supported by the state. Because the current government is positive towards the church this is not a large problem. However, if a government comes to power which is not so inclined, the churches will be forced to give up some of their projects.

Over the years the Lutherans have been involved in a few projects. For example, for a few years during the 1990s, they supported a Finnish woman in Marseilles who worked with Arab children. Each year they sent around Ft50,000 (approximately $200). They were able to raise around $500 to buy Bibles for Papua New Guinea. These projects gave them the feeling that they were partners in missions. At the same time, their missionaries in Papua New Guinea are supported almost totally from Germany. The missions pastor reports:

> Some churches give a small bit, I don't want to say nothing. I'll give a small example. I visited thirty churches with the Balints. We raised enough for his flight tickets, not more. That was a big enough sum (3000 DM), but still not much. Nothing for the work. This shows how weak we are in financial readiness, that thirty churches could only raise enough for the flight. Not more. (PG).

His point is not that the churches could not give more, but that they were not ready to give more. He perceives financial weakness as a symptom of an overall weakness. "If our churches would experience revival, then would come a financial responsibility" (PG). He spoke repeatedly of "sleeping churches" who do not take financial responsibility, but who could give a lot more if they were properly motivated.

> Our churches could afford a lot more. When we have a specific goal, example for flood problems, then we gather and give a lot. They see a big need and they give a lot. We need to motivate them, give them information, what is important, what can we gain, when we have missionaries overseas. It's a two-way street, not only we give, but we also receive, spiritual treasure. (PG).

His conclusion is that financial resources are available if people catch a vision.

Nevertheless, a realistic view needs to be taken about what Hungarian churches can manage. It is a lot easier for them to send missionaries to neighboring countries than to parts of the world which are further away and more costly. Andras Jo comments:

> But there is more scope for missions within the neighborhood. Ukraine, Albania, Balkans, Romania. So much need and so much need for partnership and help from us. Maybe more opportunity in that direction. I'm sure the church would appreciate anything that doesn't cost too much money. (AJ).

As noted above, Hungarians often give generously when they see a concrete need, particularly as it affects other Hungarians. When floods struck the Ukraine, affecting Hungarians there in particular, the people responded generously. The general consensus of respondents is that this willingness to help needs to be encouraged, that people need to be educated, to be taught how to give, and to see that if they give in small regular amounts much could be accomplished.

Political

The revolution of 1989 forms the natural background to all that is discussed here. Without the revolution, foreign missions activity, at least on the scale which is now developing, probably would not have been possible. Newly won freedoms – to gather, to engage in large scale Christian activity outside church buildings, to travel, and to publish Christian literature – have opened the door for many new initiatives. However, the effects have been different on different groups.

For the older generation, those who have very clear memories of the oppression and persecution experienced in the 1950s and 1960s, the freedoms are almost inconceivable. For the younger people, including the missionaries themselves, life before the revolution is ancient history. They were young teenagers when the revolution came, and they came of age in the new era. Their education is largely Christian, which was not possible before the changes. For them, the changes are simply part of everyday life, and the freedom they enjoy is a matter of course. They have taken advantage of the freedom to travel, having spent extensive time in Scotland and the United States, as well as India.

Ecclesiastical

The question here is whether the structures and politics of the churches themselves are a contributing factor in the rise of interest in missions. While these issues arise very often in conversation with the respondents, the discussions

5. Hungarian Reformed and Lutheran

usually focus on problems and difficulties, rather than positive influences. Three problems are mentioned frequently: a lack of vision, the lack of appropriate missions-related structures, and the lack of leadership.

The first problem mentioned by participants concerns a lack of vision. One missions leader says:

> Our biggest problem is with the pastors. They are over-worked, don't want to hear anything about missions. Mission seems for many pastors to be unimportant. They say, that's for the Scandinavians, the Germans, for Americans. They have a lot of money. We have too few pastors. (PG).

The missionaries themselves see the same problem.

> Another group in both of our churches who don't care. This is related to setup of churches. Doesn't change too fast. Everything is done by the pastors ... pastors do everything, especially in countryside. The minister has all the power, decides everything. ... The pastor has the power to point, this girl was confirmed here and now she's in India. (AJ).

A common ministry philosophy, which is reportedly taught in some of the seminaries, is that the pastor does everything. Says the husband, "the revolution of the church still needs to come ... same old sleepy institution, providing marriage and burial services."

The pace of change in the churches is seen as a big problem. "Things change quickly in Hungary, why not this? But the church is slow, it's a big sleeping elephant which needs to be wakened up" (AJ). People who have not grasped the vision and church bureaucracies which delay even the simplest procedures lead to lack of activity.

The second problem has to do with a lack of appropriate structures. The complaint of the lack of mission structures seems at first glance to be misplaced. Both the Lutherans and the Reformed have official structures which have responsibility for missions. However, the presence of *official* structures does not necessarily mean *effective* structures for missionary sending and care.

Immediately after the Revolution, in 1990, the Lutheran Missionary Society (LMS) was reconstituted. This existed in the years following WWII, but was closed by the Communists in 1952. During the Communist years, although it was not officially permitted, members had continued to promote interest in missions, contributing money where possible and encouraging prayer for missions. They had published *Samizdat* documents, sharing information regarding the world missions situation and giving items for prayer. Small groups met regularly to pray for foreign missions.

Most of the members of the LMS still have memories of the old, pre-Communist days. The average age of these members is over seventy. Their philosophy is that missions is what one does in foreign countries, and primarily focuses on church planting and evangelism, although helping the poor is very important. Some of them are concerned that the Jos are not doing real missions work because they are teachers. After the Jos arrived in India, those involved with the LMS wanted to know where they could send money and Bibles, and encouraged the Jos to become involved in social projects, like distributing medicine and food to the poor and visiting orphanages. "They wanted addresses where they could send bibles, clothes, money. But we are staying in the school" (AJ). The Jos, however, feel that the group is beginning to understand the difference.

The members of the LMS recognize that they are old, and feel that they have lost influence. The young people do not listen to them, and they do not know how to communicate with a younger generation. The current secretary of LMS speaks of a

> younger generation who are not very active. People of my generation are involved. Never start where you finished. People tried to carry on where it was finished. In terms of world mission, this may be why younger people are not ready to respond. Need for a new start. Tradition has been a positive thing, but can also be a hindrance. Had it been not the other generation who started this society, but if it had stemmed from youth movement it would have reached younger generation. Since started by retired people, unable to reach younger people and activate them. (AB).

The Lutheran Mission Center (LMC), in contrast to the LMS, involves a younger generation. A Lutheran pastor, Peter Gancs, is the director. Its focus is more local. Although the LMC sees the need for a cross-cultural involvement, this occurs primarily in Hungary or countries nearby. The center publishes a monthly mission magazine and is involved in radio outreach. The magazine includes articles about foreign missions, including reports about the Jo and Balint families.

The LMS and LMC together sponsor five missions conferences for children each year during the summer where children ages ten through fourteen learn about missions first hand. Each issue of the magazine *Misszioi* has something for children as well. Both groups see the need to reach the youngest generation if missions interest is going to take hold in the churches in the coming years.

The Reformed situation is even less clear than the Lutheran. The Reformed Missions Department is viewed with great suspicion by most people. Under the Communists it was the department of the church the government used to control what was happening in the churches. Even though it no longer has this function, the effects of the past are not easy to throw off. In addition, because of its institutional history, a pro-clergy bias exists. The missions director at the time the Jos were sent off is reported to have said, "We can't send him (Jo Andras); he's not a minister." Apparently they were sent over his objections. Nevertheless, he still claims, "We'll never send another non-minister" (DZ). A new, younger director of the missions department has been appointed, who seems to have more of an international viewpoint and is not so established in the bureaucracy. Exactly how things will develop is not yet clear.

The missions department of the Reformed Church at this point concentrates almost exclusively on matters within Hungary. It sponsors drug rehabilitation programs, a handicapped children's center and Reformed schools. It sees the schools as their way to reach the society. "One pastor says, 'we have 20,000 young Reformed students in our high schools. They are an army'" (AJ). Others contend that just because the schools are Reformed, that does not mean that the students are Reformed, or even Christian. In fact, one of the bishops does not agree that mission is enhanced through the new or reopened religious schools. "Some say mission is through the new or reopened religious schools. I don't agree. Can we see that as preparation? Maybe, but not missions" (BB).

No official missions body exists in the Reformed Church which focuses on cross-cultural missions. Some people have been agitating for two or three years for the Reformed church to develop its own sending structure, and the prospects of it coming into existence seem to be good. The process is slow. The bishop sees the need for a sending agency in the church, but nothing has yet developed. As things currently stand, if someone wants to be sent as a missionary, he or she needs a recommendation from the missions department to the General Assembly, which has the responsibility to fund the missionary. However, the missionary would probably relate primarily to his or her local church as the main sending body.

The question was posed, "what would a potential missionary have to do in order to get sent?" The answer is that nobody knows. Many different ideas were given, but none demonstrated clarity of policy or procedure. Some informants said they would need to develop a contact with a foreign agency, either German or Finnish or maybe Swedish.

> We don't have real means, either financial or personal, means to help these people appropriately. Contacts with Bavarian church, through which an appropriate person could be sent, like Balints. Other contact is Finnish (FELM). We could send people first to mission school and then to mission field. If someone is trained, has some missionary training, in principle, because we don't have such people except the Balints. It they speak language of the target country, he or she could be sent right away through Finnish mission. (AB).

A colleague within the same church agrees. "It's possible, but only with foreign sponsors. We might be able to find a partner, with Finnish and Bavarian.

I can imagine that we could write a contract with them. I doubt if we could do it alone." (PG).

Another said the churches needed to send potential candidates to PIMS to see what could be done. Kool says, "But they have no experience, so they need to be encouraged. Well, this is, it is for them very easy to defer to us, oh, they think, she is Dutch, and he is American, they will do it." (AMK).

Angelika Jo feared that, although they themselves had been sent out jointly, and another family by the Lutherans, a new candidate would need to start out almost at the beginning again. She says:

> I wonder if they would need to restart over again. Don't have mission budget, nothing like that, no framework, no organization, no institution set up. Without it it's very difficult to say they could go anywhere. (AJ).

Some hope that in the near future the kinds of sending structures will be able to be developed which will allow the question to be easily answered, with clear steps for appointment, employment and financial backing.

Although there is no official sending structure in the Reformed Church, other acceptable mission agencies exist which the Reformed Church can use. For example, Liebenzell also reestablished in 1990/1, and functions primarily within the historic church environment. Several missionaries have been sent through them. Foreign contacts also provide opportunities for Hungarians to serve, particularly through German and Finnish agencies.

The question of who is actually responsible for the Jo family, or more precisely stated, for Angelika Jo, is a complicated one. The LMS certainly sees her as their missionary, although she understands this less clearly. The church where she grew up does not recognize her as one of their missionaries. She says:

> My family belongs to Lutheran church, but one branch of family is Baptist. Those cousins are more enthusiastic about me than my closest relatives in the Lutheran church. And the Baptists invited me, and I'm scared of a conflict, that I may go the Baptists church with our slide show, but not Lutheran. But how can I go if they don't invite? (AJ).

Some people in the churches and the missions societies want to help, but they have no experience in caring for missionaries, and little practical knowledge of the world situation. For example, the Lutheran church had no procedure whereby Angelika Jo could be employed as a missionary. This made the issues of insurance and pension complicated and uncertain. The Reformed, on the other hand, even though they had no sending structure, found it easy to employ Andras Jo as a missionary.

In general the churches seem to look to PIMS to give supervision and help them. At PIMS they see experienced missionaries, people with outside contacts, and a paid staff, and feel that the PIMS people are more qualified and capable to take care of the sending details. Zomer did the most to get the Jo's prayer letters distributed, although the LMS helped, and their letters were occasionally printed in the Lutheran missions magazine *Misszioi*. He also handled their schedule when they came back to Hungary for a few weeks after their first year in India. A difference of opinion between Kool and Zomer was apparent here. Kool wanted to encourage the Hungarians to learn to handle these things themselves, while Zomer saw the need and simply did a lot himself. However, to be fair, he is also very concerned about helping the Hungarians to learn how do things for themselves and to take ownership for their own missionaries. He asks:

> how do you get the local churches involved? He who pays owns, that's money really from the safe to the church to the missionary. How do the Hungarians see this structure, this mission committee sending body, so that there's ownership? (DZ).

The third problem reported is a lack of leadership. I requested an interview with the Lutheran bishop, but could not get an appointment. This seems not to be unusual. For a year the Jos had the problem that he did not answer letters, phone calls or faxes. He is an older, more conservative leader. Members of LMS feel that church leadership is open to missions, but it just has not been worked out very well. "We don't have real means, either financial or personal, means to help these people appropriately." In some ways a carry over from the Communist days still exists. Under Communism it was often the church leadership which was the most restrictive. After the revolution in 1956, "the word 'mission' not allowed to be pronounced. The Bishop didn't allow word to be uttered" (AB). It is certainly a change that the church leadership is open, at least in principle, to missions. Kool speaks of a new Lutheran bishop who is very missions minded. He invited her to speak at a pastors conference. "New missions strategies are being developed. Enthusiasm and commitments are there, although not yet missionary minded congregations." (AMK).

The Reformed bishop is different. He is younger, and good friends with the pastor of Andras Jo's church. The personal relationship seems to open doors. He has been influenced by Kool and her book (Kool 1993). He has responded positively to her suggestions that a mission agency be formed in the Reformed church, although nothing has yet been done. Here the issue is less that people are not interested as that the leadership has failed to set up the appropriate structures.

Networks

Examination of the various networks involved in this cooperative effort of sending a missionary family is very instructive in showing how complicated the task of sending missionaries can be. Andras and Angelika Jo, being themselves ecumenical, and having been sent out as part of a four-way partnership, sit in the middle of several national and international networks.

One network in which they participate is the Reformed Church worldwide. Andras Jo is a member of the Hungarian Reformed church, which belongs to the world-wide body of Reformed churches, and has as well relationships with a variety of missions organizations, such as Liebenzell in Hungary and Neuendettelsau Mission in Germany, through whom some Hungarian Reformed missionaries serve.

David Zomer, an American missionary to Hungary with the Reformed Church of America (RCA), teaches at the university where both Andras and Angelika studied. He also offered seminars through PIMS as well. He created the contacts between the Jos and the RCA, who paid for their plane tickets to and from India. The RCA helped start the school in Kodaikanal 150 years ago, where the Jos now teach.

Anne-Marie Kool is a missionary with the Reformed Missionary League (RML) in the Netherlands Reformed Church. She was the Jos teacher at PIMS and influential in all aspects of coordinating communication between the churches.

A second network is the Lutheran Church worldwide. Angelika Jo is a member of the much smaller Lutheran church in Hungary, but which also has worldwide ties. Particularly through the LMS, the Lutherans have cooperated with missions agencies in Germany and Finland, supporting missionaries serving in France, Zimbabwe and Papua New Guinea.

A third network is PIMS. PIMS was founded by the Reformed and Lutheran Churches of Hungary and the Gaspar Karoli Reformed University, and thus has official ties with both church and recognized Hungarian universities. PIMS is a body which brings different networks together.

A fourth partner is the Church of South India. This is the sponsoring church for the school where the Jos teach. Itself an ecumenical body, it participates in many networks throughout India and the world. The school is the meeting point between churches in Hungary and India, and between Christian and non-Christian worlds. Although at one time a school for missionary kids, it now has mostly students from non-Christian families.

Cultural Factors

Five specific cultural factors will be explored here. These are 1) the biblical and theological understanding of missions and whether this has changed since 1989, 2) the extent to which there was mission vision before the revolution, 3) the effect of education, particularly theological education, 4) openness to others and ethnocentrism, and 5) contact with Western missionaries. When asking the question of culture change, it is well to remember that deep culture change takes time, sometimes a generation or more. Therefore, we can not expect changes at the level of attitudes, values and worldview in only ten years.

Biblical and Theological Understandings

How people understand the theological and biblical basis for missions affects their practice. Three main questions will be examined. The first concerns the nature of mission. This question is both theological and strategic. Theologically, two basic views were found; one which reflects the years of Communist control, the other which attempts to take biblical and theological foundations seriously. The strategic question is how should mission be done, where, and with whom? The second main question is also a theological one, which deals with the legitimacy of requiring conversion. The third main question is, to what extent has people's understanding of mission changed since the revolution?

First, what is mission? How do people understand their church's missions responsibility now and how has it changed since 1989? Here again, we can discern several streams. For some, the missions challenge and understanding remains the same as always. For others, the vision for missions has come since the revolution. Most people interviewed see the need for an increased understanding of the biblical mandate for missions within the church.

Naturally the coming of political and religious freedom does not automatically bring with it a change in mentality and worldview. It takes time for these things to change. So clearly the effects of fifty years of Communism can be seen in the holdover of old patterns of thinking about mission. The restrictions which were placed on any kind of missions activity, whether within the country or cross-culturally make it difficult now to think about reaching beyond the church walls. The Communist era paradigm of mission as almost equal to all regular church activities did not really have an outward component. Reports the Lutheran missions pastor:

> We went through difficult decades. Forty years of dictatorship. "Mission" was almost a forbidden word. I studied theology in Budapest, and in five years study I never learned missiology or missions history. The official ideology said, "The church will die out step by step. You can do something in the church, worship services, but outside the church you can't do anything." (PG).

The effects of this attitude persists among some people.

Another group of people has given new consideration to what a biblical theology of mission might mean. Despite the repression of the Communist years, where "mission" was a forbidden word, these people recognize that the church exists, not just for itself, but for the world. A Reformed bishop says, "Church without mission is no church" (BB). A Lutheran pastor declares, "the church isn't for itself, its first task is to pray for revival, taking seriously that the church isn't for itself but for the world" (PG). Some church people misunderstand the word mission, thinking of it either politically ("NATO bomb attacks on Serbia") or referring to the way Western missions have acted in Hungary.

> Maybe we need to be a little careful. People think we want to win something, with force. "Mission" has a bad aftertaste in some people's minds. We have to be very careful how we use the word mission, clear about how we understand mission. Many people understand the word wrongly; the word has been misused. We have to always begin with the biblical foundation. What does mission mean? Mission is also here. ... First of all a clear biblical, theological understanding of mission. (PG).

According to this pastor and others, the church needs to give a high theological priority to questions of justice, the importance of theological rethinking, and the need for theological clarification of the nature of mission. Following this rethinking will come the strategic questions of how to do this in a secular society. There is a lot to be learned. "Mission is a two way street – not just giving" (BB).

Regarding mission strategy, we can discover two sets of contrasting views of mission. The first contrasts missions between foreign and local. The second contrasts mission between working primarily among Hungarians and working cross-culturally.

One view is that missions means going to a foreign country. To be a missionary means to cross geographical boundaries. Related to this is a concern for the poor. Doctors or nurses, those working in orphanages, helping in practical ways constitute legitimate missions work. Angelika Jo describes this view, speaking of the older people of the LMS:

> They accept pastors as missionaries, accept nurses, civil engineer in PNG, helping the poor, helping the needy is familiar. ... Rather take ideas like, prefer going to orphanages all the time, spending our free time serving among the poor, that is not the basic idea for everybody. Maybe for some people, but not for everybody. (AJ).

This is contrasted with the view of missions as local ministry. Maybe a distinction between *missions* and *mission* is reflected here. These people see outreach to Hungarians as equally valid. A generational difference comes into play here. In general, the older people who were involved in the missions school and prayed for missions throughout Communist times hold to the "missions as foreign" paradigm. Younger people see missions as equally home and foreign. Angelika Jo says of her generation:

5. Hungarian Reformed and Lutheran 79

> Individuals, even in our youth group, people we know, find their own way of serving God wherever they work. Like in school or computer job or whatever. Look at it as service. They understand how it can be service. (AJ)

Those who see mission as everywhere conclude that the "foreign only" paradigm does not correctly understand the biblical teaching on missions. Further it does not necessarily reflect the actual needs of the world. A Lutheran pastor speaks of the "older generation who think only foreign mission. Africa, Asia where the pagans are. Totally false. In PNG ninety percent are theoretically Christian, in Hungary only twenty percent are really Christian. That's the older missions view" (PG).

The second contrast concerns the cultural distance involved in missions. Most people, when they think of missions, understand it to mean work among Hungarians elsewhere. The first view says, "We should help Hungarian speaking peoples worldwide, especially the Hungarian minorities in the neighboring countries: Romania, Slovakia, Serbia, Ukraine" (AMK, quoting JB). Even when they stretch the distance a bit, they still think of Hungarian-related peoples. The LMS secretary says, "We still have opportunity to support Finno-Ugric speaking tribes or small ethnics in one-time Soviet Union. We consider we have special responsibility in this direction rather than towards the Arabs" (AB). A contrasting view is that, even staying closer to home, Christians should reach out cross-culturally. This second view says, "Ok, maybe we can't travel great distances, but why not reach out to Romanians, Slovaks, Bosnians, Albanians, or Gypsy people" (AMK). This group points out the number of hidden groups within Hungary: perhaps 600,000 Roma (Gypsies), 10-20,000 Chinese in Budapest, Jews, Arabs. Someone remarked on the need for a paradigm change, that mission is not just crossing geographical barriers, but also cultural ones. Kool reminds her Hungarian friends:

> Mission is not only to Hungarians, but to all peoples. We need to read the Bible from a multi-ethnic perspective. Matthew 28 is not just a command to baptize, it is a command to reach the whole world. (AMK).

Some of the respondents see a romantic stereotype of missions among those who first get interested. These young people see missions to be to those far away and less privileged. "For many people, when you say mission, it immediately means third world people of color" (DZ). It reflects a romantic view of missionary history, of "sending the white brother to the dark brother" (DZ), of helping those less fortunate. Missions is to the third world, which is very primitive. Some romantic excitement about going there can generate missions involvement. Kool gave the example of a theological educators conference, where one of the speakers had worked in Africa and used African examples.

"Oh, people could not take it in – you are comparing us with those primitive Africans." It was necessary to help them understand the actual situation in the African churches, especially how large they are and how quickly they are growing.

The second main question of biblical and theological understanding of missions concerns the question of conversion. Is it legitimate to demand that someone change his or her religion in order to get to heaven? Can one not be a good Hindu or Muslim or Buddhist and still be acceptable to God? In some ways, the phrasing of the question reflects the post-modernism which has quickly overtaken the Marxist philosophy of past decades. The question is asked within as well as outside the church.

The people of the older generation are concerned that this philosophy has led to a lack of interest in missions. LMS participants perceive that the current generation of young people considers illegitimate the desire, or demand, that someone convert from his or her own religion to Christianity. "They have this idea of honoring other people's ideas. Leaving people in their own beliefs. Young people see this as violation of human rights (IR). One of them related her conversations with "intelligent youth," who ask, "why are you trying to change other people's faith? If God wants to save them he will, even in the state they are in" (IR). To her this shows that the missions commandment is not working, that it does not speak to the current generation.

The Jos responded to this concern by agreeing that the view is common, and that they themselves struggle with it, even though they serve as missionaries. Angelika Jo recalls writing her thesis.

> I started my thesis on teaching world religions in Lutheran church school situation. As I started it I just looked at it as a challenging topic. But when I reached the middle of it I was completely confused what to believe. Who am I and why am I a Christian. Should I be a Christian at all? I tried to verify everything in order to be able go to India. It was a step I had to make in order to be ready to go abroad. It was such a difficult, so dramatic process, I still remember it. Still today, as I interact with children of different religions sometimes I got really confused. Should I just talk about Christ and love? Should I be more strict about only Christ, he's the only way? Or should we just listen our hearts and search for God in our own way? Still a very difficult questions for me, as we read the writing of Hindus, and missiology in India, everything clears out. We had misty ideas of interreligious dialogue, sounded really fancy and interesting, but now we see how it really happens, what is really going on there, what are the issues. Missiological and theological writings, some magazines, our ideas keep changing. (AJ).

5. Hungarian Reformed and Lutheran 81

Now, serving in a multi-cultural school, where several different religions are present, further complicates the problem. The Jos are convinced that conversion is necessary, that Christ is the only answer. The challenge, however, is to know how to promote it. Andras Jo says:

> We don't say conversion is not necessary. It's not a good statement that our generation doesn't see conversion as a major issue. We just don't see how to do it properly, where I don't abuse my opportunity as white person, with money, attractive ... . I have to search for the way where I only offer Christ, and don't offer popularity, the shiny [advantages] of the West. (AJ).

Their work in the school also makes the problem acute. In that setting relativism is rampant. They hear from their colleagues, "Everything is possible, everything is good, let's embrace all other religions." They recall attending a wedding of a colleague which took place at a Zen meditation center run by Jesuits. It had a cross, but with a Buddha in front. They struggle with the question of pluralism, but their Christian commitments remain firm. Nevertheless, the question of conversion and related issues of contextualization and interreligious dialogue are a challenge. Before they went to India their thinking was clear. Now it is not clear because of their interaction with children of other faiths. "One of the reasons we still want to be there, because the questions [of ultimate truth] are still not answered" (AJ).

Others who are involved in missions, or are exploring missions possibilities answer the questions differently. For them the question should be answered, "Mission equals service rather than evangelism" (DZ). To what extent this reflects the liberalism of theological education rather than post-modernism is difficult to determine. Particularly among the students at the Reformed University, evangelism is not a high priority. They desire to help people, but "public evangelism isn't their way" (DZ).

The third main question in this section regards the degree to which people's biblical and theological understanding of mission has changed since the revolution. More particularly, did a change in biblical or theological understanding of mission since the revolution contribute to new missions interest? Here the answer seems to be negative. Strategic questions about who should be involved in mission may have changed, but not biblical ones. Once again, generational issues may come into play.

One of the older people said, it is "not a change in theology, rather lack of interest. Theological students can learn about mission if they want to" (AB). The Jos agree, and also say there is no change. This may reflect their age. They grew up after the revolution. Their theology has been developed under new conditions and in the context of missions training.

In fact, the Jos may be responding to the questions whether the understanding of mission has changed in general, not whether it has changed among people with missions interest. The Jos say the gospel and missions command themselves have not changed. "I don't think there is much change. The proper mission is of the gospel. Very important to propagate. You need to look at scripture as it is and understand it as it is. There's nothing new about it." What may have changed is the understanding of service in the church. They see a "generation which believes pastor is main servant, and a generation which believes all are servants in their own ways, who take conversion as missionary task in everyday life" (AJ).

Others say, however, that their theology did not have to change, but that they had to overcome their lack of teaching and a paradigm that mission was just within the church or just among Hungarians. They had to learn that mission means partnership. "We have studied missiology, the older ones haven't. For them the mission program means to have drug rehab center here, and the handicap children's center and schools" (AJ). Therefore, the change came at a strategy level, not primarily a theological one.

Interest in Missions Before Revolution

To what extent were people interested in missions before the revolution? We find evidence which points to an interest waiting for opportunity. This is seen primarily in the fact that several mission societies began again so soon after revolution: the LMS (1991), Bible League, Maria Molnar Foreign Mission Society (1992). This leads us to the conclusion that mission interest existed, at least among the older generation, and that the advent of freedom opened the door to new expressions of that interest.

Almost without exception, conversations with respondents began with history. Several times I was asked, "What do you know about the historical situation in our church regarding missions?" The older generation had lived that missions history and kept it alive among themselves. When I met with the members of the LMS, one of the original students at the missions school in 1948 brought out well-worn pictures of her class and her student identification card. The younger ones had read Kool's book and discovered Hungarian historical roots in missions commitment and activity. Only the youngest respondents did not begin with history, although they got there eventually. A Reformed bishop said, "Anne-Marie learned more than we knew, and taught us what we did not know. She found the history of mission is a very exciting story. In some sense we lost this memory" (BB).

Education

The nexus of activity related to missionary awareness and motivation is the conjunction of educational institutions. In particular, the Reformed Seminary in Debrecen where Janos Bütösi taught, PIMS where Kool teaches and the English Department of the Reformed University in Budapest where Zomer teaches, all came together to provide major impetus to missions vision. In general, one gets the impression that students come to the schools and discover missions, rather than that they come to the schools to be trained for missions. As mentioned above, the number of missiology courses being offered is growing, as is the number of students taking missions related courses (Kool n.d.).

Although most faculties do not have a missiology department or many missions courses, these are increasing, and PIMS provides a unique function in providing resources for the various schools. Those who are doing short-term projects are coming from the context of the universities and seminaries rather than the churches. Some people observe a contrast between seminary and university students, in that the seminary student seem to be a bit more willing to accept the church status quo, while the university students are more willing to ask the difficult questions about why things are done the way they are. Zomer says:

> our humanities students are a lot more intelligent than our theology or pastoral students. When they have questions ... The Pastor says, 'you shouldn't ask those kinds of questions.' Well, fooey to you. The humanities students have a healthy disregard of the church. (DZ).

He sees the university students as having a greater potential for missions than seminary students.

The newly reorganized mission societies certainly have played a role outside of the educational circles to raise interest and awareness, but the fact that they involve mostly elderly people mitigates against them having a significant role with young people. The biggest exception to this is the summer camps for children run jointly by the LMS and LMC.

Ethnocentrism/Openness to Others

To what extent is ethnocentrism a motivating or hindering factor for mission? Do superior attitudes give the confidence that Hungarians have something to offer to others? On the other hand, do negative attitudes keep them from going to peoples they see as inferior? Must certain attitudes be overcome in order for missions to happen?

Mission for Hungarians has typically been either to other Hungarians or to third world peoples to whom they are clearly superior. This has made it difficult to conceive of mission to their non-Hungarian neighbors. Hungarian attitudes towards the surrounding peoples are generally negative: Romanians and Roma (Gypsies) are strongly looked down on. This attitude is compounded by the fact that following WWI much of Hungarian territory had to be surrendered to Romania, Slovakia, and Yugoslavia. This nationalism had to be overcome for missions to occur before WWII, and, according to respondents, needs to be overcome again. Kool notes:

> So therefore, it's I think so important to always focus on the cross-cultural element in mission. And speaking about what is your responsibility to the worldwide church of Christ. And I'm always in my lectures challenging people, God not only loves the Dutch and the Hungarians, but also the Gypsies and the Jews, and the Romanians and the Slovaks. (AMK)

Missions as popularly conceived is to those less fortunate and far away. People in India, Africa and Latin America ("third world people of color," DZ) are clearly in need of help. Hungarians imply, "We have something to give them, to teach them. They don't have anything to teach us."

Role of (Western) Evangelical Missionaries

The attitude of most of the respondents toward the influx of Western, primarily American, evangelical missionaries in the past ten years is mostly negative, despite the very significant role that two missionaries have played in the development of missions involvement. This attitude does not seem to be related to ethnocentrism or prejudice against Westerners, whom Hungarians generally like. It relates rather to their perceptions of how these missionaries have operated. These newly arrived missionaries are seen as those who did not do their homework, who did not recognize the historic churches as legitimate, and who did not start with the Christians and churches who were already there. A Lutheran pastor says, "Many Western missions came without learning. They didn't learn Hungary. They acted like they needed to start from nothing. Ignored churches" (PG).

Respondents see Western missionaries as having an incomplete view of Hungarian church situation, and lack an understanding of the true needs. In contrast, Anne-Marie Kool and David Zomer were people who came to the historic churches with the desire to learn from them and to help them. Kool did a major service by uncovering their own history and teaching it to them, while Zomer provided connections with a like-minded denomination in the West. He even expressed a desire to protect his students who will go on short-term missions projects from the American evangelical students with whom they will work. "I tell them they can go 'Shine, Jesus, Shine' somewhere else, when they ask if they should bring their music with them" (DZ).

The churches are concerned about proselytism. The Reformed Bishop confesses some sympathy with Orthodox Churches in Romania and Russia who complain about the presence of evangelical missionaries who evangelize those the church considers to be already Christian. "It's very difficult to have these people here. They seem to think this is a white fleck for the gospel. It's important for us, for all people to have connection to history" (BB). This point is made regularly in the literature as well. (See Kool 2000; Borowik 1997; Barker 1997.)

Interaction between Factors

The description of the various factors which have contributed to the development of missions interest and involvement gives insight into specific aspects of spiritual, social or cultural life. Equally useful can be the interaction between the various factors. Here the questions are of the impact of social factors on spiritual or cultural ones. The same can be asked of the impact of spiritual or of cultural factors on the other two areas. Even more specifically, the interaction between economic capability, spiritual vitality, theological reflection, political freedom and openness to others can be explored. Each of these factors can exist in isolation, but what happens when they come together? Not all cases will show the same kinds of interaction, and not all kinds of interaction will be equally important. Nevertheless, they prove fruitful in opening doors to fresh analysis.

The lines between factors are never clear. The distinction between spiritual life and missions interest, for example, although separated here for purposes of analysis, is fuzzy. It seems clear that a relationship between spiritual vitality and missions interest exists. However, the exact nature of that relationship is not clear. Revival, in conjunction with other factors, seems to lead to missions, but sometimes the inverse seems also to be the case. Revival in pre-Communist times clearly led to mission which in turn fed the revival.

One area of interaction between factors is in the relationship between spiritual vitality and financial strength. Internal issues, such as a lack of vision, work themselves out in a lack of commitment to giving. "Out of my bitter experience I must say, without revival there is no mission. From here, from above we can't awake the sleeping church, without God's Spirit." (PG). Revival does not lead inexorably to cross-cultural missions, but according to respondents, without a certain level of spiritual life missions will be impossible.

We can also see inhibiting factors to mission involvement. To the extent that difficulties lead to the perception that it is not worth the effort trying to go, then less will be done. These social factors of economic weakness and lack of structures and policies impact the cultural factors of motivation and personal desire.

A further area of interaction between factors is the relationship between a key person of influence (Kool) who helped the Hungarians change their self-understanding. Whereas before they might have had some kind of general interest in missions, but never thought they could do much themselves, she helped them see that they had been involved in missions before and could be active again. Their self-perception was that they were too weak and too poor to have any influence. That is changing to one of a certain self-confidence that God can once again use them in a strategic way.

A final area of interaction is the degree to which previous activity in local mission can ease the way to a theology of missions which includes a cross-cultural component. Peter Gancs, the Lutheran missions pastors, for example, speaks of his earlier ministry.

> I was active in youth work before the revolution. Had big youth conferences. To be honest, only after the revolution have I had contact with missions. Radio work. Heard occasionally from missions, but really a new thing. A surprise from God that I got involved in mission. (PG).

It seems much easier for someone to think about cross-cultural ministry if he or she has been already involved in ministry outside the church, than it is for someone whose ministry experience is confined to the church context.

Conclusions

The sending of the Jo family to India takes place within this wider social and cultural context. While they are the only missionaries specifically involved in this case, they are not isolated from the larger church and missions community. Many more people are promoting missions interest and are recruiting and training missionaries. They must all be seen in order to understand how the one family was sent.

Why did this case occur? Two primary factors seem to be the most important. First, several key people began talking about missions, trying to spread the idea within their circles of influence. The development of missions training programs by these people contributed to the spread of the idea. Second, the publication of a history of missions in Hungary alerted Hungarians to their heritage as a missionary-sending country and church. History is very important to Hungarians, as evidenced by regular and constant references to their own history and how it has motivated them. Political freedom opened the doors for people to travel and put legs to their mission vision, and the beginnings of financial support for missions demonstrated a growing desire for ownership of their own missions enterprise.

Clearly certain individuals and a few local churches are developing an interest in being sent or in sending missionaries. The number of people expressing interest in missions is growing regularly, as evidenced by increasing enrollment in missions related courses at various educational institutions and growing attendance at missions conferences.

However, these seem to be isolated cases, resulting from the interaction with certain foreign missionaries, rather than arising out of the spiritual life and dynamic of the churches themselves. A concern for personal comfort and the renovation of church buildings overrides concerns for non-Hungarian peoples outside the borders of Hungary. However, new, younger, more missionary-minded leadership in both the Lutheran and Reformed Churches has recently been chosen, which could change this pessimistic picture in the years to come. The churches have to gain a vision for mission in both its local and cross-cultural aspects, rather than relying on the influence and abilities of either foreign missionaries or a church related educational institution, if a major movement towards missions is to begin. If this happens, if the vision and the will were there to reach beyond normal church life, then the necessary financial resources could probably be found.

6. Aletheia Church, Timişoara, Romania

The second case involves a single local church in Timişoara, Romania. In contrast to the national church involvement of the previous case, here a small free church sent a single family to Albania. It illustrates the way a missionary sending impetus can arise even within local church situations. Instead of large ecclesiastical bureaucracies needing to be developed or coordinated, personal relationships and vision are key. The descriptions are not as detailed as in the Hungarian case, because the context in which it developed is much smaller, as are the number of people interviewed. The story is a compelling one, and one which in my experience is unique.

Seven people were interviewed. These included one of the Romanian missionaries who has served long term, the pastors and missions pastors of the supporting church, and American missionaries who have had a large part in supporting the Romanian missionaries. The missions policy manual of the church was examined, as was personal correspondence from the Romanian missionaries involved. I have known the church well from the time of its inception, and the pastor has been a long time friend and colleague, so personal contact and observation could confirm the accounts of the participants. That relationship opened the door to friendly and open conversations with the participants.

In general, the respondents agreed on most questions, even to the point of sometimes telling the same stories. Small details of fact concerning dates and numbers sometimes conflicted, but these could usually be reconciled by consulting the person most closely involved with the incident described. However, we can note a second type of response. I interviewed a Romanian missionary in Albania, who is not directly involved in Aletheia but was somewhat involved with the church's missionaries on the field. He offered a somewhat different perspective on the care and guidance the church gave to their missionaries. In addition, the former missions pastor, who was involved at the very beginning and who now has another ministry, gave a contrary opinion on many points. It is difficult to evaluate the nature of his contributions. Certainly every story has two sides, and the need for balance and realism is always necessary. At the same time, the possibility that other factors play a part here is great. Issues of personal, perhaps strained, relationship with church leadership, difference of vision, jealousy of a successor's success, or the impact of a changed role in the church can all come into play. As examples, and as a foretaste of what will come, this respondent disagreed on such points as the level of commitment to missions from the whole church, the impact and participation of visits to Albania, the church as a model of missions sending, and the effectiveness of the missionaries involved.

Background and Historical Development

In 1995 a young couple, Marcel and Felicia Hoban, came to Aletheia church to share their vision for missions in Albania. The church caught the vision and decided to adopt them as their missionaries. Although the church was very young (only a year old) and very small (twenty members or fewer) it committed themselves to support the Hobans, both financially and spiritually.

How did this come about? In 1988, Marcel Hoban, then eighteen years old, was a member of a youth group which met regularly for prayer and Bible study. Someone had visited the group and encouraged those attending to pray for countries where there were very few Christians or where they were persecuted. This brother showed them statistics, and then pointed out that Albania had recently declared itself the first officially atheistic country in the world. Hoban, together with his group, began to pray for a Bible translation and Christian response in Albania. Through this prayer, he began to get a vision and motivation for that country. One day, while praying and studying the Bible in his parents' house, Hoban received a vision ("before my eyes"), in which he saw a scene of some mountains and some darker skinned people, and heard an inner voice which told him "There you will be a missionary." He was totally surprised and thankful to God for the vision, but he did not know where the place was or what the vision meant.

A few years later, in 1992, he tried to go to Albania, but could not because of a lack of funds. Finally in April 1994 he was able to go for a visit of several weeks. While traveling around the country with some other Romanians, they came to a certain mountain. As they saw the needs of the villages, it suddenly became clear to him that this was the same mountain and these were the same people that he had seen in his vision. However, this time he got a different message from God. This time the message was "This is the place."

Marcel and his wife Felicia were sent as missionaries to this village by their church, Agape, in Timişoara. However, after six months their church let them know that there was no more funding for them. They then responded to a previous invitation to come to another church in Timişoara, given to them from Cornel Marincu, the pastor of that church. This church, Aletheia, despite being at this point just a year old and with just 24-26 members (someone else says 15-20), took on the Hobans as their missionaries and have been supporting them since.

In 2001, Aletheia sent another couple to serve in the same village in Albania. The missions pastor says the church prayed for a year that someone would come along who could replace and/or work with the Hobans. When a new family began attending the church, the church leaders quickly recognized that they would be good people to send. "It was a fit like a glove when they came to Aletheia. They are zealous and an encouragement for us" (MI). This family had already had some theological training and had been involved in the southern Romanian region of Oltenia for six months.

A church now of around one hundred members, it wants to send missionaries to Serbia, and has someone preparing to go to the Muslim world. After six years of mission activity in Albania, the church evaluated their ministry progress as follows:

> We could see six people born again, a great respect for our people and for the Christian values they have presence there, a Community Center where we can serve the people of Pinet. The entire community of Pinet has been exposed to a practical Gospel and we are about to began [sic] Christian services in our facility. (Iliesu 2001).

Themes and Factors

We will examine the spiritual, social and cultural systems, before looking at the interactions between them.

Spiritual Factors

The reports of God at work in this case are ubiquitous. Although differences of opinion occur in other areas of the church's involvement, no one disputes the view that this missions vision comes from God. Hoban's initial interest, burden and vision all took place within the context of prayer and Bible study. A group of young people was praying for nations without the gospel, especially for Albania, before the revolution, before there was any opportunity for them to do anything personally. They saw that their prayers could have an effect on people responding to God, even if they were not involved themselves in spreading the gospel.

Hoban's vision itself is the clearest evidence that God wanted to do something new. Coming before the revolution as it did, before anyone was talking about the possibility of Romanians becoming involved in cross-cultural missions, the supernatural nature of God's intervention is even more clear.

A number of statements make it apparent that participants see God's hand in their development of missions involvement. The missions pastors says,

> When you can see how God is working to put things together, it's wonderful … . It's God's way to do things. He prepared it all … . God commanded us. We know we've been called by God to do it … . God made us do missions. (MI).

The church committed to support their missionaries and have been able to do so "by the grace of God, by miracles" (CM). "We responded and by the grace of God, he supplied the needs. We followed the visions; God supplied the need ... . We decided to listen to God" (MI). I regularly heard such terms as "faith", "prayer", and "God's provision" from the respondents. They clearly feel that God is the one who initiated their involvement, who maintains the vision, who gives the gifts which allow them to fulfill their missionary commitments, and who will continue to send out other missionaries from their church.

Finally, when informants are asked the advice they would offer others coming after them, their language reflects the same emphasis. "Be sure God called to do it." "You have to have faith." "Be led by the Spirit." For them, God is without any doubt the one who has brought them to missions.

Social Factors

Among the social factors explored are the role of the key people in influencing a movement, the economic, political and ecclesiastical structures, and the variety of networks in which the Aletheia missions program has to work.

Key People

As can be seen by what has already been described, Marcel Hoban was the key person in helping Aletheia develop their missions vision. It seems safe to say that without his impetus, the cross-cultural involvement of the church would only have come much later.

Daniel Matei was a Pentecostal pastor, who immigrated to the States some years before, and then served as missionary in China. Immediately after the Revolution he returned to Romania and shortly thereafter helped start a new style church, Agape. This church is charismatic, as opposed to the traditional Pentecostal churches of Romania. It emphasized a more contemporary worship style, ministry training, and outreach. Matei had a heart for missions and it was part of his desire for Agape to become involved in missions. He helped Hoban get his vision accepted in the church and sent out. He eventually went back to pastor a church in the States, leaving a large hole in the church leadership.

Cornel Marincu was the founding pastor of Aletheia. He was one of the original members of Agape, and was director of church planting and missions, but left the church over differences in philosophy of ministry and practice. He started Aletheia to recapture the original vision which led to the starting of Agape, but which he felt had been lost. He may not have had a particular vision for missions until Hoban came along, but he soon caught the vision and helped the church to adopt it quickly. Although he is no longer the pastor, and works now with the church's denomination, he is clearly still the key person in the church.

While not referring to a specific person in this specific case, responses also pointed to the importance of the pastor in determining whether a church will develop a missions vision or not. In general, a pastor with such a vision will be able to motivate his church to adopt that vision. If a pastor does not have the vision and someone comes to the church with vision or a desire to go as a missionary, generally difficulties occur. Often such a pastor will see the person as a rebel or as someone who only wants to condemn the church for not moving in that particular direction. In many situations in Romania since the revolution, people with missions vision have had to leave their church and find another which is willing to share their desire to be sent. So the pastor can promote or destroy any missions vision by his attitude.

Economic

Does the difficult economic situation in Romania inhibit the rise of missionary interest and capability, or has the openness since the revolution promoted new possibilities? While one might expect that the difficulties would make it hard to think about giving for something which does not immediately benefit the people, I did not hear such talk from leaders at Aletheia. Naturally, the situation is challenging,[7] and seen from a human point of view nearly impossible, but the conviction that God will provide comes across clearly.

The people involved in this project are united in the view that, if the church has the vision, there will be no problem with the money. Noting the fact that Romanians complain about money, one respondent observed that everywhere he has traveled, including the United States, people complain about money. Therefore, the difficult economic situation in Romania should not prevent them from giving. He said the church has to teach people about money, that it all belongs to God. He spoke passionately about the relationship between giving and vision.

> We are never too poor to do ministry. If it's his mission to go on the mission field, then he will provide and you need to go. If we believe God is the provider, then he will provide. Start small and grow. Know what direction you are going. That's much better. Financial – comes from vision. We need to be taught to give in proportion to what we have. Economics is not biggest problem. People think first thing is you have to have money. Not true. Money is only money. Most important is vision. (II).

This response characterizes the views of the leadership as a whole. Although they acknowledge difficulties, no one implied that they, even as a small church, could not give significantly to fulfill their vision. When the second family was sent to replace the Hobans, they were "sent even though we didn't

---

[7] A prayer letter from an Austrian missionary serving in Romania reports that "The prices have once again been raised drastically – especially for heating and warm water. The monthly living costs have about doubled in comparison to last year. According to the statistics, during communist times the living costs took about 14% of an average income, today they are (in the city) around 85%!!"

have money. We were committed to them. Money has always been there. Money shouldn't be decisive factor" (MI). Another said:

In my perspective, the finances are not the most important, finances should not be the reason to bring back a missionary. If someone has the vision to go, that's most important. Money doesn't need to play the role in missions. We have always received what we needed. By the grace of God, he supplied the needs. (CM).

The church as the sender has the responsibility to find the support. It committed itself to find the money, either from the church or from somewhere else, either within the country or from outside. In the church leaders view, the missionaries should not have to run around to find supporters, then have to answer to many different people. They should answer only to the church; the church should protect them. When the Hobans came to Aletheia, Marincu told Hoban they as a church did not have the money, but that God would provide. He promised before the Lord that if Hoban came back, it would not be because of money.

The church committed themselves to $250 a month, and "by the grace of God, by miracles", (CM) the money has always come in. Respondents say they have never missed a month. At times, they could not get money into Albania, but they still collected it. They invested $15,500 in Albania in the year 2000 alone (Iliesu 2001). The offering of the first Sunday every month goes to missions. People have sacrificed to help. Some have given up their car; others have given up their vacation money. "It isn't walking through the roses" (MI) to be involved in missions, but they have persevered.

The missions pastor says that Aletheia supplied sixty to seventy percent of the funds. Marincu says it covered all but fifty dollars a month last year. According to a written report, it has outside sponsors for about $3000, but has to find the rest itself (Iliesu 2001). At the beginning, the church apparently had Western contacts who would have connected them to a mission board which would have taken care of Hobans. However, the leaders decided not to take advantage of this offer. They felt God had called them to do it, so they asked God to supply the needs.

Several Romanian businessmen from outside the church have become regular donors. These men, some Orthodox and some Evangelical, have responded positively to presentations of the needs in Albania, and have given generously. Aletheia recruited them when it wanted to send a second couple, but did not have the necessary resources itself. The church had to learn to deal with issues of communication with donors as well as legal issues like taxation. No law is currently in place regarding sponsorship, which makes the collection of donations complicated. In addition, it has lost some sponsors (both within Romania and from outside) because of poor communication. Regular giving is not a habit for most Romanians and if they do not receive regular information about the work in Albania, they sometimes forget. Therefore, the church has instituted a process whereby someone visits these businessmen each month to share current information and to collect the money.

Aletheia also had to learn what it means to care for their missionaries. In the opinion of others involved at the edges, the care with which the church supported the Hobans was not as complete as the church leaders implied. Was the church really so faithful and consistent as claimed? The missions pastor says in 1997 they as a church could not send money for three or four months, but the Albanians took care of the Hobans. A Romanian missionary in Albania says, "We [he and his wife] did what we could to help, but we couldn't do everything. The church didn't support them very well" (GD). Another missionary attributes this to the fact the Romanians have a mindset that "ministers should suffer for Christ, including economically" (BF). Therefore, the church may not see the situation as a lack of care, but rather the legitimate consequence of serving the Lord.

At times, things were very difficult for the Hobans. They lived at the same level as those of the village. They hauled water by donkey, and for three years they did not have a car. They returned to Romania twice a year. Someone from Romania had to go and bring them to Romania, then take them back to Albania. Travel to and from Albania was very difficult. It included transit through Bulgaria and Yugoslavia, neither of which were particularly friendly towards Romanians.

Regardless of how well the church actually applied their principles, their bottom line conviction is that it has the responsibility to support its missionaries and that God will help it meet that commitment. The missions pastor says, "as a church we are prepared to pay the price to establish a strong church there" (MI).

Political

Is the freedom to travel outside the country a motivating factor for the people of Aletheia? The pastor says that this is not a reason those in the church are interested in missions. They know that when they go on a mission, they go to work.

> They understand that what missions means, and know that if they go somewhere they're not going for a walk, they're going for missions. We haven't encouraged people to go just for the love of trying something new. They know the church won't send them just to take a walk; that if they go it's for missions. Those who have gone have gone with the purpose of doing mission. (LC)

This is especially true because Albania is not an attractive place to visit. Stories of trips to and from Albania include accounts of very difficult border crossings, broken down vehicles, nights spent in the car with the temperature below freezing, and many other difficulties. Nobody would mistake mission to Albania with a vacation to Western Europe.

The fact that Romanians were totally isolated under Communism means they have had to learn much in a short time. At the same time, their experience also helps them relate to the Albanians who were in a similar situation.

Ecclesiastical

Ecclesiastical factors here mean primarily local church structure and vision, and to a lesser extent inter-church relations in Timişoara.

The Hobans were initially sent out by Agape Church. Even before the Hobans left, Marincu predicted that they would have difficulties, and that they should come to Aletheia when that happened. Agape had the position that if people came in with vision, the church would send them. There was no structure in place to help them stay on the field. Marincu says Agape was enthusiastic, but ultimately did not really stand behind the Hobans.

Aletheia began with people from Agape. It started with the intention to be a new kind of church for Romania. It wanted to start small, grow slowly, and grow deeply, in contrast to Agape, where the concern was for fast growth, big show, huge building. Those who started Aletheia wanted to learn from what they saw as Agape's mistakes. In addition, the church had a multi-cultural character from the very beginning. Among the initial team of ten persons were an American missionary and an African student, giving the church access to multiple perspectives in the founding stages.

The important point here is that Aletheia as a church was open to new ways of doing ministry, and therefore it was able to respond to a need and a vision and adopt it as its own. No inherent resistance to doing something new and challenging existed. Marincu as a visionary and initiator certainly made this easier as well. The consistency of Aletheia's support for the Hobans probably reflects that same philosophy of ministry. It has been constant in its support, even though it is small and has faced difficult times financially, whereas Agape gave the Hobans a big send off but quickly forgot them both spiritually and financially.

According to Aletheia's philosophy of ministry, the church, not a mission agency, is the primary sending body. Several people talked of situations where people were sent by a missions agency or a *filiale* (regional association of churches), and the difficulties these people experienced, both financially and spiritually. These respondents felt these problems could be avoided if the local church takes primary responsibility for their own people.

Since Aletheia began with no experience, church leaders had to learn everything from scratch. For example, they had to learn to what extent the church should get involved in on-field issues. Aletheia's leadership style can be characterized as directive and somewhat authoritarian, but the church leaders learned it was better to let those on the field make the decisions related to local ministry issues. They also had to deal with issues of missionary care, communication, and preparation. Critics, such as the former missions pastor and other missionaries in Albania, claim the church did not do a very good job in any of these areas.

Regarding missionary care, the former pastor says "the most important job [of the church] was spiritual cover and prayer for Marcel" (CM). The missions pastor said, "the main problem was financial. We are a small church and we had to support them" (MI).

Respondents spoke of the mistakes they made in communication – with the missionaries on the field, with the church itself and with outside supporters and partners. The missions pastor said, "We made mistakes in communication with our missionaries – how we maintained communication and made them feel a part of the church. We had to go through that to understand it" (MI). The current pastor remarked, "Our experience as a church is that we lost some good sponsors because there was a period in which we didn't communicate. We neglected them" (LC).

The church also had to learn about missionary preparation and transition. The church leaders see it as their job to prepare the new missionaries to go and to support them. However, in the opinion of a Romanian missionary active in Albania with another agency, the new family probably will not last long. He sees them as having no (or little) theological training and no Albanian language, and thinks they are being abandoned alone in the village.[8]

How does foreign mission fit into Aletheia's overall ministry plan? It has planted three churches in the Timişoara area and others farther away. It is starting a church among Gypsies, and is helping churches in Oltenia, primarily with training. This gives people a chance to get involved in outreach that is somewhat cross-cultural, but not as far away as Albania. It has a group of eight to ten people who are interested in missions, and are preparing for a short-term trip. The philosophy of ministry calls for every member to be active in ministry. Foreign missions, therefore, is simply a geographical extension of its local and in-country cross-cultural vision, not something that is a separate outreach.

---

[8] Since their deployment, they have returned to Romania to have a baby. At this point it is not clear how soon they will return to Albania.

6. Aletheia Church, Timișoara, Romania

Through the six years that the Hobans served in Albania, people from the church visited them regularly. About twice a year, a group would travel from Romania to Albania to visit and encourage them, and to help with practical issues, like bringing money and supplies. Ten to fifteen people have been on those trips, quite a large percentage of the members of this small church. Church leaders say they sent both mature and not so mature people. One purpose of these trips was practical, to help. The other purpose was to challenge people. The missions pastor says of those who participated, "They have now lived there for a week and they understand better. The impact was significant. They got the heart for missions" (MI).

In addition to sending people to Albania, the church also sponsored a group of twenty (Marincu says ten) Albanian children to visit Romania. They came as a choir and visited a number of Romanian churches. A worship tape by the Albanian kids choir was produced which was used to help Romanians understand Albania better, and to get a heart for Albanians and ministry in Albania.

Since the initial interviews were conducted, Marcel Hoban has become the missions pastor of Aletheia. It is unclear how this development will change things, both in the church and in Albania. The Hobans did not have a vision to stay in Albania indefinitely. They favored a strategy of gradual disengagement, but they did not necessarily feel their time there was over.

The church now faces the question of what is a missionary. When Felicia Hoban was home for two months she was not considered a missionary and had to find a job. It is not clear whether the Hobans came back because they felt the time was right, or because the church said it was time to come home. Other respondents feel that the Hobans will not stay in Romania for long. If they do not return to Albania, they will likely go somewhere else. Their time in Albania was exhausting, and they need time to rest, but later they will probably return.

The respondents in general claimed that God has used Aletheia in a significant way, and that it is perhaps a model for how a local church can become involved in missions. However, contrary opinions exist. The former missions pastor says the church was not a good model of a missions vision, but that it was blessed that the Hobans came to them. He is skeptical that the vision is widely accepted throughout the church.

> I don't think the church cares so much for missions, maybe when Hobans came and shared. Maybe when we pray. But no one is there to communicate with the church about missions. Leadership in the church. They have to communicate the vision and they don't. They don't present it. Names don't mean anything. Pictures don't mean anything. Present a piece and try. Missions is not throughout church. Need to communicate – doesn't happen enough. (II).

He faults the leadership for not communicating the vision or presenting missions in a way that means anything to people. Although people from the church have visited Albania (including himself several times as missions pastor), those trips were not planned as part of a strategy to develop vision, but rather in response to emergencies. The church needed someone to drive, someone who was a good mechanic, someone who was good with children. Contrary to statements from other church leaders that the church prays for their missionaries every week, he implies that this may not be the case, or else that the prayer is formal and not serious.

As with most issues of perspective, both aspects are true to some extent. The leadership seems serious about promoting and praying for missions. The reality of that commitment may be less intense than the leadership desires.

Networks

Despite the relative simplicity of the situation under consideration, an analysis of the networks involved is complicated. These include networks within Romania – both within and outside church circles, networks within Albania – again both within and outside Christian circles, and relations from outside Romania, which, however, touch both Romania and Albania. By setting Aletheia church and the Hoban family in the center of these networks, we gain a picture of the scope of relationship involved in a new missions situation. In this context, communication and accountability are important and daunting tasks.

Romania

Both the Hobans and the church have a somewhat uneasy relationship with some other churches in Timişoara with whom they regularly interact. Cornel Marincu, the Hobans and the initial core group of Aletheia all came from Agape. The current pastor came from Exodus Pentecostal Church, which he helped plant some years earlier. Aletheia has relationships with the Pentecostal churches in town, which typically look at it with distrust because it is not typically Pentecostal and has not joined the Pentecostal Union. However, Cornel Marincu has developed a reputation and trust which has overcome many of the barriers. At the same time, Aletheia has recently joined a new denomination of unaffiliated churches with which Marincu now works. The Pentecostal Missionary Society (PMS), one of the earliest mission agencies to start after the revolution, is also associated with this denomination. The Hobans had the choice to go through the PMS or the church, and they chose the church.

As noted above, in addition to the church circles within which it works, Aletheia has also developed a group of Romanian donors outside the church. Important issues here include the flow of information and the accountability of the donated funds.

Finally, at the broadest level, the church interacts with the Romanian government. Leaders have had to learn, and are still learning, about how taxes, pension and health insurance work for people who mostly live outside the country.

Albania

In Albania, the Romanians are naturally embedded in both Christian and non-Christian networks. The Hobans initial contacts and cover were under the auspices of the Albanian Encouragement Project (AEP), a consortium made up of all the mission groups who work in Albania. They have more recently switched their affiliation from the AEP to the Albanian Evangelical Alliance, feeling it is a better partnership fit for them. In addition, they have contacts and working relationships with other Romanian missionaries in Albania, as well as with non-Romanian missionaries, who have helped them in many ways, especially when communication and funds were not able to come in from Aletheia. For example, World Relief helped build the new community center in the village.

The village of Pinet, where the Hobans lived[9] and the new couple now lives, provides another network. When they first went there, they established a relationship with the mayor, who was at that time twenty-two years old. Because of their commitment to the people of the village, with whom they have lived a very simple lifestyle, such as working the fields with them, the village has adopted them. More recently, the Romanians have contributed to the welfare of the village by building a community center (which they hope will eventually house a church) and dug a community well. They have been able to accomplish these projects through the financial contributions of many people, both within and outside of Romania. In addition, they are faced with religious issues. They are Christians in a totally Muslim village. Because of the nominalism of its Islam, Albania has been targeted by Muslim missionaries from outside the country, and some of these have been active in Pinet. The mayor and his nephew (and four other people) have become Christians. The Romanians hope this will open the door for more people to believe, and perhaps lessen the impact of the Muslim missionaries.

Finally, the missionaries have to deal with the Albanian government. They have had difficulties getting visas. Only tourist visas have been possible, making regular, and usually very strenuous, trips to Romania necessary.

---

[9] The fact that the Hobans are not currently living and working in Albania complicates the report which follows. "They" will be used to refer both to the Hobans when they were there and the new couple who are there now. The Hobans see themselves as still involved, even if they are not in Albania at present, and they remain part of the ministry team.

International

Aletheia has not been able to fund their missions program totally from their own resources. This has required establishing relationships with partners outside the country. Exodus Fellowship in Maryland is listed on the church letterhead as the contact for the USA, some church in N. Carolina has also been a partner, and donors come from N. Ireland and Germany as well.

Cultural Factors

The cultural issues include the biblical/theological understanding of missions, the extent to which missions interest existed before the revolution, a look at the way the people of Aletheia view others and themselves has affected their missions motivations. In addition, several themes regarding missions motivation which arise out of conversation with participants will be discussed. It is important not only to understand their current state of thinking, which may give too static a picture, but also to understand the more dynamic process of how thinking has developed and changed.

Biblical and Theological Understandings

The questions to be dealt with here are: 1) how respondents developed their biblical and theological understanding of missions, and 2) what that understanding is. As we will see, their current view has developed over the years, and has been influenced by personal experience in mission.

How did members of Aletheia develop their Biblical and theological understanding of missions? Before the revolution, and in many churches still today, mission has no connotation of cross-cultural activity. Mission was seen in the first place as almost anything that took place outside of one's own church. Visiting another church for an *evanghelizare* (evangelistic service), sending the youth choir to a neighboring church, visiting the old people in the hospital, sending a deacon to hold a worship service in a church without a pastor, were all seen as *misiune* (missions). After the revolution, as new opportunities suddenly appeared, mission came to include church planting. In the years right after the revolution doors were wide open for church planting and many churches grew rapidly. An understanding of mission that included a cross-cultural component came later.

New political conditions opened the door to ministry outside the country, and some people began to catch a vision for these new possibilities. However, objections arose on many fronts which had to be overcome for missions vision to take root in the church. Many Romanians still see the great needs of their own country, and cannot understand why they should send someone somewhere where the need does not seem as great. Further, missions is expensive. It costs more to support a missionary than it does a pastor at home. An American participant observed, "Missions is a strange concept. They ask, why travel to

6. Aletheia Church, Timişoara, Romania

other country when needs are greater here. It's more expensive there. There's a need for hard currency" (BF). Finally, a receiver mentality is common which says, we are poor, we have suffered, we need help. We have earned the right to receive. Missionaries are rich Westerners, not poor Romanians. Aletheia's vision developed in this environment.

At Aletheia, Marincu's philosophy of ministry, influenced by the BEE "Church Dynamics" course, contained a growing awareness of the need for mission outreach. When Hoban came, the church adopted his vision. However, church members did not just accept his vision. They caught it for themselves and owned it. The current missions pastor took the position because there was a need. The previous missions pastor was moving into another ministry and the pastor asked him to take it over. He did not want the position and felt it did not fit his gifting or interests as a teacher and trainer. He felt he would never be a missionary. Nevertheless, he caught the vision because he was doing it. He relates, "I said to myself, I will never be a missionary. I didn't really care. But God changed me. As missions director, my life was changed" (MI). Since then he has gotten involved in foreign ministry, traveling to Vietnam with BEE to teach courses to others who now experience under Communism what the Romanians had lived through. The vision is the church's vision, and church leaders encourage everyone in the church to be involved in it.

Marincu traveled with the Hobans when they moved back to Albania after Aletheia began supporting them, to see the situation for himself so that he could share it with the church. He says of his experience:

> Experience in Albania caused me to see passages differently – studying Acts, preaching gospel as lifestyle. Evangelism is part of the mission. It is not the all and it is not the end. But perhaps the beginning. Going on the field and seeing the needs was important. We started a Bible study on Acts. Mission was not strategy; it was a lifestyle. Preached gospel as a lifestyle. Sometimes in our seminars we give a different idea. It's good to organize, but that's not all. (CM).

Missions is more than just evangelism. It is certainly a large part, but not everything. Missions is "to carry Jesus with me in everything I do." Marincu recognized how his experience gave him a different set of eyes, both for how he read Scripture and how he did ministry. Jesus is the great example of missions.

> He didn't care about numbers, he just went to share. He listened to the people. Mission field is to have Jesus in my heart and develop him in a country. The right mission strategy is sharing in the marketplace, listening to people, being willing to share. (CM).

The church has a written manual, which includes a section on multiplication and mission. All church members have to read and understand the vision. In addition, it developed a mission constitution, which outlines policies on finances, communication and partnership.

What is the Biblical and theological understanding of missions that Aletheia has developed? It defines mission as the "proclamation of the gospel to unconverted people everywhere, conforming to the command of the Lord Jesus" (1998, 14). The supreme objective of its missions is

> to make the Lord Jesus Christ known to all people in all countries, as Lord and Savior, such that they become his disciples and become engaged in indigenous local churches, which are self-governing, self-maintaining and self-multiplying. (Manualul bisercii "Aletheia" 1998,14).

From this Aletheia developed its own strategy informed by that of Jesus, the Great Commission, the early church, and Paul. That strategy is not to save as many souls as possible over as wide an area as possible, but rather to plant and assist a local church in the process of maturing, so that it will be able to do evangelism and missions as one of its functions (Manualul bisercii "Aletheia" 1998,14).

Church leaders tie their view of missions to their understanding of what the church is and what it should do. Mission is the job of the local church. This conviction helps to explain the concerns expressed about other missionaries. For instance, two girls from Oradea serving in India, and a man from Satu Mare serving in Afghanistan, were sent and cared for, not by a local church, but by the PMS or *filiale*.

The church leaders understand missionary sending as an act of God. The church was not dreaming of missions when the Hobans came to them. Marcel Hoban summarized this view.

> I believe God is the one who calls, not the church. The church's role is to discover, to confirm those that God has already chosen, to prepare and send into service those God has already called. (MH).

Interest in Missions before Revolution

All respondents agree that they did not think about the possibility of foreign missions before the revolution. Hoban and his group prayed for other countries, but with no idea that God would use them outside the country. The current pastor outlines at least three reasons why Romanians had no vision for missions outside the country. First, they were isolated from the rest of the world, without information and knowledge of what happened outside the country. Second, they did not believe there was a need for them outside; they thought it was enough to stay there, and they did not believe they could do mission outside. Finally, nobody encouraged them to think about missions. "Pastors didn't ever talk about it, or talk about how the world needed us, or that there are other peoples to which we could go. Until the revolution we were simply closed, locked inside" (LC). They were concerned about evangelism, but only within the country. In the context of Communism, missions seemed impossible and unreachable.

Educational Factors

None of the Romanians involved in this case have a formal theological education or studied at university. Several of them have extensive experience with BEE, a church-based leadership training and theological education program. Therefore, education does not seem to have had much impact on their missions vision. Hoban took some courses at Agape before he went out, but he already had his vision. Marincu was influenced by BEE, which helped him think about the nature of the church and ministry, and helped him determine the kind of church he wanted to start. However, it did not really impact his vision for missions, which came more from Hoban.

Ethnocentrism/Openness to Others

Respondents see the question of ethnocentrism and openness to others as an important issue for them to consider. They have experienced some of the negative consequences of missionaries from outside who had arrogant attitudes, and have seen some positive models of those who came to serve. They recognize the advantage of living in Timişoara, a multi-ethnic city in southwestern Romania near the borders with Yugoslavia and Hungary. In some parts of the city, Romanian, Hungarian, and Yugoslavian schools are close together. The missions pastor comments on their relations with Albanians.

> Albanians and Romanians have good relationship. We don't have problems. Similar cultural background, similar economic conditions. Albanians receive the Romanians much better than say, Americans or other Westerners do. We are similar. They live at the same level we do. That was God putting the things together. (MI).

Although the Romanians feel they have something important to bring to the Albanians, they see they have a lot to learn from them, for example in area of hospitality. Romania has a strong reputation in this area, but "We don't know anything compared to them [Albanians]. They give you everything" (CM). They recognize the possibility and the danger of an attitude of superiority and pride, of being full of themselves. They know they need to be humble and to see others as "like us". Marincu talks of BEE as being a role model for them in this, in that BEE staff came in and recognized they had things to learn from the Romanians, and not just to teach. Finding the balance between having something to offer and something to learn is important.

Tied to respondents' view of others is naturally their view of themselves. The years under Communism had drained them of the courage to dream. They looked to outside missionaries to do the work. "We have the potential, but we have a poor image of ourselves. That poor image affected us very much. It made us think we were too weak, that we couldn't offer anything" (CM). Before they could begin to get involved themselves, they had to learn to think in a new way. The transition came as they were able to change their mental picture of themselves, to see themselves in a different light, and see that God could use them to be missionaries.

Role of (Western) Evangelical Missionaries

Aletheia and its leaders have had much contact with Westerners through the years, starting even before the revolution. Western missionaries are seen as having both a positive and a negative role, but even the negative was an encouragement to them in developing the courage to do missions themselves.

On the positive side, some missionaries have been very helpful. The training offered through BEE helped Marincu develop his own ministry skills and philosophy of ministry.[10] Missionaries from the West came and modeled missions to the Romanians, helped them to see missions first hand, and encouraged them to think about missions for themselves. Others came regularly and encouraged them in their vision. An American missionary family with BEE was in the church from the beginning, encouraging the church's vision and personally supporting the Hobans. This fit in with their own vision of ministry in Romania.

On the negative side, participants saw some missionaries who were not good models for them; people who came in and were not willing to learn Romanian culture and language, and who created problems with their condescending attitudes. Nevertheless, this was still seen positively. Romanians looked at missionaries from the West with whom they were not impressed and thought:

> oh, if this is what a missionary is, we can do that. We have people who are more mature, better prepared, experienced, able to teach. We can do a better job than they do. So it helps, even if they are weak. We rise to the challenge and say, hey, we can do that. (CM).

Having Western missionaries in Romania is seen as positive, even if those missionaries are weak. This allowed the Romanians to see that missionaries are people just like them. So they rose to the challenge and said, "we can do it too. We can be missionaries" (CM).

Role of Ministry Involvement

All of those who give leadership to the missions program of the church were involved in outreach activity before they caught a vision for cross-cultural missions. The Hobans were involved in mission as they understood it at the

---

[10] Marincu served for several years as a part-time BEE staff member in the middle 1990s.

time, for example, visiting sick people in the hospital (MI). Felicia Hoban describes their experience.

> We had been involved as young people in what was understood at that time in Romania as missions. Visiting other churches, visiting hospitals, visiting old people, evangelism in other churches. We had been active in ministry so when we started thinking about cross cultural ministry it wasn't something new in terms of the work, but new in terms of the place and language. We'd been involved in ministry all along. (FH).

The pastors had helped start a number of churches in neighboring and more distant areas of Romania. People did not first have to be convinced of the necessity of evangelism, because they were already involved in ministry. Only the geographical distance was new.

The church has a number of people active in outreach to the surrounding area, and it sends teams to Oltenia to help develop some churches in the south of Romania. Sending short-term teams seems to have helped leaders develop their missions vision.

Importance of Story as Motivating Factor

Different people in different contexts repeatedly retell two stories, showing that they have become a part of the church's missions folklore and identity.

The first is the story of Hoban's vision about Albania, told at the beginning of this case. The second is a recurring story of how God protected the Hobans in Albania. They moved into the village of Pinet, simply to establish a Christian presence in the village. They went as newlyweds, and as such, were adopted and protected by the village. During the troubles in Albania in 1997 when foreigners had great difficulties and many were evacuated, they had to stay. The villagers told them "you'll be the last to die. First we will die, then our children will die. Only then would you die." Another time, when Muslim missionaries from Pakistan came to the village, they told the Albanians that they should kill the Hobans, because they were Christian missionaries. The villagers told them to go away. "They are Christians, but they are *our* Christians. They are one of us."

These stories are told regularly and serve as motivations for others who are praying for or considering missions, to show how God can take care of them if they have the courage to move forward for him.

Interaction between Factors

After describing the various systems, it is instructive to try to understand the way the different systems interact with one another. No system operates in isolation from the others, and in this case, it is often difficult to determine into which system a particular issue fits most appropriately.

Which normally takes priority, a new practice which leads to a new way of thinking, or new thinking which leads to new practice? In this case, the former is more often true, but we can detect a certain cycle. Following the revolution new opportunities came for Romanians to travel outside the country. They were able to participate in international conferences and to travel to potential mission countries. These experiences allowed them to see the world in new ways and caused them to rethink their old understandings of the Bible and their philosophies of ministry. For example, the practical experience in Albania helped changed the way Marincu read the Bible. The experience of one the pastors in Sweden showed him that the world needed Romanian missionaries to come and evangelize. The principle seems to be that personal experience leads to a change of thinking, more than the other way around. On the other hand, study with BEE had caused reflection on current practice which led to a new philosophy of ministry which helped them be open to new practice.

Spiritual affects social which affects culture change. God spoke directly to a key person, who came with a vision and changed the direction of a group, including structures and culture (visions, philosophy, and Biblical understanding). Looking at it another way, using the language of diffusion studies (Rogers 1995; Gladwell 2000), an innovator influenced an early adopter who was able to then make the message understandable to the group so that it adopted it.

Vision and economics are closely related. However, the nature of this relationship is complex. Vision impacted willingness to pay, but is this an aspect of the cultural system affecting the social system, or is vision here an effect of spiritual vitality? We can see the spiritual system working into the cultural to bring about change in the social. At the same time, vision did not actually change the economic system. It changed instead the way that the people involved understand their capabilities and made them willing to use their financial resources to further a specific cause. This makes the economic system the stage on which culture change takes place. It is not so important to determine in which system a particular factor fits as to recognize that interaction between systems does occur.

In Romania, a new way of thinking often comes from the pastor to the church, but in this case it happened the other way around. A new pastor came to Aletheia with a vision for church planting but without a cross-cultural missions vision and caught it from the church. Because of his involvement as a church planter he was easily open to their vision.

Conclusions

Why has Aletheia become a missionary sending church? The process can perhaps be summarized in three stages. First, someone came to the church with a compelling vision for cross-cultural missions, given by God.

Second, the pastor of the church was open to something new and was able to help the church adopt it. That openness can be traced to at least three influences: the impact of BEE courses, considerable interaction with Westerners, and the influence of negative experiences at Agape. He had a theological base and a philosophy of ministry which was open to missions.

Third, the church was open to the missions vision and adopted it as their own vision. At first people saw a need and wanted to help a specific family. Gradually, however, they became convinced that supporting missions was what God wanted them to do. Aletheia had been a multi-cultural community from the beginning, and had been encouraged by its contacts from outside the country to be open to God doing something new through it.

The missions pastor summed up his understanding of how things had come about, showing how all the systems come together.

> It's God's way to do things. He prepared it all. You have to have courage and be a little crazy and step out into the dark. You have to have faith. We didn't have enough money to buy them a nice car, nice work things. But we had faith and we had a pastor crazy enough to send them. Then we became as crazy as him! The church has caught the vision! (MI).

Aletheia is a small church with a large missions vision. It was one of the first churches in Romania who sent out missionaries without support from some outside organization. Although the level of help from outside sources is probably larger than implied by the main participants, they nevertheless have devoted themselves to providing for their missionaries as completely as they can. Certain long-term issues must still be clarified, including the status of the missionary at home and the possibility of long-term foreign assignments. Nevertheless, they seem to have the vision and the will to be used by God in Albania and elsewhere in the future.

7. Biblical Mission Association, Poland

Biblical Mission Association (BSM)[11] is a Polish mission agency consisting of four branches: Mission to the East (MttE),[12] Wycliffe-Poland (W-P), Mission to Poles in the East, and Ministry to Ukraine. In 1995, the first two of these branches were small missions initiatives, which independently were trying to get legal recognition from the Polish government. They became aware of each other and decided to combine forces in order to simplify the registration process. They have a common board, with a common office and accounting, but, in terms of ministry focus and direction, they operate independently. Mission to the East focuses on the former Soviet Union, specifically Central Asia, with a primary emphasis on evangelism and church planting. Wycliffe-Poland has people spread more around the world, from Mali to Central Asia and Australia. It concentrates on Wycliffe's Bible translation and literacy promotion.[13] The third branch, Mission to Poles in the East, focuses on Polish minorities in Lithuania. The fourth and newest movement, Ministry to Ukraine, has recently joined BSM, and its official relationship is still being clarified. The impetus for this ministry came from the president of BSM (currently also director of Wycliffe), and involves ministry to several Gypsy churches and villages in western Ukraine. They provide clothing, support schoolteachers, provide meals for schoolchildren, and fund church buildings. Wycliffe's specific involvement relates to the literacy programs in the schools. The emphasis in this case will be on the first two branches and touches on the fourth as it relates to the first two.

Twelve people were interviewed. These included the officers of BSM, including the key people of both branches, American and British missionaries who are members of the mission, the president and professors from the Seminary where most of the missionaries have been trained, missionaries who have served both short and long term with MttE, lay people who have been involved in the ministry to Ukrainian Gypsies, and the pastor of the supporting church of the first missionaries. In addition, I traveled to the Ukraine with a group of Poles, where I observed the ministry among Gypsies. I also participated in a conference in which the director of Mission to the East (MttE) gave a presentation, and shared a room at a Europe-wide missions conference with

---

[11] BSM in Polish is Biblijne Stowarzyszenie Misyjne, which in their literature is alternately translated Biblical Mission Association or Biblical Mission Society.

[12] Mission to the East in Polish is Misja na Wschod.

[13] Either of these branches could be examined as a separate case, especially Mission to the East, which corresponds most closely to the indigenous model which was sought. Nevertheless, because they are legally one organization, and because they are unique in Poland, together they show a wider range of missions involvement in Polish churches.

the president of BSM. These occasions allowed me to update the information obtained at interviews with both of them conducted earlier. Promotional literature was available in English, and articles in German were consulted.

Background and Historical Development

The story of this mission is really two stories, each with its own roots and developments. The two stories do not intersect until 1995, when someone introduced the two parties to each other. MttE, based in Wrocław in southwestern Poland, had primarily Baptist and Navigator roots. W-P, with headquarters in Ustron in south central Poland, had primarily Lutheran and Wycliffe roots. Although the different people involved knew of each other, they were traveling independent paths until they came together to form a common mission agency.

The first missionary couple went from Wrocław to Central Asia in 1993, before any missions organization was in place. They joined an American team already in place there. A few friends gave them a few dollars and they went with no guarantee that more money would come. They were followed in 1994 by single woman. BSM was founded in 1995, in part to care for these missionaries already on the field. By the summer of 2000, BSM had twelve full-time missionaries serving in a wide variety of places, such as Tanzania, Mali, Lithuania, Kazakhstan, Russia and Uzbekistan. Others were in England and Australia, preparing for further ministry. The mission has around fifty members, who pay an annual membership fee and attend periodic meetings. In addition to sending and supporting missionaries on the field, BSM has sponsored several projects. The largest of these was to publish portions of the New Testament in one of the languages of the Tuareg people in Mali. Other projects include humanitarian and educational aid to Gypsy communities in the Ukraine. In Central Asia, BSM missionaries have started an English language school and some businesses, through which they partially support themselves. They publish a regular magazine, *Idźcie*...

Mission to the East was formed by two men associated with Biblical Theological Seminary (BST) in Wrocław. These two, through their travels around the Soviet Union, both before and after the revolution, saw the potential for Poles to be involved in missions in that part of the world. The first Polish missionaries went on a short trip to Central Asia in 1992. There they caught the vision for long-term ministry. The next year they returned with a one-year commitment. They went with almost no money, traveling six days by train, with no idea of what to expect. MttE gradually developed as a way to provide support for this couple and the other missionaries who began to join them. The name "Mission to the East" emphasizes the direction in which they see their call. The director said, "This was to disassociate ourselves from any false mission associations of evangelizing Chicago or Milwaukee" (MC).

Wycliffe-Poland grew out of contacts that a Polish evangelist made with the director of Wycliffe-Germany at a conference for evangelists in East Germany in 1990. He invited this man to Poland and the two of them traveled around the country, speaking at churches and student groups. In 1992 they offered the first mini-SIL course, with around twenty participants from all of Poland. Eventually a missions organization was started to motivate and encourage missions from Poland, which was loosely associated with Wycliffe International.

Themes and Factors

Spiritual, social and cultural factors form the framework for the investigation of the question why missions began to happen in Poland. The lines between the factors are never totally clear, and at times somewhat arbitrary choices are made as to which category a specific theme belongs.

Spiritual Factors

To what extent can we see God's hand in the rise of missions interest and involvement? Some respondents see God very clearly at work, both in creating the movement itself and in creating the conditions in which Poles could be effective in mission. They understand this at least partly as the answer to prayers through the years. God is seen as working in small groups of people and awakening their hearts towards missions, rather than bringing revival to the evangelical churches at large, which they characterize as slow moving and lacking in vision. Further, the question of God's call is considered.

God Is at Work

Several people attribute the emergence of Polish missions to the fact that God is specifically at work in their situation. The BSM vice president felt the first reason missions interest has grown is "a spiritual factor and God's influence" (AH). God was at work, first in a few people who had been involved in evangelistic ministry together in Poland. "God's influence on our thinking in our circle of friends" (AH) stimulated them to start something. He started a prayer group at BTS, which was influential in getting a number of students interested in missions. The following statements illustrate the viewpoint that God was specifically at work.

> God started it. It was one avenue of God working, awakening in people's hearts the desire to minister particularly in the East. I would guess that's God's working in a way, in the country and the people, and whether that's through Communism, or the Catholic Church, or the Holy Spirit or whatever, I don't know. But I would guess the bottom line is that God's at work in the country. Most of the people who come around to us are people who God is awakening it [missions interest] into their hearts. It's not from the churches, I can only suspect it's from God. (MC)

Those statements came sprinkled through one interview, but reflect the views of several others. Another missions leader attributes "mainly God's influence on our thinking and he stimulated us he would like to start something, even if we weren't conscious at this stage about it" (AH). An American missionary speaks of the fact that young people can now build homes and begin to prosper a bit. "So for those who pass on that, now that it's possible, it's the love for the Lord that drives them. Sense of God's work in the world" (CM).

Respondents see God at work in creating the context for Polish missions, in the development of Polish culture and even through the imposition of Communism from the Soviet Union. God is also seen to be at work in a larger way, in his supervision and creation of a people's culture. "Poles are extremely enterprising, initiative takers. That's something God's put it in them" (MC). They are able to look at things positively, even when things are not going well. "Probably something God's put into Poland, in Polish nature" (MC). Other respondents also attribute some of the advantages that Poles bring as missionaries to the way God made them and placed them providentially into a place where they can be used in an effective way.

Respondents also see God at work in the preparation of the conditions for missions on the field. Under Communism, Polish people were required to learn the Russian language in school. Poles (along with the other eastern Europeans) hated Russian and usually did not give their studies much attention. However, now that freedom has come for Poles to work in Central Asia, Russian is the common language. BTS's president says, "ironically God has a great sense of humor, ironically the oppressing factor became a factor that helped those guys to plant into the new situation and share the gospel."

Role of Prayer

Although Poles could not consider personal involvement in missions prior to the events of 1989, some people did begin to pray for mission. People would tell one of the leaders, "I've been praying for missions for years that someone from Poland would become a missionary. Maybe what is happening now is an answer to those prayers." He says, "If something is going on, it's also result of the prayer of this group of people" (JM). He would not claim that all Christians were praying for missions, but some of them had been praying faithfully for many years. In certain circles, already in the 1960s, young people were encouraged to pray for those outside their circles and outside Poland and to pray for the world.

> They [missionaries from the West] brought in a new mentality for evangelicals in this country and they were teaching was to consider the responsibility for the world. And distinguishing a few phases: Phase 1. To notice that there is more than our circles and our country. So we started

to pray for the world. I remember for years and years, back in the 60s we had calendar tricks, Monday we would pray for one thing and the next day for somewhere else, et cetera. (ZK).

Another leader encourages other groups who are considering missions to focus on prayer. "I strongly believe God can use prayer in the lives of people who pray. He can call them and create the right kind of motivation and interest. I saw this in my life and in the people I'm involved with." (AH).

Question of Revival

Is the emerging missions movement the result of revival occurring in Polish churches? The general response of interviewees was that, although there have been pockets of revival in the country, missions motivation is not primarily a result of these revivals.

In the early 1990s a revival movement among students occurred, and in parts of the Catholic Church today it continues. While the comments above indicate an awareness of God's specific work, that work is seen as happening in small circles. "Revival is only on a very small scale, in our immediate context" (AH), says one respondent. Another does not see revival in Poland, but rather a "slow and creeping process" (CM) of movement. Taking a more historical perspective, one leader notes that those who were involved in evangelism in the old days were "those who were awakened spiritually, were those people who would go out and share the gospel. It was from a spiritual rather than a social conscience" (ZK).

The fact that the first missionaries in Central Asia have stayed so long indicates something more than purely human motivation. "God obviously is real and at work in their lives, but that's not the impetus for everything that's happening" (CM). In summary, then, respondents do not see revival in the church as a driving force in missions, but recognize that small-scale revival within individuals and small circles of friends helped provide the impetus and endurance for missions efforts.

Question of Call

The question of a call to missions shows up regularly in interviews. Two basic viewpoints were heard. The view of the majority of respondents is that the sense of God's call is very important. One of the early missionaries talks of how important it was for him and his wife to have a call, because they were doing something new. He says of Polish church people, "They keep expecting me to come back and become a pastor. They have no concept of long-term missions. I think I never will. I have missions calling, whether in Central Asia or Poland or elsewhere" (ZP). He trusts that God will use him to call more people into missions service. Another leader speaks of someone who was really moved by a short-term experience in Central Asia and "God called him to go there." (WT).

Some pastors preach that a person must have a specific call from God. Another pastor, however, speaks of the idea as something of a mystery, specifically when the call involves a specific location. He says, "I couldn't do this. I don't understand it. But some people have it." (DT). A young woman who has done a short term in Central Asia struggles with this question. While open to another short-term trip, she does not see a long-term commitment possible, because she does not have a sense of call and is still waiting for it. Another person said his call to missions came with his conversion when he was sixteen years old.

On the other hand, a few respondents feel that a call to missions is inherent in the gospel. For them, what is important is to follow God however and wherever he might lead. They see people who want to go into missions because they read the Bible and recognized the command to go into the whole world, and "for them, this statement is enough for them to be ready to go." (JM). The BSM president sees a danger in the ways call is taught and practiced.

> The teaching in churches is you must have call from the Lord, but how are we to define, identify this call. Some people defend call on the basis, 'Jesus said go, so I want to go, why don't you let me go.' They will ask, you have to have a call, what do they mean with this call? The issue of call can become a platform for manipulation. (JM).

On the one hand, if someone is interested in missions, they may be asked if they have had a call, which may lead to uncertainty on their part. On the other hand, people can use the claim of a call to avoid responsibility to get training, or be approved by a mission agency. "'God called me; who are you to question that?' Pastors may manipulate those who want to go, and those who want to go invent events which prove they have a call from the Lord." (JM).

Social Factors

Social factors include key people and their role in the social system, and economic, political and legal, ecclesiastical and network factors. In addition, organizational approaches taken by the two main branches of BSM are compared. The question here is to what extent structural or relational factors promote or inhibit the growth of cross-cultural missions activity.

Key People

Among the key people in this case are two non-Poles and three Poles. One of the non-Poles was very influential at the beginning, the other four continue to be very active leaders in the missions movement.

Malcolm Clegg is a British missionary who has lived in Poland since 1983. He serves with Navigators, teaches missions at BTS, and is president of MttE. Malcolm, or Marek, as he is more commonly known by his Polish name, has a positive reputation among Poles. They characterize him as different from most Western missionaries, because he speaks Polish well and understands Polish culture. As one example, a colleague says of him:

> He really helped it [promoting missions]. Being able to travel there regularly, his commitment to help Poles in mission, his understanding of Western culture and Polish one, concerning problems of cooperation on mission field. Helped to understand each side, help manage conflicts, what kind of presupposition lie behind kinds of thinking. His influence is exceptional. (AH).

As a student in the Soviet Union in 1977, Clegg met Poles who were smuggling Bibles into Russia. One of the first Westerners who saw possibilities for Poles to be involved in missions, his participation at BTS from its inception has given him influence with a wide variety of students. The seminary president recalls that "we started this seminary. From the very beginning we knew mostly by Marek Clegg that we would change mentality of young leaders and we would push them out of the country." (ZK).

Burkhard Schöttelndreyer was the director of Wycliffe-Germany in 1990. Jerzy Marcol (see below) met him in Germany and through him caught a vision for Bible translation. Schöttelndreyer later traveled around Poland and other Eastern European countries, encouraging young people with the vision of peoples who did not have the Bible in their own language. It is not clear how influential he was to the country as a whole, but he was a key person in motivating Jerzy Marcol, one of the crucial Polish leaders.

Jerzy (Jurek) Marcol is the president of BSM and director of W-P. Jurek became a Christian in 1981 through reading the Bible. The motivation to serve came along with his conversion. He immediately wanted to go to Bible School in Switzerland, to be trained for missions. However, as he and his wife were preparing to go, martial law was imposed in Poland, destroying any chance of their leaving the country. His love of languages and his love of travel were both motivating factors for him to consider missions. He learned German and English with a view to the possibility of using them in cross-cultural ministry. Contact with the outside world opened his eyes to the needs in the world. In 1991 he went to a conference for evangelists in the former East Germany, where he met Burkhard Schöttelndreyer and learned about Wycliffe. This opened his eyes to the needs and possibilities for Bible translation work. He worked as a Wycliffe representative for a few years before deciding to start a Polish organization with an emphasis on Bible translation and literacy. Although he originally desired to be a missionary himself, he came to see that he could be more useful if he stayed home and promoted missions than if he himself went as a missionary to another country.

Andrzej Horyza teaches practical theology at BTS and is vice-president of BSM. He was active in evangelism before the "breakdown",[14] and after 1990 became curious about how the Christians in the Soviet Union were doing. His interest in missions was kindled primarily by reading about persecuted Christians around the world.

> A particular kind of literature stimulated our thinking at this stage. Someone gave me a copy of Open Doors magazine before 1989. Really something for me to read this. It was totally impossible to get these materials before '89. Afterward we got a regular information flow from missions magazines about persecuted Christians, situation in different countries. (AH).

As a result of attending an Open Doors conference in 1990, he was motivated to spend a summer traveling around the Soviet Union, east of the Urals. There he met a wide variety of people, following one contact to the next. After this, he regularly made such trips and took students with him. A number of them caught his passion. He began a prayer group at BTS, which eventually about half the student body attended. One of his former students, who named him as a significant influence on his own decision for missions, said, "at first I thought he was kind of strange, but I saw his vision and commitment. He was willing to think, and not just accept what others said." (WT). Another leader spoke of "his passion for the mission to the east. He was bringing young people, our students every occasions and he just took them with him to the east. They never came back the same." (ZK).

A final key person is Zbyszek Pawlak, the first Polish missionary sent out by MttE. He, along with his wife Asia, first went to Central Asia in 1992 to explore possibilities there. In 1993 they went with a one-year commitment and have stayed nine years so far.

> We felt a calling. We were willing to destroy the wall. There was a need for someone to lead the way. But we also wanted to be committed to living a godly life as normal person. We saw possibility of doing that in missions. (ZP).

While desiring to be a model for Polish missionaries, he does not know whether their time in Central Asia is long-term. He says people keep expecting him to come back and become a pastor.

---

[14] This is his term for the revolution in 1989. This point will be discussed in more detail below.

> They have no concept of long-term missions. I think I never will. I have a missions calling, whether in Central Asia or Poland or elsewhere. Maybe we'll work in Poland as mobilizers and trainers. We trust God will use us to call more people. (ZP)

Economic

To what extent do economic conditions and attitudes either help or hinder the missions impulse in Poland? Polish mission leaders recognize that missions agencies must be self-sustaining if they are to continue to grow. Missions agencies must deal with the reality of a difficult economic situation. However, attitudes toward finances play an important part in whether missions outreach becomes a truly Polish movement and whether missionaries can be supported from within Poland. The relationship between these two aspects will be explored, as well as some of the practical aspects of financing missions.

The reality is that, while a few people are doing very well financially, for most people the economic situation is difficult and probably getting more so. In real terms, many people are getting poorer. In many churches unemployment is high, sometimes up to half the congregation. Evangelicals, where the missionaries have their contacts, typically belong to the poorer part of society.

In addition to this difficulty at home, missions abroad is getting more expensive. As one example, when the first missionaries went to Central Asia, their support needed was $150/month, now they need around $750/month. Before, travel was very cheap; now it costs around $2000 to get a family there. Consequently, the percentage of income coming from Poland is getting smaller. Currently MttE draws around $200-$300 a month from Poland (25-30%), obviously making partnership with outsiders necessary.

While acknowledging that the economic situation is difficult, respondents also note some positive realities. They note that people have more than they used to, even if some things are more difficult. Says the BSM president, "We are not poor anymore. We have less than those in West, but we have a lot more than people in East. Now is time to help those who have less." (JM). In addition, they compare themselves with the wrong countries.

> But unfortunately we never compare ourselves with really poor countries. We tend to compare our situation with Germany, Switzerland, Norway, the good developed countries. Never looking to Kazakhstan, Nepal, or several other places. (ZK).

It is important to understand the actual economic situation, but the attitude toward finances and giving is also important. The respondents in general felt that a clear missions vision and motivation would allow significant giving, even given a difficult financial reality.

Before the revolution, financial weakness made missions seem impossible. The typical Polish attitude was always "we are poor and need help" (JM). At times they truly needed outside help to survive. Nonetheless, this attitude of dependency makes it difficult to think about reaching out beyond themselves and their own programs. Poles have no tradition of regular giving outside the church context. Pastors typically are not paid very much and the expectation is that ministers should be poor. Trying to find regular, monthly support is difficult.

Materialism is a growing concern, both in its positive and negative aspects. Positively, people now have the chance to build houses or buy apartments. Incidentally, this also makes it difficult for young couples to consider missions. An American missionary observed:

> They have the chance to own their own home. Asking them to give that up is different than asking young Americans to give it up. Americans have always had it, here they're seeing possibilities for first time. They're not looking for toys, but basics which they couldn't get earlier. People have to work for years and years, and get help from family, because bank loans are overpriced. Chance to have simple secure home for family. So for those who pass on that, now that it's possible, it's the love for the Lord that drives them. (CM).

At the same time, people are becoming more attracted to what money can buy. As one leader says, "if you come on Sunday to the service you will see that we struggle with the same problems of other churches – lack of parking spaces." (ZK). Another leader sees this as one of the negative impacts of revolution.

Although most Poles are not in the habit of giving regularly or systematically, they do exhibit great generosity when they see needs, responding spontaneously and practically. They have generously supported projects like flood relief, helped provide Gypsy villages in Ukraine with Bibles and clothing, and funded the publication of new Bible translations in Mali. This can perhaps be traced back to the days under Communism, when, in order to survive, one had to receive help from others, and be willing to give help in return. In addition, Polish Christians spontaneously support missionaries when they realize they have a need. When a report is given in church about a missionary, someone may come up to the person responsible and give ten or twenty Złotys.[15] Although some people may give out of a sense of guilt, most are motivated by compassion. A BSM leader says:

> We received lot of help from West. Average church members have a kind of interest. Want to bring humanitarian help, but they don't know where needs are. Want to help. Example, helping after floods in Ukraine two

---

[15] At the time of writing, the złoty (PLN) was worth 4.2 to the US dollar.

years ago, Gospel of Mark or Luke in Taureg, Bibles for Gypsies. People want to help, maybe feel guilty, once they received a lot, now they have much. Result of compassion. They experienced poverty in past, understand it for others, know how meaningful help from West was for them. Want to help others if they can give it further on. (JM).

BSM desires to see this form of generosity grow. Their goal is to encourage giving which is "compelled by compassion." The missions leaders recognize that the Holy Spirit is the one who motivates to respond to needs, but that he often speaks directly to the interests and strengths of a people.

The missions agencies feel a tension in teaching about missions. They do not want to appear to be advocating something which will take away money and people from the local church. Yet they feel it is crucial that Christians in Poland understand the Great Commission, and see that the job of the church is greater than just to have programs in the church building. They feel it is the job of pastors to teach about missions, so that they can concentrate on the details of helping people be sent. The BSM president says:

> Agencies are in awkward position. Teaching about missions, supporting and praying for missions, should come from pastors. If we as interdenominational organization come and tell the people should give, we are accused of being arrogant and trying to get money for themselves. We are taking money away from pastors and churches. Pastors should do the teaching on how to sacrifice, not only in parish but other places. Very delicate issue. Requires transformation. (JM).

Since few pastors teach or preach about missions, the agency people feel they must. This raises the question of competition.

Some churches are starting to support their own projects, which might take away funding from the mission agencies already in place. The agencies are determined to not allow the competition to divert resources from the church. For this reason they try to promote any kind of missions efforts. The BSM president says:

> We want to publish anything we hear about new initiatives in our bulletin. If churches start their own initiatives, they may stop supporting BSM. Because of our publications people start supporting missions. (JM).

All the missionaries are supported through churches, rather than through the agencies, and churches can demand as much accountability from their missionaries as they choose. Some churches have begun to see that they also get a benefit locally when they invest cross-culturally. "We don't want to exempt Polish churches from supporting missionaries. The church begins to learn that they get lot of blessing from supporting and sending missionaries." (JM).

A few practical issues have either had to be faced or will need to be faced, in order for missions support to continue. First, BSM had to answer the question of where support for Polish missionaries would come from. The director of MttE reports that currently, major support comes from a few Christian businessmen who give large gifts. A few dozen individuals give smaller gifts, maybe ten to twenty Złoty,[16] and a few churches give relatively small gifts, 100-200 Złoty. The mission would like to see more giving coming from churches, as a sign of growing ownership of the vision.

Second, the agencies are dealing with the relationship of structure and communication to giving. They have seen the difficulty of keeping support because of lack of communication from the field. People tell them they do not know how to pray, and they do not know whether their gifts are still needed. This comes in part because of a lack of financial accountability from the home base. MttE's president says:

> People here are starting to get frustrated. A, that they never communicate, never is extreme word, but they extremely rarely communicate with Poland, maybe 1-2 times a year we might get some news from them, on average, so people are getting frustrated, both givers and prayers. Everybody says, why don't we ever hear from them. We've seen it doesn't serve either side, people start to drop off. Second, people don't know whether they need money or not, because there's no review that they're accountable to send to office yearly report. (MC).

To try and deal with this lack of connection between field and home, MttE has set up a system of advocates, or friends, who are responsible to make sure that the message about and from the missionaries is kept before the church. Their periodic reminders usually have the effect that people come up to them afterward with some small gifts to pass along. They have also begun requiring their missionaries to report regularly or lose their support.

We can make a final observation. Some people who give to projects out of compassion become regular supporters of missionaries. This dynamic is similar to the observation that personal involvement in evangelism often leads to missions involvement. The general feeling among respondents is that Polish missions could be self-sufficient. The money is there if sufficient vision exists. "I think the Polish church could be very easily self-supported and could easily support 100% of missions efforts, but we as many other sinners start to feed up ourselves first and eat." (ZK). This is not to deny true financial difficulty, which makes it difficult for Polish Christians to think about supporting something outside the country. Nevertheless, one missions leader says,

---

[16] Around $2.50 to $5.

Now is time to help those who have less. This requires transformation. We shouldn't expect to say to those in West, please help us any more, because we need help. We should think about who we can help too. (JM).

Political/Legal

In asking about the political and legal ramifications of the events of 1989, the first thing one has to clarify with Poles is the nature of the changes that took place. In general, people do not like to speak of a revolution here. One pastor claims there was no revolution, and Horyza spoke repeatedly of "breakdown", never using the word revolution. Someone else spoke of the "changes". Here, less than in the other countries, it was seen as a more gradual process which brought increased freedom, but "this freedom might have come anyway, as it did in former Yugoslavia" (AH), even without a "revolution".

The first major benefit of the "breakdown" was the ability to travel. The Wycliffe director says Poles could always travel more than other Eastern Europeans. In 1986, he traveled to Denmark and Egypt. However, for most people, true freedom to travel occurred only after 1989. At that time, many people began to travel, both to the east and the west, and these experiences helped them gain a vision for what Poles could do in missions.

The second major benefit of the "breakdown" is the practical possibilities that are now available. The possibility of actually organizing as a missions organization, the possibility of getting passports stamped as "missionaries", and issues related to taxation and social security are now possible which were not previously. Reforms beginning in 1994, which brought about tax breaks for donations to charitable and social projects, were one of the reasons for agencies to organize more formally. However, some things have not changed. One of the primary reasons for the two organizations to register as a single organization was due to the difficulties caused by bureaucracy and corruption. Roman Catholic opposition to non-Catholic religious organizations exacerbates this difficulty (Borowik 1995).

Certain legal issues connect directly with ecclesiastical issues. Legally, missionaries must be sent out by a church rather than a mission organization. Because of the power of the Roman Catholic Church, favorable tax and social security provisions are in place for missionaries. They pay a very small flat tax each month, and do not have to pay health or social security when they are out of the country.

Polish law sometimes seems to work against simple missions administration. One leader comments on their need to learn how to operate a mission agency, while doing it. Sometimes their attempts to do something the way they thought it should be done ("sober-mindedness said, do it this way" [JM]), but which were not allowed under Polish law. This seems to be especially true in the financial area, where laws are regularly changing, as the government itself learns to adjust to a market economy from a socialist one.

Ecclesiastical

In contrast to the two previous cases, where church-related issues were very important, here respondents had less to talk about. Some of this relative silence certainly has to do with the parachurch background and leanings of some of the key people. Some is also due to the state of the Polish evangelical churches. While some respondents saw grounds for cautious optimism, the overwhelming opinion was pessimistic about the condition of the church and the missions interest to be found there. Nevertheless, leaders caution that it is important for missions to try to work closely with church leadership if missions momentum is going to increase. Both negative and positive aspects of church life can be noted.

Negatively, according to several respondents, many Polish churches are nearly moribund. Statements such as "Churches are still pretty dead down the line" (MC), and "The church needs to wake up" (CM) characterize the responses. Most churches and most pastors are not interested in cross-cultural missions, although a few exceptions can be found. Many young people are frustrated with the state of their churches and desire to see more active ministry outside the church. Some churches have difficulty seeing the need to minister cross-culturally, especially if there is no church of their denomination in the next town.

Complaints about control issues were also common. The charge is made that pastors want to control both any program they may be involved in as well as the private lives of the people in their congregation. If they can control it, they may support it. The head of MttE observes:

> The Church is highly control oriented. People tend to be, not only church, people are generally highly control oriented. People tend to be interested in what I can control. So if this is my thing then I'm interested in it and I'll give my attention to it. If not my thing, then I'll not give much attention to it, or my effort. Very much true here. If I'm to be involved I want the say in it. And that's what most pastors are about, unfortunately. So I would say, that's probably an issue too. If it's our deal, then I'll do it, but then I say what goes. If it's our deal, and I don't say what happens, then, well ... (MC).

In addition, pastors often seek to control the finances of people. "Pastors want to be minister of finances of their church members pockets" (JM). The issue of perceived competition also comes into play here.

Strong denominational thinking is a concern. Churches have no tradition of cooperation. Pastors are often suspicious of programs that are not sponsored by their denomination. One respondent called this a result of "post-socialist thinking" (AH). Another leader notes:

> There's not much colaborship in Poland between churches and organizations, people aren't used to working together. Rather great fractions in church. Pentecostals don't work with Baptists, and certainly don't work with Catholics. Nobody works with Lutherans, cause they're sort of half-Catholic anyway. So what's this, who's behind this? Who controls this? Is it Baptist? Not Baptist, then I'm not really interested in that then. (MC)

Since BSM is not a denominational program, it usually takes longer to break down suspicion and build trust with church leaders.

The question could be asked to what extent missions interest among young people is a reaction against an unsatisfying church situation. They say, in effect, "I can't do anything here, but maybe there, outside the country, I can." A leader said:

> People are bored with what pastors are doing. Do this, buy this for the church. Those who want to do outreach are frustrated. They want to help where real needs are. People come to office. I hear bitter remarks about situation in local churches. People are dissatisfied with what pastors are doing. It's painful to hear. (JM).

A more positive view can be heard as well. The church in Wrocław where most MttE leadership is involved sees itself as being missions-minded. Missions outreach is part of their vision statement.[17] The church has employed and sent out several missionaries, which has broadened their vision from one of only local ministry to include foreign missions. Other churches have also benefited by sending out missionaries. The church involvement with a missionary has helped change their thinking and their praying. Another way churches have benefited has been through their direct involvement in ministry in the Ukraine. One respondent reported that "this initiative is bringing new life into the churches. I don't want to say that they were stagnant, but they weren't very lively." (P1).

A second area where missions has had a positive impact has been through the promotion of projects. The publication of parts of the New Testament in Taureg brought together churches which rarely have contact with each other, including radical Charismatics and conservative Lutherans, Adventists and Baptists. Sometimes missions representatives have been criticized by groups in the churches because they talk to other groups. In this case, a common ministry has made theological differences less divisive.

---

[17] One member of the church, however, asserted that while it is one of the liveliest churches in the country, it has little mission vision.

We might suppose that concerns about the health and level of missions interest would lead mission leaders to ignore the church and concentrate on interested individuals. However, this is not the case. These leaders recognize that the church is God's final instrument for mission, and that church leaders must be respected. When asked to give advice to newer movements, at least two missions leaders included suggestions to respect church leaders and submit to the church. Says one, "The first principles of recruitment and church relations is to respect church leadership." (JM). Another one noted how personal experience had shown him that if churches do not feel a sense of ownership it will be difficult to go far.

> My advice would be to be submissive to Polish church, spiritually and financially, and not to do something aside from the church but from the church or with the church. This is out of my own experience because we went so far putting into place this school [BTS] we found out ourselves. Next to the church and not under the church. So church doesn't have this ownership mentality of ours and we have to struggle and fight. If there's not ownership mentality in place, then the competition comes very easily. And this can destroy the best programs or burn you out because you always have to fight, fight, fight. (ZK).

He feels that BSM has this positive relationship to churches because the people involved in BSM want to serve the churches.

Networks and Partnerships

To survey the networks in which BSM is embedded would require a separate paper. Describing the networks within and outside of churches in Poland, the organizational network of Wycliffe International, and the support and financial networks with the West would itself be daunting. Adding the various networks in which missionaries (serving in ten or more countries) are involved makes the task almost impossible.

However, the issue of partnership is a useful one to explore, particularly as the Poles themselves are now working partners in relationships, not only with Western mission agencies and donors, but as active (and "senior" partners) in various mission endeavors. As this develops, Poles as senders wrestle with the same issues that they struggled with as receivers. They are attempting to come up with a style and method which will allow them to help, while avoiding the problems they perceived when they were "helped". Two situations, in particular, require careful thought. The first is MttE's ministry in Central Asia where they partner with a Navigators team made up mostly of Americans. A prayer letter from MttE's president reports increased communication difficulties. This has required that training focus more on issues of intercultural teams. The second is the ministry among Ukrainian Gypsies, where the mission is in a position to offer significant material help. The dynamics of these relationships will be explored below.

Basic Approach to Organization

Because Poland has no missions tradition or models, Wycliffe-Poland decided to adapt the Wycliffe model to the Polish situation, which includes making sure it fits Polish laws. However, in contrast to other Eastern European countries, like Czech Republic or Hungary, Wycliffe-Poland has not become a full branch of Wycliffe International. They are, rather, a "cooperating organization" with Wycliffe International. Their approach is to learn all they can from Western models and to adapt these however they can. They have chosen not to become a branch of Wycliffe in order to have more flexibility and control over financial and strategy decisions.

MttE, on the other hand, deliberately decided to *not* pattern themselves after any Western models, seeking instead to find a truly Polish way to do mission. Structure has followed need from the very beginning. The president uses the metaphor of "flesh and bones". They have established policies and structure only as needs have demanded it. Issues of financial accountability, communication and reporting from the missionaries, taxation and insurance and legal responsibility vis-á-vis the government have all been dealt with when occasions demanded it. He says:

> We've tended to go the way of, OK, let's let them learn, they need to learn for themselves, to give the minimum of bones until we see the bones are necessary, and when Poles wake up to the fact that bones are necessary, we'll put bones in there. And we'll put in the bones they see are necessary. (MC).

They want to develop structures that are Polish rather than the structures of Western organizations. Later he repeated the point.

> We've seen bones as a necessary evil, a necessary support, but not the driving force. This needs to come from people's heart and desires. We're not looking to control in any way, we look to support as we can. (MC).

The goal of MttE was actually to create an alternate missionary network, which would be non-Western funded, using non-Western methodology. "This was our desire from the start. What we do will be eastern. Eastern methods, eastern approach, eastern mentality. Reproducible." (MC). Adds a colleague:

> We're trying to do something which has our Slavic atmosphere, that it's ours, rooted in our culture. One of advantages as well, because those culture are relational cultures. They are interested in relationships rather than business contacts. Things operate differently here. (AH).

This non-traditional approach has opened doors to them where Westerners might not be welcomed, or where outsiders need more time to adapt and be effective.

Occasional tensions have arisen between the two branches regarding the level of support and structure that is necessary. As can be seen, MttE has favored an absolute minimum of home country administrative support, preferring to send all the money to the missionaries. Wycliffe, on the other hand, while also desiring to send the maximum amount possible to the field, has seen the need for more office and bookkeeping help. The two sides also vary in their approach in how much support is required before a missionary can leave for the field, and how much training is necessary. Nevertheless, these differing policies do not appear to damage the working relationships.

Cultural Factors

Culture factors include symbols, rituals, beliefs, attitudes, values and worldview. Most of the issues handled here belong to beliefs, attitudes, and values. Included is not only an examination of the particular issues, but also the degree to which these things have changed over the years, in particular since the "breakdown" in 1989.

Biblical and Theological Understanding

Most Polish believers before the revolution, and still many in the churches, see missions as internal, local ministry. This may involve handing out tracts on the street or starting another church in the next village. Fear was an inhibiting factor before the changes. In those days, "obedience to the state" was the law. Now freedom exists and people can take advantage of more opportunities. However, according to the respondents, most people have not experienced a change of understanding of missions. In fact, one said that "missions is not yet a movement in Poland because the theological understanding of missions is not yet there." (ZP).

On the other hand, those who are involved in missions now have learned that their previous understanding was inadequate. These changes have occurred for a variety of reasons.

For some, a reading of the Bible made clear that they had a greater responsibility than they were aware of. One lay person involved in the ministry in Ukraine spoke of a Bible study in Romans 15 which showed members of his group that they should help those less fortunate than themselves. "We became convicted that we should do something practical to help others. We had been thinking we should do something since aid stopped coming to Poland. The Bible study made it concrete." (M1). Another lay person spoke of how a similar long process of reading the Bible helped people in his group see that they should act. "We had prayer meeting for six years. We used to focus on ourselves and their needs – asking God to bless us. Through God's word we began to see that we should focus beyond ourselves." (P2). Still others read the Bible and came to understand the Great Commission and accepted it as speaking to them personally.

Others had their understanding changed through personal experience and reflection on that experience. Some people began to get involved out of a sense of compassion and a desire to help.

> Later they realize not enough to give bread. Sooner or later, the Holy Spirit begins to speak to people or churches, to be involved in sending missionaries with purpose to make disciples, preach gospel, teach. What I observe, people who are willing to meet humanitarian needs spontaneously became regular supporters with purpose to support missionaries who want to go, preach, teach. (JM).

Others became involved in a short term ministry and came to see that their old view of missions needed to change. A missions teacher who took students on trips commented that one of the goals of the trips was to help students change how they saw the world.

> These first hand experiences which students had helped them understand what paradigm they have, and how narrow their understanding of missions is. What can God do? What is culture? What kind of freedom do we have to change forms and approaches? They changed in their thinking. It was a combination between first hand experience and reflection after a while. (AH).

This emphasis on practical experience was the most common reason given for a change of theology. Those who were taught and active in evangelism had an easier time having their vision stretched to include cross-cultural ministry.

Even for those who have grown in their understanding that missions involves cross-cultural ministry, the theological reflection may be shallow. One missionary spoke of a pastor, for instance, who only seemed to be interested in the number of baptisms and quick results. "The first and only question was 'how many people have you baptized?' They had made the decision not to baptize. When he heard the answer his interest was over. He had no interest in pursuing the reason for it." (CM). He was not ready to discuss issues of contextualization, or cultural or religious difference, or necessary preparation time. This is not that surprising, though, given that the entire missions involvement was less than eight years at that point.

Missions Interest before Revolution

There are two different opinions regarding Polish interest and involvement in missions before 1989. Some say there was no thought given to missions; others claim there was. The differences lie in the personal experiences of the respondent.

On the one hand, a few people say that there was an interest in evangelism but not missions. Poland had no missions tradition or missions models. This lack of interest could be traced to two factors in particular: Poles had very few opportunities to travel outside the country, and Polish income was very small (Marcol 1998). Nevertheless, some people began to pray for missions.

On the other hand, some people were interested in missions before the changes. After 1990 people promoting missions began to hear statements like "I've always dreamed about missions, but always thought it was impossible." Others would say, "I would like to go, but who will support me?" (Marcol 1998). Marcol spoke of wanting to go with his wife as missionaries in 1981. They were planning on going to Bible School in Switzerland, but martial law came and the borders were closed. The opportunity passed.

Some Baptist or Pentecostal people became involved with international organizations like OM or YWAM, but they had to leave the country to do so. They were seen by some as merely fortunate, but they had no support from Poland. The motives were usually mixed. Often these people emigrated to be involved in missions, but the motivations may have also included the desire to escape Communist oppression. Marcol said, "the way to missions was through emigration." (JM). Another leader spoke of his cousin who had left Poland to join a Lutheran Mission to work in Peru. He evaluated her motivations positively.

A few Poles smuggled Bibles to the Soviet Union before the revolution. Others gave Bibles to Russian soldiers in Poland. Both of these activities were risky, but show that some Poles were determined to reach out beyond themselves.

A certain generation of young leaders, influenced by contacts with the Navigators and BEE, began to push out beyond the church walls, to do evangelism. These foreign missionaries challenged the young men, both by teaching and by personal example, to pray for the world and to reach Poland itself. Some of these young Poles made plans to start an underground seminary (BST). When the changes came they were able to operate publicly. The leader of the seminary comments, "We're jokingly saying in that time we were using scout's principle and it's much easier to ask forgiveness than to just go out. Just going and doing." (ZK). A whole group of leaders was prepared to act when it became possible. A few of them led the way into missions involvement. They had prayed for other countries, had thought about mission, and had laid the organizational base before the revolution.

In summary, conditions of isolation and oppression kept most people from thinking about mission possibilities. A few people, mostly those who had had more contact with missionaries coming in secretly from the outside, had begun to pray for the world and to do outreach however they could. When political changes came and brought freedom to act outside the country, they quickly took advantage of the situation. In 1989 no one perceived a great groundswell of missions interest, but many of the conditions were in place for missions involvement to develop.

Education

Polish general education provided one significant advantage for mission involvement. All the people were required to learn the Russian language. "Everyone had to sing in the same choir in our country." (ZK). Consequently, the first missionaries to Central Asia could already speak the language of the people.

At the time of the political changes a key group of young people seemed to be waiting to move. BST opened in 1990 and a group of dedicated and gifted students entered. Several of these students soon were gripped with the possibility of missions service and, impatient with the training process, decided to go immediately after finishing the two year program. An American missionary says the school looks back to that first group with affection, as probably the best group they have ever had. BST was started as an alternative to traditional theological education and probably attracted a more adventuresome type of student at the beginning. These students were already predisposed to be open to new ideas. The first missionary speaks of his experience there. "I finished two years at BST. I came to BST expecting to become pastor. That seemed the only possibility to minister." (ZP). There he met Marek Clegg and Andrzej Horyza and was motivated by them to explore missions. He feels that the seminary classes he took did not prepare him for cross-cultural life. "Classes in seminary, no, but Malcolm talked to us about various things; culture shock, and so on." (ZP). For a time there was a missions school as part of the seminary, but this has not continued, nor was its program integrated into the seminary curriculum. The biggest influence of the school was to provide the context where Clegg and Horyza could have an influence as teachers. Now, as part of MttE's training process, candidates are encouraged to come and take some classes at BST.

Role of Western Missionaries

As one might expect, various opinions, at times totally conflicting, were heard on the question of the influence of Western missionaries on the Polish missions movement. Three different answers can be distinguished. Some respondents speak of the time before the revolution, when they interacted with missionaries with OM, the Navigators and BEE. These Western missionaries did not necessarily talk about Poles being involved in missions, but they impressed on a generation of young leaders the fact that they needed to be active in sharing their faith and trying to reach their world. The missionaries provided models of people who were willing to make great sacrifices to help people of other countries.

A second view is that of someone who claimed that Western missionaries have had absolutely no influence, either positive or negative. He made one significant exception for Marek Clegg, who is not seen as a typical Western missionary.

The third view is that missionaries have been a big factor. A pastor cited SEND and CBI (now WorldVenture)[18] missionaries, noting one single woman in particular who has modeled missionary life for a whole group of young women.

View of Self and Others

How do Poles see themselves in relation to other peoples? Two attitudes were found. According to respondents, some Poles see themselves positively, as having something very significant to offer to the world. On the other hand, many Poles seem to suffer from an inferiority complex in relation to other nations.

The question is not one of individual personality, but of national self-perception. Some people think of Poland in very positive terms. Poland as a country has suffered tremendously through the centuries, including over a hundred years during the eighteenth and nineteenth centuries (1795-1918), when it disappeared entirely from the map of Europe. This has given Poles the feeling that their sufferings have prepared them to live for others and to take the problems of others on themselves. As a strongly Catholic country this image has taken a religious cast. Poland is the messiah (or the Madonna) of Europe. Europe needs Poland and Polish people (Byrnes 1996, Babinski 1995, Mach 2000). BST's president notes:

> Many Poles feel they are the center of all other nations. We are the best. Somehow an unexpected development or deepening conviction that this is true carried through persecution over the past time because of Communism and because of WWII and exterminations by Nazis and then by Communists, developed kind of a proof that this kind of mentality is in place. (ZK).

The other extreme to this messianic complex is a national inferiority complex. Poles have experienced strong prejudice over the years, especially from Germany, which has affected their self-image. They see themselves as a Western

---

[18] The possibility must be taken into account that, since the respondent knew that I serve with CBI, he spoke with more kindness than might be warranted, so as not to offend. That being said, the woman in question does have a very positive reputation.

European nation, as an important bridge between East and West, but they have been cut off from the West for so many years they no longer have much self-confidence. Many, particularly within evangelical churches, have an inferiority complex in comparison to missionaries from outside the country. They say, "Missions is for the Westerners, we don't have anything to offer." They see themselves as having no abilities, no financial resources, nothing to offer to others.

> But at the same time a new factor we feel inferior to other missionaries, evangelicals, we are talking about less-educated people, poor people, simple people, by simple fact that some one came from abroad, particularly from America was the best proof that he was right. Whatever this person was saying, he was right. So you can see the inferiority complex developed in Poles. This developed a mentality or attitude of who we are, we cannot do anything. We do not have finance resources. We don't have abilities. We don't have anything in place to help out others. (ZK).

In order to be willing to go out in missions they must be motivated to overcome this attitude. In contrast to Western missionaries, who often come with a self-confidence that they have the solutions to the problems of the world, many Poles are convinced they do not know very much and will not be able to do very much. They have not experienced great success in ministry at home and so do not bring many ready-made answers with them to new ministries.

These two mentalities are contradictory, and describe the extremes. The feelings of each individual fall somewhere on a continuum between the two points.

> It contradicts each other those two factors that I think this would be the scale and you will find all sorts of different kind of mentalities and attitudes and understandings between those two extreme points. (ZK).

Nevertheless, both attitudes, and the interplay between them, have an effect on how they will actually carry out ministry on the field.

Issues of Partnership

Poles are now partnering in all of the fields where they work. How will the two attitudes of national pride and national inferiority effect how they function as missionaries?

Poles have been in partnership with Western missionaries in Poland for a number of years. Not all these experiences were positive. One missions leader said:

> From one side, I appreciate foreigners coming here. Others wanted to do what Polish people could do. Missionaries depended on translators. Usu-

ally these were pastors or other church leaders who could do ministry themselves. They expected we would help them voluntarily. We had families, kids, needs. (JM).

Polish leaders reported being treated like cheap labor, of having to translate for outsiders when they were capable of preaching and teaching themselves, of feeling manipulated or watching others be manipulated by the promise of money or the threat of losing money. They saw missionaries living at a much higher level than they could, and saw how much more it cost a missionary to live in Poland than it did for them.

Now that Poles are missionaries themselves, they have to wrestle with the same issues from the other side. Now they have the money and resources to help and serve in poorer countries. Particularly in the Ukraine they are now the rich ones, who come in for short trips from the outside and use translators. They are attempting to avoid the mistakes they perceived when they were the receivers, but recognize that the issues are not as clear-cut as they previously thought.

How to Separate Gospel and Culture?

Polish society is very monocultural, so most Poles do not have much experience dealing with people who are different than themselves. They are learning how to distinguish between their own cultural biases and background and a biblical perspective. In Central Asia, for instance, the missionaries have been very careful not to impose a particular form of church polity on the people, but to help them, through Bible study, to develop a form which will be truly indigenous. For the same reason, the missionaries have not hurried the process of baptism. At the same time, I noticed areas where they have not yet thought clearly about cultural differences.

Two examples can be noted as illustrative of the issues involved. Polish missionaries are trying to teach the people in their country[19] that, according to Genesis 3, when a couple marries, they should leave the groom's family and start out on their own. They have not asked whether this a biblical model or a cultural one. Moreover, they cannot explain why are they encouraging this, but not baptism and starting churches. In a second case, the Polish missionaries say that they themselves must learn to work because Communism killed that in them. They are also trying to teach the men of their people group that they also should work. These two examples, coupled with the theological and strategic ones of church development, demonstrate how complicated the process of contextualization is.

---

[19] For security reasons the country and people will not be identified.

Role of Personal Experience

Most respondents feel that personal experience is very important in developing a missions vision. This has at least two components: personal experience in the home culture which prepares one for cross-cultural missions, and some kind of cross-cultural experience which allows one to see needs and ways to help meet those needs.

Local ministry can lead to cross-cultural missions. People who were involved in local ministry, particular those doing evangelism, found it easier to think about cross-cultural missions. This is a logical extension of what they were already doing. One missions leader says, "we'd been involved in evangelism, but did not think about missions. The 'breakdown' in 1989 gave us the opportunity to travel across the border and see what the needs were elsewhere." (AH). He was then motivated to try to meet those needs.

One leader of a seminary sees the other side of the issue. He claims that if someone is not involved in local missions, he probably will not be a good missionary.

> It's like with the experience of going out on the streets sharing the gospel. If you have this kind of experience, that is the right way of preparing for missions. Because two thousand kilometers and an expensive ticket doesn't make you a missionary. If you aren't a missionary with experience of sharing the gospel at home and if your experience doesn't help you in it, there is very seldom that this attitude can be developed away in a faraway place from your home. But I do not want to say it's impossible. (ZK).

While it can happen that some people find new courage or motivation away from home, more often this does not happen.

Short-term experiences are valuable. After the changes Poles began to travel abroad. As we have seen, some traveled to the West and met missionaries who opened their eyes to new possibilities. Others traveled to the East, especially to the Ukraine, and saw great needs. They saw people who were worse off than they were and wanted to help. Several respondents emphasized the compassionate dimension of their response. They also wanted to pass along what they had received. They were helped when they were poor; now they wanted to help when they were not so poor. Still others discovered that they as Poles had something unique to offer, which other nationalities could not. Many of those who made short term trips returned with changed perspectives, even if these did not lead them to choose missions for a long term commitment. They viewed their own church situations differently, and they often had a new perspective on how blessed they were living in Poland. One leader gives this advice to groups which are considering missions involvement.

Get first hand experience. They can travel there, join our team for vacation. Create soil in their thinking ready for new kind of seeds. Learn what you don't know. They will learn answers. They will learn to ask right questions. (AH).

He feels that this short term ministry will open people's eyes to new ministry possibilities, which a person staying at home will not see.

What Advantage Do Poles Have?

Poles have a number of inherent advantages as missionaries. Poland forms a bridge between East and West. Poles want to think of themselves as Western, but they realize that they have many cultural similarities with those further east. One outside observer (speaking about Eastern European Christians in general, but with specific application to Poland) notes that their experience under Communism allows them to offer comfort to others who have experienced the same oppression. They frequently have an excellent education, and they bring new strengths into teams because of their cultural backgrounds and the languages they have learned (Schöttelndreyer 1998).

Respondents enumerated several of the advantages they have perceived, especially for those who go to Central Asia. For instance, Poles speak the Russian language.[20] This allowed them to move rapidly into ministry. In one Central Asian situation the American missionaries with whom they were working saw their effectiveness and switched places with them, putting them in charge of the local mission work.

Second, the living standard was not so different, at least when they began in the early 1990s. It was relatively cheap for them to live in Central Asia.

Third, the cultural gap is not so big as for Westerners, and, because of historic political ties, Poles did not need visas. They simply need an easy-to-get stamp in their passport. Further, Poles are very relational, which allows them to get along well in those cultures where relationships are important. Since Poles do not have much money, they need to focus on relationships. The people they serve with do the same; they have little money, but they have built many relationships.

A British missionary with years of experience in Poland observes that Poles do not need much structure and time is not very important. Therefore, travel-

---

[20] This is true at least for the generation older than their mid-20s; the younger generation, who have not had to learn Russian, will lose some of this advantage. Polish and Russian belong to the same language family, which makes learning the language relatively easier for them than for non-Slavs. Nevertheless, they will have to work to learn it, not simply have it already.

ing several days does not bother them. They are compassionate and respond to the needs they see. He says of them:

> [Poles have an] entrepreneur spirit means that they cross borders. Practically, they're no richer than Hungarians or Czechs, maybe than Romanians, but certainly compared to Hungarians or Czechs, but they've got enterprise to get up and go. Wherever you see, if you travel to States or Turkey, you'll see Poles, they're there. Wheeling and dealing their way through life. So they're an ambitious people. That's one reason I'm here. I see there's a tremendous potential in the people. (MC).

Finally, Poles' experience under Communism has prepared them well for ministry in certain countries. They are able to come into Central Asia as fellow sufferers under the Russians. One leader speaking of the missionaries there summarized:

> But again, the same factor in [the country where the missionaries serve] for example, helped them because here an oppressed nation sends people to oppressed nation against the big imperialistic regime, bad guy, Russia. So again the inferiority or the oppressed mentality was one of the helpful factors starting up mission points in [this country], because those guys were able to appeal to [the people] as those bad guys who don't know anything. We do not want to do anything in common [with the Russians], but the level of complexity in this part of the world is so strange that they were using Russian language which both sides hate to share the gospel. (Laughter) At the same time they were received as good guys because Poland was oppressed as [this country] was oppressed. (ZK).

Personal Motivations

What has prompted Poles to get involved in missions? A mixture of motives, both human and spiritual, can be heard from respondents.

On the one hand are factors which do not seem to have any particular spiritual component. These motives, however, have taken people into new experiences where their motivations often change to more "spiritual" ones.

Some people speak of a desire for adventure, going out of a love of travel, or a desire to see a situation first-hand. Some were attracted to missions for social reasons, because friends and others in the church were going. Sometimes they knew the missionaries they were going to visit and wanted to see how students serve the Lord after seminary (GS). Still others were motivated by an interest in languages.

On the other hand, one hears what might be considered spiritual reasons. For example, some wanted to be role models, so people could see that Poles can be missionaries. The desire to help is heard frequently, a motivation grounded in compassion for others. They show a desire to help others who had less than they had. Here was an attempt to repay the help they had gotten when they needed it.

A participant in several trips to the Ukraine desired to use his art to do something more fulfilling. A young missionary to Central Asia expressed the desire to do something great for God. His call to missions came together with his conversion to Christ. He wanted to be a "Christian hero, a Christian knight" (WT). A final motivation is seen in the desire to be obedient to the command to go into all the world and preach the gospel.

Interaction between Factors

It is important to outline the specific spiritual, social and cultural factors that have had an impact on the rise of this Polish missionary sending movement. Equally useful is to look at the interaction between various factors, either within one of the larger categories, and between them. Four in particular are striking in this case.

First is the feeling that prayer influenced the political situation. Marcol notes, "As more and more Christians began to pray for missions, God brought movement in the political and economic situation in the country. Changes began to take place" (Marcol 1998). Further, prayer helped change attitudes and expectations within the church, so that people developed the willingness to move beyond their own immediate circle and reach beyond the borders of Poland. People prayed that God would use Poles in missions, and God has begun to answer those prayers.

Second is how personal experiences can change both cultural factors such as mindset and attitude and social factors of structure. Polish missionaries originally went out with little financial support, with few preparations and no structural backing. Eventually they came to realize that structures were necessary to provide support for them. The positive benefit of building structures contributed to a more positive outlook towards structures themselves.

Third is the interplay between spiritual and human factors. God created Poles in a certain way. He supervised the political process to allow freedom and to force Poles to learn Russian. He placed particularly open students in contact with particular professors, which opened the door to new ministry possibilities. BSM's vice president summarizes:

> The human factors provided the room, the context in which God could work. It showed us possibilities and abilities. The moving power is the spiritual factor, but the human factor created the context which could close or open the door for the spiritual factor which influenced our mindset here in Poland. (AH).

Fourth is the recognition that money may influence beliefs, maybe negatively. People who wanted to keep money coming may be willing to compromise on their beliefs to match those of the donors. This compromise may encompass specific aspects of theology, philosophy of ministry, convictions or values, styles of ministry, and the willingness to allow people to teach or preach in churches who are not really acceptable. Integrity is the ultimate sacrifice to such compromise.

Conclusion

Why is missions occurring in Poland? A tentative appraisal is possible at this point, while recognizing that other factors may be present not clearly stated by the respondents.

A few key persons had a vision to see Poles become involved in missions. They found an environment where some people were prepared to hear the message. This environment was created by the fall of Communism, which opened the borders and allowed free travel. Poles visited other countries and discovered that they were richer than some others, and that they had some unique things to offer. A natural compassion and a national self-perception that they were put in Europe to help others, compelled them to service.

The experience of life under Communism opened doors of ministry to others who had suffered similarly, and languages learned out of compulsion were able to be used to advantage. A newly established theological seminary provided a context where young people who wanted to serve God were put in touch with teachers who wanted to see them used cross-culturally. Finally, the entire process was supervised and directed by God, who answered the prayers of people that Poles be used in mission, who created Poles with certain strengths and advantages, and who pulled the various factors together at the right time.

A Polish leader attempted to summarize his perception of why missions activity had begun. He concluded:

> I can share with you my guesses and presupposition ... personal experience, the main thing ... talking about mission abroad, discussing spirituality, biblical basis, motivations, excitement of going outside to see new situations, factors sometimes are selfish or a natural gift from God pushing you out. Sometimes this is the mentality of you being frontier out in front of everyone in the immediate circles. (ZK).

BSM was the first Polish mission agency within evangelical Protestant circles which had the specific purpose to send cross-cultural missionaries from Poland. Since then other smaller initiatives have begun, but BSM is still the leader.

7. Biblical Mission Association, Poland

The first BSM missionary claimed that missions is not yet a movement in Poland, because a theology of missions is not yet present. However, it does appear that a movement has truly begun, even if it is not widely spread through churches around the country. Estimates of the number of people who have participated in longer or shorter term trips within the context of BSM range from dozens to several hundred. Given the small size of evangelical churches in Poland, this is significant. A number of people are in the pipeline, either preparing for or considering missionary service. The number of individuals and churches who support missionaries is growing. The prospects for further growth appear positive.

8. Romanian International Mission, Romania

Romanian International Mission[21] (MIR), based in Cluj, Romania, is the final case. It has the broadest scope of the four cases, encompassing the missions initiatives of a variety of churches, denominations, foreign and national missions agencies and concerned individuals. It would make a fruitful study in organizational development, but that will not be the focus here. Instead, MIR can be seen as a picture of the developments of missions interest and activity in the whole of Romania. MIR, as such, has not sent any missionaries, but many of the groups in the country who have sent missionaries participate in MIR.

Interviews were conducted with nineteen people, from the following categories: Romanian officers of MIR, American missionaries who have had extensive contact with MIR and related missions organizations, Romanians who have participated in short-term missions trips, Romanian long-term missionaries, members of organizations who are associated with MIR, even if not direct participants themselves, pastors of missions-minded churches, the president of the largest denomination in the country, directors of missionary training schools, and professors at seminaries where students are preparing to go into missions. In addition, I participated in three MIR meetings, using participant observation to confirm (or disconfirm) accounts of participants. Further, relevant documents were collected, including minutes of all MIR meetings, the constitution of MIR, minutes of meetings which took place which led up to the development of MIR, publicity materials, reports and motivational papers.

Selection of the Case

In September 1999, I attended a meeting in Cluj, Romania, which resulted in the establishment of a new Romanian cross-cultural missions agency, METRO. For a variety of reasons, I was not able to continue my involvement, although I watched developments from a distance. I considered the case for inclusion in this study from that time, at least as a practice case, but because it had not actually developed far enough to send missionaries, I did not pursue it. According to several friends, it looked as though not much was happening. In the fall of 2001, I made a trip to Romania to research one of the missions agencies related to METRO. I had been told that METRO and this other organization had gone separate ways due to philosophical differences. Upon arrival, I discovered that the philosophical differences did exist, but that they had not parted ways. It took me some time to become aware of this. Therefore, I got maybe more information on the one agency than I might have, and then needed to change direction somewhat.

---

[21] In Romanian this is *Misiunea Internațională Română*.

Many people are involved in MIR (as METRO has become), which allowed a wide range of possibilities for interviews. It would have been good to travel to București and Sibiu to talk to a number of people. Probably this highlights the difficulty of communication. I had apparently not communicated clearly my desires. My contact thought I was just interested in missions in general, so sent me to Timișoara and Arad to talk to people who had some general interest or involvement in missions, but not to MIR people. These interviews were helpful in giving me a broader picture of missions activity in the country as a whole. For the case itself, it would have been more helpful to visit with people more directly involved in MIR, for example, the president, two vice-presidents, commission leaders, and founding members. I was able to connect with several of those people later, some through telephone interviews and correspondence, but face-to-face would have been better.

On a methodological note, this also shows advantages and disadvantages of having someone else set up an interview schedule. The advantage is logistical – someone else has to deal with the telephone and calendar, and knows the right people to talk to and has the connections to open the door for the interviewer. The disadvantage is strategic – the other person does not necessarily understand well what is wanted or needed. It also highlights the inherent difficulties of intercultural communication, showing how easily misunderstandings can occur.

During that trip, I was able to attend another meeting of MIR, and could hear and see first-hand some of the discussions and meet all the people involved (several new people had joined since the initial meetings).

Description of the Case

In September 1999, Gavi Moldovan, the president of the Romanian church-planting agency *Misiunea Mondială Română* (MMU, United World Mission in English), invited a variety of Romanian leaders and expatriate missionaries to a meeting in Cluj.[22] He called this meeting to explore whether a Romanian cross-cultural missions agency should be founded. The participants were invited because they were "missionaries with cross-cultural experience and pastors with vision and influence in the churches." (GM). This *Bordul de inițiere* (Initiating Board) had two tasks: to discuss the Romanian situation, and to decide what should be done and the best way to do it. By the end of the meeting a new Romanian missions agency was born: Misiunea Evanghelistică Transculturală Română (METRO).[23]

A second meeting in November 1999 continued the discussion. This included reports by the various organizations that had an interest in sending missionar-

---

[22] I was one of those who attended.
[23] Translated into English as Romanian Evangelistic Cross-Cultural Mission.

ies from Romania, and reports on the progress of assignments from the first meeting. These included proposals for a training curriculum, research on other mission organizations in Romania, development of publicity materials and the draft of a constitution for METRO. The critical question in this regard concerned the form the association would take. On one side were those who felt a legal organization was useful and necessary. On the other side were those who saw the benefit of an informal association, and felt the development of the apparatus of an organization was premature. This second group preferred to develop a network of organizations and concerned individuals. The group did not reach consensus on this question. Further meetings and further discussions of this issue were planned.

Despite a continued lack of agreement on the questions of how METRO should develop, whether as an organization or a network of like-minded organizations, the group made the decision to seek legal registration. To do this according to Romanian law, a detailed constitution was necessary, complete with task forces, departments, several vice-presidents and other administration. Over the course of the next two years much time and energy were spent working on the process of becoming an officially recognized legal organization.

Soon the name METRO was changed to *Misiunea Internaţională Română* (MIR), partly to avoid confusion with a chain of large wholesale outlets of the same name which had entered the country. The word *MIR* was also chosen for its positive meaning. "In Romanian 'MIR' is also the word used in John 12:3 for the perfume that Mary poured on Jesus' head. Just as that perfume filled Lazarus' home with it's [*sic*] fragrance, MIR desires to see Romanian missionaries going out to be 'the aroma[24] of Christ among those who are being saved.' (2 Cor. 2:15)."[25]

MIR was founded with a double purpose: spiritual and social-humanitarian. The spiritual purpose was to motivate churches, along with other people and groups within and outside Romania, in the selection, preparation, sending and sustaining of Christian cross-cultural missionaries. The social-humanitarian purpose was to organize projects of material and social-humanitarian help for people living in different countries of the world (*MIR 2000*). This purpose worked itself out through five main areas of activity: research and documenta-

---

[24] In Romanian, the connection between the two verses is clearer. The word "aroma" in Romanian is *mireasmă*, a cognate of *mir*. Some respondents also point out that *mir* means "peace" in Russian, making it a non-threatening word for missionaries desiring to enter the former Soviet Union.

[25] This statement forms a significant part of MIR's self-identity. It can be found on an English language promotional brochure, a Romanian brochure for MIR's missions school in Sibiu, and in the constitution.

tion, promotion and motivation, training and equipping, raising funds, and sending missionaries. This fifth purpose was only an emergency measure. MIR was prepared to send missionaries only if no appropriate church sending structure was available.

Because of the loose nature of the association, different people attended each meeting. Consequently, much time was spent reviewing the developments of past meetings and helping the new people to understand why they were gathered. The participation of a wide variety of people was positive in that it demonstrated the growing interest in missions around the country, but it came at the cost of progress towards the accomplishment of the group's goals.

Much time was spent on organizational matters. One missionary respondent noted that "they didn't work from the concept of form following function. Developed the forms, then tried to figure out what it should do." (DP). MIR decided very early to develop structures, hoping the structures would eventually facilitate ministry.

The current activities of MIR include the work of five commissions and a missionary training school *Şcoala de Misiune M.I.R.*, based in Sibiu. Forty-five students participated in the first session, which lasted one and a half years. A second two year session began recently with twelve to fifteen students.

In the opinion of several respondents, MIR is currently not doing anything significant. Much energy and activity has gone into gaining official registration. As one participant said with ironic pride, "We have a stamp!" (MC). However, many issues remain unclarified, namely, the nature of the organization and how it will function. The major problem most identify is the lack of someone who can give full-time effort to the project. All the participants are heavily busy with other activities, especially within their own churches and organizations. They see the need for a full-time secretary who can concentrate on getting things moving, but no one is available, and the cooperating organizations lack the financing for such a person. This absence of activity is difficult for many participants to tolerate. After one particularly frustrating meeting of MIR, in which the central question was again one of purpose and structure, one of the participants asked another, "Is MIR dead?" The answer was, "No, it's not dead, but I think it is in a coma." (DP). This relative lack of activity, however, does not disqualify MIR as one of the important cases in East-Central Europe, because many of the key people in MIR are important players in the developing missions scene across the country.[26]

---

[26] Since that meeting I received an email from the person asking the initial question. He reports the positive news that things seem to be moving forward again, with some of the leadership and structural issues having been worked out.

In the meantime, groups affiliated with MIR continued to develop their own programs. Several missions schools were started,[27] some new missions societies either began or received new life through the personal engagement of a person with vision,[28] and several churches sent their first missionaries, usually in cooperation with a missions agency.

MIR includes many of the foreign missions groups who are most involved in missions in Romania, as well as all the major denominations. Members of MIR include the director of an official mission in the Baptist Union, *Sociatatea Internațională Baptistă Română* (SIBR), members of the leadership of the Baptist, Pentecostal and Brethren Unions, the director of the Mission and Evangelism Commission of the Romanian Evangelical Alliance, MMU, some local churches, and the evangelical student movement. Western missions agencies who participate with MIR include the Alliance for Saturation Church Planting, BEE International (now Entrust), CBInternational, Church Resource Ministries, Evangelism Explosion, Greater Europe Mission, International Teams, OC International, Pioneers, Shield of Faith, and United World Mission, among others. Some non-Western missions are participants as well, notably from Korea. In fact, a list of those who have participated in, or who belong to MIR, reads like a Who's Who of Romanian evangelicalism.

What follows will not be an organizational history of MIR. That would be a fascinating study of organizational development, cross-cultural communication, inter-denominational relationships, leadership styles, understandings of the relationship between form and function, political maneuvering, among other things. However, these topics are outside the scope of this study. This research will focus not so much on MIR itself, but rather on the conditions which culminated in the need for MIR. MIR can be seen as the reason for the study, but is not the focus of the study. In this case we will examine the context of the churches in which missions interest is developing, and which resulted in people seeing the need for something like MIR.

Major Impetus

Almost all missionaries from the West came to Romania after the revolution, after the third world missions movement was well underway. A few of these missionaries and mission organizations came to Romania with the idea to help Romania become a missionary sending country. Others quickly saw the potential and started working to bring it about. This contrasted with traditional missions, where missionaries preached the call to missions in their home

---

[27] Mission schools have been started in Constanța, Sibiu, Arad, and Timișoara. In addition, the Baptist Seminary in București has begun a missions department.

[28] For example, a mission society in the Baptist Union has become active.

churches, but neglected that message when they planted churches on the field. Within a few years a number of missionaries were talking about the need to promote missions in Romania.

In November 1997, a group of (mostly American) missionaries and Romanians met for the first time to establish what they called Partners in Mission Training (PMT). They wanted to establish a network or partnership that would assist what they saw to be an emerging movement of missions sending in Romania (minutes from PMT meetings 1997). They shared what they were each doing, and planned ways to encourage Romanians to expand their missions vision and activity. They also started to develop a curriculum for a missionary training program. This network eventually merged with MIR.

One of the results of this desire to promote missions in Romania was "Mission for Romanians", a paper written by OC missionary Russ Mitchell (1998).[29] This paper was frequently mentioned by respondents as a significant factor in opening the eyes of Romanians to their potential for mission. In this document, the author outlined the potential and opportunities for Romanians to mobilize for missions, and calculated that Romania has the personnel and financial resources to send at least eighty Romanian missionaries, without a great stretch of faith. At least one key pastor was gripped by the potential expressed, and began to distribute this paper to other leaders. The Missions and Evangelism Commission of the Romanian Evangelical Alliance eventually published it, which gave it an even wider audience.

Key People

In a movement as widespread as MIR has become, it is difficult to single out all the key people. However, two groups of key people can be determined: missionaries coming from the West, and Romanians who have caught and spread the vision.

Western Missionaries

When asked about key people, the names of several American missionaries showed up regularly. People like Stan Downes, Dwight Poggemiller, Steve Farina and Tom Keppeler are mentioned by different respondents. Each of these men has had an influence in his particular circles, encouraging the Romanians with whom he worked to consider the possibilities and potentials of Romanian missions. What seems to be more important than the specific individual is simply the presence of outsiders who have seen what Romanians

---

[29] This paper was first presented at the November 16, 1998 meeting of Partners in Mission Training. It was later printed and distributed in Romanian as *Misiune pentru Români*. This Romanian version was first presented and adopted at a meeting of the Evangelism and Mission Commission of the Romanian Evangelical Alliance, on January 22-23, 1999.

could do and have encouraged them to pursue it. They all, in one way or another, provided links to outside resources as well, either financial, or through literature or through relationships with other sending missions.

Romanians

Several Romanians were influential in promoting a vision for cross-cultural missions. They all have stories of how God grabbed them with a vision for missions. One of the first times the topic of foreign missions became public was at a national missions conference for Baptist pastors in the fall of 1998. Vasile Taloş, the president of the Baptist Union, spoke several times, passionately and convincingly, of the need for Romanians to start thinking about cross-cultural missions. He exhorted those Baptist pastors present to move beyond their old paradigms of ministry within the church, and pushed them to think about outreach beyond their walls and their borders.

Other Romanian leaders have been very influential. The following are only small examples, chosen from among those involved with MIR. Gavi Moldovan, a Pentecostal layman, desired to see God use him in evangelism. After he led several people in his workplace to faith in Christ, the factory supervisors told him not to talk to people anymore about Jesus, or they would punish him. His response was, "If you tell people to stop asking me questions, maybe I'll stop telling them about Jesus." His vision was to plant a church in a village. After the revolution, his desire grew to see churches planted throughout his province. Gradually, through the ministry of MMU, he encouraged church planting all over Romania. Finally, through exposure to the outside world, and hearing pleas for Romanians to come and help their brothers and sisters in the Balkans, he saw Romania's potential as a missions force. Moldovan's vision led him to issue the invitations to the first consultation, which ended up in the initiation of MIR. He is now MIR's secretary.

Beniamin Poplăcean, an influential Baptist pastor and leader of a Bible school, was initially resistant to the idea of missions, seeing how great the needs in Romania still were. However, after reading the paper by Russ Mitchell and being challenged by missionary colleagues, he, too, began to catch the vision. As the leader of the Missions and Evangelism Commission of the Romanian Evangelical Alliance, Poplăcean spread the vision through a variety of channels. He is now the president of MIR.

Gelu Paul, leader of a student movement in Timişoara, returned from theological studies at Gordon-Conwell Seminary in the United States with the vision to see Romanians involved in missions. One of the first young Romanian leaders to begin talking about missions, he worked for ten years to see the *Perspectives on the World Christian Movement* course translated and published in Romanian. Now he is the pastor of a new Baptist church in Timișoara. The church has already sent one young woman to India, and has another woman preparing to go with Wycliffe. Several other people are considering missions, particularly in East Asia. Several other such people could be mentioned, each of whom has had significant influence within their own circle.

What is important to note here is that each one of these men already was a leader with a broad national platform for spreading the vision. When they began to speak about the urgency of the moment to become involved in missions, they had a ready audience.

Current Situation

Important for an understanding of the contemporary situation are such issues as current Romanian involvement in missions, the advantages they bring to the world missions scene, and reasons for their involvement.

Current Involvement

Since the Revolution in 1989, Romanians have been sent to a wide range of countries, including the following: Iran, Afghanistan, Albania, Kenya, China, Israel, Spain, Turkey, Pakistan, Vietnam, Moldova, Russia (particularly Siberia), Ireland, Uzbekistan, Ukraine, Egypt, India, Libya, and Macedonia. In addition, several people are working cross-culturally within Romania, particularly with Turks and Gypsies.

No one knows how many Romanians have been on short term missions trips, or how many are now serving longer term. The number of short-termers is undoubtedly in the hundreds. Many young people have served with OM and YWAM in various projects, and many of the missions schools and seminaries are encouraging or requiring a short-term experience as part of their program. The estimates of respondents regarding long-term missionaries[30] vary quite widely, even among those whose primary ministry is to promote missions. Two colleagues teaching in the same missions school gave different numbers. One said, "under a dozen, certainly under twenty" (DP). The other guessed, "maybe fifty serving long term" (MC). Another respondent gave the same figure (GM). In between came one definite opinion of twenty-eight (RT), and "impossible to say" (SD). This respondent, an American missionary whose primary ministry is research on church growth, listed a variety of reasons why accurate statistics are difficult to find. He says that manpower is lacking to do detailed research, many people are sent by small organizations or local churches who are not networked as completely as the larger ones, and some

---

[30] What constitutes long-term is a matter of discussion. Very few people have gone as missionaries with the assumption that they will do this for a lifetime. Most "long-termers" probably envision serving three to five years.

groups do not advertise much, due to security concerns of missionaries serving in delicate situations.

A growing number of (particularly young) people are gaining an interest in missions. This can be seen by increased attendance at regional missions conferences, and by the attendance of around fifty people at the TEMA missions conference in Holland (despite difficulties in getting visas). Further, around 500 students participated in the missions conference Explo Domi in Timişoara over New Year's 2000, and the large numbers have participated in short-term trips.

United World Mission (MMU), a MIR related mission, has developed a three-pronged strategy for deploying missionaries. Its leaders plan send mission teams to countries such as Turkey, Moldova, Serbia, Bulgaria, Albania and Ukraine.

> We planned this ministry in three stages. First: in European Countries and more specific in South-Est context. Second: in the Arabic countries where Romania had very good economical and political relations before 1989, relations still kept nowadays and where Romanians can get easier. Third: up to the end of the world. We are not very strict in sending missionaries only in this order. (Moldovan 2001).

India seems to be another country with whom Romania is developing relationships, and where they will likely send missionaries. A group of pastors and missions leaders associated with MIR spent three weeks in India during the summer of 2001 and came back enthusiastic about the welcome they found there and the prospects for ministry to which they were introduced.

Advantages Romanians Bring to Missions

One of the motivating factors for Romanians is that they have several advantages relative to Western missionaries. One of these is their educational background.[31] Many already speak three or four languages. Further, Romanians benefit from political ties with the Muslim world continuing from Communist days. A large number of people have experience in the Middle East and North Africa, where they served as engineers or technical consultants. They have a wealth of knowledge that they can share with potential missionaries. Because of past historical ties, Romanians are not seen as a political threat, and do not come with any "colonial" or power baggage.

---

[31] Although this may be changing. The assistant dean of one of the Christian universities says that the cultural and educational level of incoming students is very low compared to only eight or ten years ago.

A third advantage concerns lifestyle issues. Coming from a poor country, Romanians are not used to a high standard of living, so do not have to learn to get by on less. They are much closer to the lifestyle of most of the countries in which they serve. Culturally they are also much closer to eastern countries than are missionaries from the West, serving as a sort of bridge between East and West.

Finally, the Romanian church has a rich history of endurance against opposition, giving them the ability to relate to those who were once or are still under persecution. The Romanian church has a good reputation, and, as one of the largest evangelical populations in Europe, has the personnel resources to offer the world.

Missions Motivations

Romanians express a number of reasons for their involvement. Some desire to obey God's call to missions, which they have understood as both internal "pressure" and as obedience to Scripture. Others want to help meet the needs of the world, fulfilling their destiny and potential as a strong and well-prepared church. An American missionary who teaches in the MIR missions school says that Romanians have been challenged to go where Westerners cannot. "They can go places we can't. Libya, Middle East, Israel. That's a strong preaching point. Romanians have caught on to that. Small group went to Serbia recently and traveled easily." (MC). Another teacher in the same school spoke of some of the motivations he has seen from students.

> They see that God has blessed Romania, has a plan for Romania. The Great Commission is for everyone, for those who go and those who stay. There are some resistant people, but young people respond quickly. They have a sense of the Lord's blessing. God calls us to share what he's doing, because he wants to bless us. It's not a hard sell. (DP).

Finally, some desire adventure and travel. As one respondent pointed out, this must not be seen in a totally negative light, because God can use it to get people into situations where they can be used. A Romanian woman who served a year in Central Asia noted:

> A spirit of adventure, something new, something different. I don't know their motivations, though. The freedom to travel, to what extent does that increase interest? Most people want to travel, but westward, not eastward! Always these two parts, there's the adventurous side and the spiritual side. God can use the small part of spiritual desire with the large adventurous part. (IA).

On the other hand, respondents also acknowledge a variety of less noble motivations. Many people want to leave Romania. One missionary says, "Everybody wants to leave" (TK) and are making active plans to emigrate. Another said, "Desire to leave Romania is a motivation. There are Romanian communities just about everywhere. It's a small part" (DP). One young pastor said that, "the motivation of some is to escape from bad economic situation. Others are going on faith." (CS).

Themes and Factors

Again we will examine the spiritual, social and cultural systems, and then some of the interactions between systems.

Spiritual Factors

My years of experience in Romania had led me to expect that most people would attribute the development of missions involvement to a special work of God. This expectation helped me see the need for a system of analysis and questioning which would go beyond this obvious answer. In fact, most people did not answer this way, which surprised me.

In the first Romanian case, that of Aletheia Church, Romanians, especially, took a while before they got to this point. On the other hand, I asked a Romanian pastor, who has been one of the major influences towards missions, why this interest developed in his church. His answer was "God must have given it directly to them, because they didn't get it from me." My response to him was, "G., that's a really nice answer, and I'm sure it might have some truth to it, but let's be serious. I know you've been pushing missions for several years." This acknowledges that a mixture of spiritual and human elements go into the development of a missions movement.

Nevertheless, many respondents are convinced that God is doing a special work in Romania today. People talk openly and with conviction that God has prepared the Romanian church especially for this moment, and that he is developing a missions movement which will become a significant force in the world.

I regularly heard such phrases as "The Spirit of God is moving here", "sovereign movement of the Holy Spirit", "I saw the Lord doing something special here." These respondents see that God has prepared the Romanian church. The church has gone through difficult times and has become a large church with major personnel resources. In this regard, one missionary wrote:

> A number of people have sensed that the Lord is telling them that Romania is to be a major missionary sending nation. The idea is that Romania has a destiny to fulfill. God wants it to become a leader in missions in Europe much as Korea and Brazil have become leaders in Asia and South America. I've heard that from only about 3-5 people, but they are people who I trust to hear accurately from the Lord. If God is speaking that way to inter-

cessors, it stands to reason that He is speaking in a similar way to church leaders and to potential missionaries. (SD, personal communication).

Others understand that the vision to do something towards missions, an internal "pressure" or call to get involved, is something God gave. While recognizing a variety of non-spiritual motivations, they see that when God gives a vision, it will control a person so that he or she cannot do anything except get involved.

Interesting is the fact that the emphasis on God's working is heard more often from Western missionaries than from Romanians, although by no means exclusively. Perhaps this perspective comes because they have entered the Romanian scene from the outside and therefore are able to see something the Romanians have a harder time recognizing. On the other hand, some of the missionaries may have a vested interest in seeing God at work, or an inherent bias in that direction, because their main ministry focus is to encourage Romanian missions involvement and to train Romanian missionaries.

Social Factors

Important aspects of the social system include such factors as economic possibilities, political freedom, ecclesiastical structures, and local and international networks.

Economic

Most respondents feel that lack of financial resources is the single factor that most slows the growth of missionary sending from Romania. Many feel that if the financial resources had been available, many more missionaries could already have been sent. Some say seventy or eighty, others even more, young people are ready to go cross-culturally right now, but do not have financial backing. On the solution to the problem, however, a range of opinions can be heard. Some feel it is a real problem, related to the Romanian economy, which will not be solved until Romania's economy is strengthened. Others cite an attitude of poverty as the real problem, not an actual lack of finances. These people are convinced that the money can be found if vision is there, because God will honor faithfulness to the vision he has given. Still others note the need to develop partnerships with Western organizations.

Nobody disputes the fact that the economy is in difficulty in Romania. Unemployment is high, real wages are dropping, and the percentage of household income required for housing, heat and electricity has doubled several times during the past few years. Many churches have difficulty paying the salary of the pastor and meeting heating and upkeep expenses.

In addition, because Romania is a relatively poor country, they often send missionaries to countries where the cost of living is higher. This presents psychological difficulties in fund-raising, when pastors and churches hear that the amount needed is several times more than the pastor's salary.

The real difficulties are sometimes accompanied by an attitude of poverty. A pastor says: "The church has human resources but not financial" (MM). Another pastor comments: "The attitude, 'We don't have money' is the greatest hindrance. 'Without money we cannot do anything' has become the motto of many. 'We need to take care of our own things.'" (CS). An American missionary observes, "Biggest roadblock is psychological more than financial. 'We're not able to give regularly. We're not Americans, we can't send missionaries like Americans.' It's a perception more than reality." (DP).

Many Romanian Christians feel that since they suffered during Communist times, they deserve to receive financial help from the West now. Since the revolution, hundreds of church buildings have been constructed, many much larger than the size of their current congregation warrants. Many of these buildings were largely financed from the outside. Romanian pastors frequently visited American, British and Scandinavian churches, as well as those of the Romanian diaspora in Europe and America. This attitude translates into the feeling that the local people are too poor to send missionaries, especially when there are still so many needs at home. Another missionary noted:

> This attitude is a hindrance to vision growing. People say, "this is great stuff, exciting to see what God is doing, but we can't do it because we don't have money." I've heard it number of times. It sets of sense of dependency on outside resources. "When we get resources, then we can move forward." Probably a bigger problem than people talk about. (MC).

Against the view that Romania is too poor to support missions stands the view that money goes with vision. These people claim that God will provide if people are faithful to the vision they have received. A missionary states, "The fact that they're worse off economically doesn't mean it's not possible. If vision, determination that this is what Lord wants us to do, money should be there." (DP).

A staff member of a MIR-affiliated mission speaks of his home church of four thousand members.

> The leadership has no vision when money concerned. I calculate if each person gave 50,000 lei [around $1.75], the church could easily support ten missionaries. I'm embarrassed when asked how many missionaries church supports and I have to say 'none'." (VP).

The secretary of MIR states emphatically:

> God speaks to you and shows you that there is a great need, and always God is faithful to provide the human and financial resources, as a function

of the vision that you have. And I look in Romanian local churches, there is not a single one that has enough money for their programs. What I see, if they don't have a building, they find the resources for a building. If they want to do a special program of evangelization, they find the resources for the special program of evangelization. If we want to develop cross-cultural missions, to the extent that the vision is there, the resources will be there. If we have vision and passion, God will give the resources. But always vision begins with the truth. Unfortunately most begin with a vision, then say they have vision but no resources. And others who say, we would do something but we don't have money. Those who have the vision find resources, because God will give them on the day they are needed. They will not be rich but they will have enough for what God said. (GM).

This view reflects the confidence that the vision for missions is not manmade, but comes directly from God. These respondents note that when a concrete need is presented and the vision is communicated, then people give. That leader continues:

When there is a serious motivation a specific reason to give, people will give money beyond their strength. When there is a reason, "Brother, let's give money for mission in Ciobobirlea", but when they say, "Brothers give money, you have to give money, they must build something", they give. "Give for this mission", they give. "Give money so that they can do this ministry", they give. For concrete reasons the church will put money at your disposal. But concrete motives are born with vision. (GM).

He does not specify where the money will come from. He acknowledges that God may choose to meet that need through gifts from Germany, American or England, as well as from Romanian businessmen. Nevertheless, he is convinced that God will provide.

These respondents point to the calculations published in the Mitchell paper (1998) which seek to demonstrate that Romanian churches could raise a million dollars a year for missions through minimal contributions of each member (around $2 per person). This would be enough to send around eighty missionaries to surrounding countries.

Confirmation of this positive attitude comes from a group of students at Emanuel Christian University in Oradea, who spoke of their experiences on a short-term missions project in Albania. In their excitement they were planning another trip the next year, but doubted that their American sponsor would want to pay for a month-long trip. However, they were united and positive in their confidence that they would have no problem finding the money. Already several months in advance they were praying and working on fund-raising, but they were certain that the money would come.

However, one respondent, the pastor of a large church, when asked about this attitude, said rather bitterly, "those who say this [that money follows vision] already have their donor sources lined up and do not have to worry about finding money." (MM).

Most respondents agree that individual local churches will not be able to support a missionary alone. Some MIR cooperating agencies are trying to network churches together. In this way, groups of three to five churches have been able to send two or three missionaries, including a woman to Macedonia.

A final note about the respondents is in order here. As missions leaders who are driving forces on the cutting edge of a new movement, all these people are visionaries with wide international experience. They have traveled widely and have a wide range of contacts with the outside world. It must be noted, therefore, that their views on the financial questions are probably more optimistic than that of the typical Romanian pastor or Christian leader. People with their vision and faith will be necessary to overcome the inherent resistance of the churches who complain of lack of resources.

Regardless of the attitude toward Romanian financing, almost all respondents agree that if Romanian missions is really to expand, partnerships with outside funding sources will be needed. These missions leaders feel that Romania should contribute as much as possible, but that costs are simply too high to expect that Romanian churches will be able to handle everything themselves. MIR has one department whose main job is to develop such partnerships.

Political / Legal

Political freedom has not brought as much freedom for Romanians to travel as for some of the other ECE countries. No longer restricted by their own government, Romanians now face barriers from the countries of Western Europe and the United States. Until the beginning of 2002, they had to have visas to Western European countries, which were not easy to get, even when they had letters of invitation and guarantees of support. Now they can travel without visas, but they have to have hard currency to guarantee that they will not become a burden to others. On the other hand, political ties to the Muslim world remain in place, which make these countries much more accessible to Romanians than to many Westerners.

Aside from the freedom to travel, however, the free flow of information and the freedom for missionaries to come to Romania have been large factors in the rise of new interest in missions. Romanians were not only restricted in their movement, but also in their access to information about the outside world. Most Romanian Christians simply had no idea of the needs of the world, nor any idea that they might meet those needs.

8. Romanian International Mission, Romania

Ecclesiastical

As noted above, a few key leaders became excited about missions and spreading their vision. At the same time, young people began looking beyond the borders of Romania. Being younger and not tied to specific church situations, they found it easier to act than more established leaders. Several respondents commented on the number of young people willing to be sent if the structures and resources were available. The MIR publicity brochure tells of students attending a MIR training session, who speak of their concern about getting trained. "We are willing to come to the training meetings and do everything you ask. Our only fear is that there will not be anyone to send us out once we are ready to go."

This fear highlights one factor which has to be considered as either encouraging or hindering the growth of missions: the willingness of pastors and local churches to support their young people who are interested in missions. In general, if pastors are in favor, things happen. If pastors are not in favor, things are difficult. Several reasons for this ambivalence exist.

Young people have little standing in the church. One young woman, desiring to go to the Muslim world, received this response from her church leaders, "Are you trying to teach us something? Don't preach God's heart for the nations to us." (IA). However, she found a ministry opportunity in Central Asia. The ministry leader spoke directly to the pastor, giving him the opportunity to decide whether the church should become involved. After the pastor endorsed the project it was accepted without question by the church.

Few pastors preach or teach about missions, and very few pastors are considering missions for themselves. Their concerns are more often with the church and the local community. Some see young people with missions vision as a threat, either to their finances, or to their work force, or to their ability to meet local needs. A ministry leader notes, "Most pastors say, 'Don't talk about missions, we are needing to teach people to tithe to the church, to support the church and other ministries'." (CS).

Pastors sometimes also feel threatened when they perceive that they may lose control. One respondent, a member of a four-thousand-member church, recalls a case where some businessmen wanted to find a way for their Italian, non-Christian partners to channel money to missions and relief projects. They wanted to establish a fund, separate from the church but managed by the church leadership, which would distance the money from the church. The pastor dismissed the idea with the claim that the businessmen did not trust him. Similar stories can be heard of pastors who do not want to lose control of the financial resources of church people who may want to give to support missionaries.

Sometimes, the young people who get excited about missions do not have good church connections. They may have not been involved in ministry in their local church, they have come to faith at the university or without a church background, so they are not known in the church. This raises the question of the relationship between ministry at home and interest in missions. Involvement in local ministries opens the door to a willingness to serve cross-culturally. This raises the question whether a lack of local experience implies that the missions interest is just a romantic one of adventure, rather than based in an honest desire to serve.

Networks

As a network of missions, MIR is the center of a network of networks. A list of the networks involved gives us a picture of how embedded MIR is in Romanian church life. On its board, MIR has representatives from the three largest denominational unions, each of which is a network of churches, schools, and missions organizations. In addition to the churches, participating missions organizations from outside Romania as well as those from within the country are involved. Partnerships with local churches outside the country form another set of networks, as do partnerships on the various fields where Romanians are serving.

Because of these internal and external network connections, MIR is positioned for growth. It has the potential to become well recognized within the country. It also has possibilities for financial assistance from the outside and of placing missionaries on international teams in various fields of service.

Cultural Factors

Those cultural factors which have had the biggest impact on missionary motivation include the Romanian understanding of missions and how it has changed, the degree to which cross-cultural missions was present in the thought of Romanians before the revolution, the role theological education played a part in the rising interest, the extent to which contact with missionaries from outside the country has contributed, the extent to which Romanians have had to overcome negative images of outsiders and of themselves, and the role of personal experience in building motivation for missions.

Biblical and Theological Understanding

For most Romanian Christians, "mission" means one of two things: either some kind of outreach to the next village, or Americans or Western Europeans who have come to Romania. *Misiune* has traditionally meant sending the choir to the next village to sing in church there or to send a deacon to care for a small village church made up mostly of old people who cannot afford their own pastor. Often it includes the aspect of *evangelizare*, of preaching an evangelistic message in the church. If one wants to talk about cross-cultural missions, one must be very explicit and talk about foreign missions, or missions in another country, or cross-cultural missions. When churches talk about the number of missionaries they have, they usually mean deacons or lay people who travel on Sunday mornings and lead worship services in small churches. Alternatively, a missionary is understood as someone from the West who has come to Romania to work with the church.

Those who have developed a more biblical understanding of missions, including the idea that the Great Commission is for all believers, have usually come to this understanding after exposure to missions from other sources. Meeting missionaries from outside the country, traveling themselves to other countries, meeting missionaries from non-Western countries, and being exposed to the needs in other parts of the world have often led Romanians to read the Bible with fresh eyes. For instance, one respondent spoke of the pastor of his home church, who after attending a missions conference, came back with a new message.

> After the conference he came to church with the materials and all his sermons were about missions. Whereas before he would always preach "we preach Christ crucified", today is it "go into all the world and preach the gospel." It's a change in his messages. Already you can see it. (DG).

This church has recently sent a missionary family to Turkey and the pastor has begun talking about the need to hire another pastor who would concentrate on missions issues. An American missionary notes how Romanians have responded to exposure to the outside.

> After they saw the possibilities, the Great Commission began to seem like something written for them. Because it was possible. Leaders have seen clearly we have the call and need to do something about it. So involvement and opportunity led to change of missions understanding, not other way around. (SD).

Most respondents say that missions is not generally taught or preached in Romanian churches. Others claim that through solid and systematic expository preaching, the missions message comes through. Says one young women who has served in Central Asia, "preach the Bible and missions comes out" (IA). Speaking of a pastor known for his teaching ministry but not for his missions involvement, she notes with surprise how often missions gets referred to. Her conclusion is that, since Bible teaching is a strength of the Romanian church, missions is taught. An American missionary agrees, saying what has changed is not the Romanian understanding of missions, but the freedom that allows them to put into practice what they already knew. "It's not a theological shift rather a demographic – an awareness of need. Some of a shift out of a fortress mentality which continues to have negative effects today." (TK).

Newly published missions literature seems also to have had some impact in helping people change their understanding of the missions mandate. Several missionary biographies have appeared, as well the *Perspectives* course and Piper's book *Let the Nations Be Glad* (1993). The publication of further books is planned. This literature has also been instrumental in helping Romanians think about missions strategy. One of MIR's secretaries emphasizes that MIR wants to focus on "E-3 Missions", reflecting the influence of the *Perspective* materials on their strategy.

Interest before Revolution

Most respondents agree that missions vision for outside the country did not exist before 1989. Most churches had a fortress mentality, concerned with their own survival, rather than reaching out. Travel, even within the country, was restricted enough that it was hard for them even to reach out to those around them. Those missionaries who secretly traveled into Romania focused on helping meet the needs of the Romanian church, not on encouraging them to look beyond the borders.

Romania has not been a traditional missionary receiving country. A few groups were active there before 1989, notably the Navigators, BEE, and groups involved in Bible and literature smuggling. However, the number of visiting missionaries was always very small, and their contacts were restricted to a small number of people. Only after the revolution was Romania flooded with Western missionaries. The Romanian believers never expressed a need for many missionaries from outside. They felt rather the need for financial help from the West. After the revolution hundreds of churches began massive church building programs, most of which were funded by churches and Christians from the West. Therefore, Romanian Christians needed to discover the potential to send missionaries, and to overcome a poverty mentality which made them feel it was impossible for them to afford to send missionaries.

One contrary opinion must be mentioned (RT), that of a pastor who says that missions was a normal part of church life and teaching.

> Vision existed for years, but wasn't possible. We could barely go to next town. Desire and vision existed. Fire existed. The only thing missing was money and freedom. The culture has changed totally. Young people got vision for missions from parents. Young people have always heard growing up of need for missions. (RT).

Therefore, he says, interest in missions is not something new, but something which could finally be released. His church wanted to send people immediately after the revolution, but did not have any money. In addition, he felt they were motivated in the first place by the Great Commission, and not because of any personal experience. "There wasn't any need for a change of theology or biblical understanding of mission, because these were already developed." (RT).

This was a unique opinion and one for which we must seek reasons. While it is impossible to determine motives, we must note that the respondent was a high-ranking denominational leader and pastor of a large church. In addition, he has just started a missions school with almost total financing from Scandinavian sources. He is used to dealing with foreigners, especially used to fund raising, is a skilled politician, and is not given to making statements which would make anyone look bad. For example, his estimate of the number of evangelicals in Romania was fifty percent higher than that of anyone else, and when asked about the role of Western missionaries, he claimed they had only a positive influence. Therefore, his response must be tempered by other viewpoints.

Educational

In general, the impact of theological education on missions motivation is seen to be negligible. With the exception of an introductory missions course, missions is not found in the curriculum of most theological institutions. Some people credit BEE and others in providing the basis for good Biblical teaching, but most students come to Bible school or seminary with an interest in missions developed elsewhere.

Education and training for missions has now taken a high priority for missions leaders. Many Bible schools were started in the first five years after the revolution. Now missions schools are springing up around the country. The School of Missions M.I.R. in Sibiu, the Dobrogea Missions and Evangelism School in Constanța, Team Action Missions School in Arad, and a new mission school in Timișoara are just a few examples of schools that have been started in the past two years to help prepare potential missionaries. In addition, the *Perspectives on the World Christian Movement* is being published by BEE and will be studied in church-based training programs across the country.

It appears to be easier to start a school than to find ways to send missionaries. The president of one newly founded school said that the school leaders want first to get the first group of eighteen students (out of eighty who applied) through the nineteen month course. Then they will start working toward creating a sending agency.

While it is far too early to begin to evaluate the effect of these training programs, a couple of observations are in order. First, as much as possible, students in these programs are being trained in the context of ministry. Cross-cultural contacts are required as part of the curriculum of most of the programs. At the same time, local ministries are not neglected to the exclusion of foreign ones. Stories are told of students on their way home from a two week training program who, while still in the train station, began to minister to street children, and who led the conductor of the train to the Lord before they got home. In another program, the students were learning Turkish and meeting with Turkish people in Romania as part of their training. This is in contrast to many Bible schools who have trained many people, but who have not produced people who are active in ministry. Second, a concern was expressed after the first session of one of the new schools. The participants came to the training very motivated, most desiring to be sent out at the end of the five month long program, but at the end of the time, most of them no longer wanted to go into missions. The leaders of this program are trying to determine the reasons for this decline of interest. They believe it could be that the participants received a realistic view of missions, particularly among Muslims, and realized that they were not sufficiently called or prepared to go right away. It could also be that the training was too stringent, or that the difficulties of missions life were over-emphasized during the training. More exact reasons are still waiting to be discovered.

Most missions training is taking place in the missions and Bible schools, and in non-formal programs run by Western missionaries. However, some of the seminaries and Christian universities are starting to adjust their programs in response to the mission interest of students. For instance, the Baptist Seminary in Bucureşti has begun a missions department, offering a double major in co-operation with the University of Bucureşti. Currently eleven seminary students are enrolled, as well as at least fifty from the university. Emanuel Christian University in Oradea has begun sponsoring short-term experiences in nearby countries, some of them led by professors. The curriculum itself has not yet been changed, but the response to interest in missions is growing.

Contact with Western Missionaries

Contact with Western missionaries is generally seen by respondents as a positive factor in the rise of missions interest, although there are naturally some more negative voices. On the positive side, two main reasons are given. The first is simply the fact that they are there. The value is not as much what they do as just the fact that they came to help. This was especially encouraging for Romanians who have visited the United States and seen what the missionaries had given up. The second and more important reason is that many missionaries have recognized the potential for missions of the Romanian church and have repeatedly encouraged the Romanians to fulfill their potential. One of MIR's secretaries noted the influence missionaries had on him. "I hung around Tom and Barry and others with missions vision. I got contaminated with missions." (CS).

On the negative side are concerns about ineffective missionaries. Two main points are made. First, not all missionaries are good models of service. Many have come who have not bothered to learn Romanian and continue after a number of years to work through translators. Often they have come with little understanding of the historical and religious context of Romania and a condescending attitude toward the churches. Sometimes they come and steal leaders from churches, offering finances and taking responsibility from Romanians. Second, economic issues come into play. Some missionaries live very well by Romanian standards. The fact that these missionaries live well creates false expectations about the lifestyle that missionaries should maintain. A Romanian missionary observed:

> Western missionaries? Positive factor or not? Touchy issue! There're all sorts of opinions about Western missionaries. How they live and how they present the word missionary. When they build huge houses, have rich lifestyles, have nannies, etc., it's negative! When they gather young adventurous Romanians around them, there's a huge problem. So some perceive missions like that. And then there are some missionaries that live simply and have more impact. I've seen the same here in Romania and Uzbekistan and Tashkent. The simpler missionaries have more impact. It means more to the people. When the people see the sacrifice, it just means more. When Romanians here see Americans and their living style, for them [the Americans], I know it's a sacrifice, but for the Romanians the way we see them, it's a luxury for them, they're better off. When young people come around, see the Western missionary, it's nice, there's a materialistic edge to it. So contact with Westerners, yea, it's good, but it depends which Westerners you contact. (IA).

In addition to a large number of missionaries from the West, missionaries from Brazil, Argentina, Korean and other non-Western countries are active in Romania. This has challenged some Romanian Christians who see other poorer countries send missionaries. For some people this has included a shame or competition factor. Romanians see that Romania has the same kind of resources as those other countries, but is doing nothing. This has motivated them to want to become involved in missions.

Ethnocentrism / View of Themselves

Romanian's view of outsiders, and their ability to tolerate difference, is closely tied to their understanding of themselves. Respondents recognize ethnocentrism and its converse, national inferiority, as issues that Romanian Christians will have to deal with if they are to become effective missionaries. Three aspects emerge from their discussions: ethnocentrism exists and must be dealt with, Romanians have the ability to get along well with people outside their borders, and they suffer from a national inferiority complex which they are beginning to overcome.

Romania, as a Balkan country, has a well-deserved reputation for inter-ethnic tensions (Kaplan 1993). Romanians are historically xenophobic, partly as a result of centuries of domination by Russians, Turks, or Hungarians. Large Hungarian and Gypsy minorities, as well as twelve other ethnic minorities, comprise over two and a half million people. Tensions and hatreds between the ethnic groups are not absent in the churches. Outsiders are shocked to see how Romanian Christians act toward Gypsies and street children, groups that are most despised in the country. "They have no understanding of the Gypsy issues. Romanian Christians treat Gypsies like they aren't human." (TK). One hears disparaging remarks not just about Gypsies, but also about Jews, Hungarians, Germans, and those neighbors on their borders. An American missionary commented on the way Romanians on short term trips in Moldova treat the Moldovans. "I see it in their interaction with Moldovans. Looking down on them." (MC).

Romanians have a well-developed sense of legalism, nurtured by years of needing to maintain a distinctive identity in a society opposed to them. This legalism allows them to become easily judgmental, viewing anything that is done differently than they have been taught as wrong, or worldly, or inferior. I have heard a Romanian pastor speaking derisively about American churches he visited, because they drank coffee in church. Such examples could be multiplied. One Romanian respondent spoke of the "national sin of pride" (IA), and said she knows very few humble Romanians. Competition is endemic in the society, starting with the earliest school experiences. In comparing Romanians with Western missionaries who have come, this person's response was, "We think we have better Bible teaching, we think we know the Bible better, we think our churches do things better. We just think we're better." (IA). One mission leader even attributed part of the missions motivation to this sense of competition.

On the other hand, it is pointed out that those who are ethnocentric are probably not going as missionaries, and that those who do go have some degree of cross-cultural ability. Those who have served in other countries report experiencing, not necessarily strong ethnocentrism, but normal reactions of culture shock when confronted with differences.

This leads to the aspect of Romanian national self-identity. Because of their historical weakness, they have developed a national inferiority complex. A young pastor observed, "It's rather inferiority than superiority. We're not recognized as equals. That's the legacy of Ceauşescu. Lack of resources is maybe only the tip of the iceberg when it comes to excuses. Maybe sense of inferiority is a stronger reason." (CS).

The fact that they are going out may be a sign that they are beginning to realize that God can use them. "An attempt of stepping out and saying, yes, we do have something to offer to other people, as a nation, as a culture, even as a legitimate partner in the task of world missions." (TK).

Role of Personal Experience

One factor that nearly every respondent mentioned was the fact that, after the revolution, leaders began to travel outside the country. There these leaders saw a world of which they were unaware. They began to compare themselves with others and began to see their potential. They saw and heard of churches which were sending missionaries, despite being poorer and weaker than Romanian churches. Moldova was mentioned as an example of this. Although a much poorer country than Romania, Moldovan churches have spontaneously sent dozens of missionaries spreading across the former Soviet Union. Romanians began to see that they had the human and financial resources to get involved.

Further, they were confronted with the needs of the world. Before, they had only themselves as a reference point. They were poor, they had needs, and certain parts of Romania had very few evangelicals. Now they heard of countries where the needs were even greater than at home.

Not only did church leaders hear and see the needs, but they received invitations to come to other countries and help. This happened most dramatically at the Hope for the Balkans conference in Sophia, Bulgaria, in 1996, where the Romanian leaders heard what they perceived to be a Macedonian call from those present, "Brothers, come and help us." (Given that it was a Balkans conference, it is likely that the call was literally from Macedonia!).

As Romanians were confronted with their own potential, with the needs of the world, and the cries for help, they began to see that God had prepared them for just such a time, and that they dare not miss the opportunities he was giving.

Previous Outreach Experience Leads to Missions Cross-Culturally

Many of the Romanian missions leaders had been involved in outreach within Romania before they discovered cross-cultural missions. One pastor said that all church members were taught of the need and importance of personally sharing the gospel with non-Christians, so the extension to cross-cultural ministry was natural for them.

Romania has had a very large church planting movement since the revolution, which has resulted in hundreds of new churches being started since 1990 (OC International and Misiunea Mondiala Unita 2001). Some of these churchplanters first were motivated to go to a different part of the country, where the number of evangelicals was small. They received a taste of cross-cultural ministry in this way. Most of them came from Transylvania in the north and west, and went to the south and east of the country, which is seen as culturally quite different. Out of this experience, some of them have seen the possibilities of moving to new opportunities outside the country. This is by no means true of them all.

Interaction between Factors

Having looked at the various individual factors, it is useful to see how some of the factors have interacted. The spiritual, social and cultural systems are not discreet entities, which we can dissect and analyze individually. Each system intertwines and affects each of the others. Not every possible interaction can be examined, but the following are some of the most notable.

Personal Experience Leading to New Understanding

Both leaders and young people report how personal experience, either in a missions setting, or in a context where contact with world needs could be observed, was instrumental in changing the way they understand their responsibility for the world.

Leaders in general did not come to a conviction about missions through Bible study or hearing messages about missions. They gained cross-cultural experience, and then the Bible made sense in a new way. Because they were convinced, that message became a central part of their preaching. Biblical teaching was not decisive to begin with, but has become an emphasis now.

Young people observed that cross-cultural experience was important for them personally in shaping their attitudes towards missions. They returned with a new awareness of the complexity of ministry. Some have used their experience to strengthen their ministry involvement at home. Their experience has served primarily to develop a pool of potential missionaries. Young people are often not accepted right away by church leaders. They have to earn the right to speak. Consequently, their influence is smaller and probably will come later.

Role of Western Missionaries

Several missionaries had an influence on a small number of leaders. The contact Romanian leaders have had with Western missionaries in their role as missionaries belongs to the social system. The missionaries themselves did not reach large numbers of Romanians with the message that they should become involved in missions, but they influenced the Romanian pastors who could reach large numbers. The contact alone, however, has not brought about significant changes. These have been facilitated by the openness to contact with missionaries on the part of the leaders. This openness is an attitude and value question which belongs to the cultural system.

Work of God's Spirit

God is credited with having created a church which is prepared to hear a certain message and to be willing to obey. He changed political systems, which gave freedom for Western missionaries to enter Romania and for Romanians to leave Romania. He worked through experience to bring changes in their attitudes toward the world and toward themselves. He gave the vision that Romanians should reach beyond their own borders and help those who have never heard the gospel. God, in his sovereignty and through the work of the Holy Spirit, is seen as the driving force for everything that is happening in missions. The various human factors work themselves out in the context that God has set in place.

Effects of Other Systems on Economics

Economics is a critical topic, and is affected by a number of factors. Economics is a subsystem of the social system, yet is influenced by the spiritual and culture systems. One of the most important interactions is between culture and social. Vision and communication of vision are cultural factors. The effectiveness with which a vision for missions is clearly and convincingly conveyed to the churches will determine how willing people are to give. An identification of their place in the fulfillment of that vision helps people to overcome true economic difficulties.

Economics is also affected by the degree in which leader and people demonstrate their faith in God's provision. The more faith, the more likely that the money will come. This faith is difficult to categorize. It belongs to the spiritual system, but as a reflection of values, attitudes and worldview is also part of the cultural system.

Finally, economic capability is affected by the nature of the contacts that Romanian leaders have with outside funding sources. The cleaner these contacts and the greater the trust which has been built, the greater will be the flow of outside money.

Role of Theological Education in Changing Attitudes and Structures

Theological education seems to have been inconsequential in the beginning days of missions interest. Missions courses were not offered in the various theological education programs, and most people came to seminary with plans to become pastors or maybe to be involved in some way as a Christian presence in society. Missions vision and interest has developed outside of theological institutions, but it is gradually making its way inside. Although not decisive at the beginning, it will be more important for moving forward. The training potential missionaries receive will hopefully make them more effective, and help them to stay on the field longer than they might have without training. Also for those not preparing to be missionaries, there should be some benefit. To the extent that students have exposure to missions courses and missions experience, they may then be more open and encouraging when they become pastors and have a role in encouraging churches to send missionaries.

Development of Structures

One final question about interaction between cultural and social systems can be asked, as it related to the way which MIR has developed. The approach to developing structures and the kind of structures developed come from an overlap between the two systems. Romanians conceive of a task and build the structure to implement that task through a certain cultural grid, created through a combination of historical, ecclesiastical and political experiences. The question that can be asked in this situation is to what extent the focus on structures has inhibited progress toward actual goals. Those from the outside, as well as some Romanians, have become frustrated with what seems to be premature overemphasis on the creation of structures. Those who are building the structures see the need for these and are convinced that greater progress will come through the structures than if they did not exist. One of the respondents, in noting this difference of opinion, spoke of a tension between having a new vision with an old way of thinking, which had been developed under very different political and ecclesiastical conditions. They have caught a "fresh vision, but are trying to implement it through old structures" (TK), and it is an open question whether this will ultimately be effective. Probably only future events will allow a clear answer to the question.

Conclusion

In summary, how do respondents understand the growth of a missions movement? MIR remains at the center of what has been discussed. Internal organizational issues have not come to the forefront, but the problems discussed affect MIR and all its cooperating organizations.

God has prepared the way and is now working to make Romania a missionary force. God had created a church which had a foundation of prayer and understanding Scripture.

A variety of Romanian leaders, pastors and ministry leaders, all at around the same time began to receive a vision for what God wanted to do through the Romanian church. This vision came as a result of

- contact with Western missionaries who were encouraging them to think about missions,
- through experiences in other countries, where they heard of or saw needs and heard of ways that they could help meet those needs,
- through seeing what other, non-Western countries were doing in missions with fewer resources,
- through a desire not to be left behind in what God wanted to do, and

8. Romanian International Mission, Romania 165

❏ through a desire to obey the command Jesus gave to go into all the world and preach the gospel.

MIR has had a catalytic effect. The kinds of issues which have been discussed, and to which answers have been sought, are critical for any organization which is beginning to involve itself in missions. Further, MIR has brought together a large number of interested parties and allowed conversations to take place between denominations and organizations, which may not have occurred without its impetus.

Regardless of whether MIR itself becomes a major force for missions or not, it seems evident that momentum towards a true missionary sending movement is growing. From certain highly placed church leaders to expanding grass roots interests, Romania seems on the way to becoming a significant missions force. Certain developments, particularly in the area of financing, will have to continue, but the people involved seem committed to doing whatever it takes to make Romanian missionary sending a reality.

9. A Thematic Comparison of the Cases

We turn now to a comparison of the different cases. The categories of analysis include those which are suggested by the literature and explored through the research questions, as well as those which were generated by the respondents themselves (Spradley 1979; Rubin and Rubin 1995). Kvale (1996) sounds an important warning that the conversational context in which interviews take place must be remembered and safeguarded. The transcripts should not be reified but should be treated simply as records of interpersonal interactions. They are not prepared texts which were written for public consumption, but are documents in-process, evoked through a specific set of questions in a specific interactional process.

One Polish respondent's very strong comments about the differences between the countries can be highlighted here. He made the point that Poland, Hungary and Romania are all very different cases: different languages, different ethnic groups, different cultures and histories. I agreed, but also noted that they at least had a somewhat common experience of life under Communism. His answer was that the Communisms they experienced were also very different. This must be emphasized. Outsiders tend to notice the similarities, especially if they look through the grid of Communist history and anticommunist ideology. Poles, Hungarians, and Romanians are very clear that each country is different. Their various historical conflicts only serve to emphasize these differences. Poles and Hungarians tend to get along very well, perhaps because they have no common claims to the same territory. Hungarians and Romanians are traditional enemies.

Some of the country differences can be seen in the religious, political and cultural areas. Only a very brief and impressionistic comparison can be attempted here. Nevertheless, enough can be said to discourage the temptation to view the region monolithically. Religiously, Hungary is a predominantly Catholic country, but with a large Protestant minority and small evangelical minority. Poland is a Catholic country with a very small Protestant and evangelical minority. Romania is an Orthodox country with a small Protestant and evangelical minority, except the Hungarian population, who are evenly divided between Reformed and Catholics, with a small evangelical community. Economically, Hungary was the most liberal. Poland experienced heady days of freedom during early 1980s during the rise of Solidarity, followed by repression. Poles probably had the greatest freedom to travel. Romania was by far the most repressed and the most isolated, experiencing an almost total lack of freedom. Culturally, Hungary is an isolated culture and language among Europeans. After a millennium of existence, it still retains certain characteristics of its Central Asian forebears. Poland is a Slavic country, with many Slavic neighbors, offering many near-language ministry opportunities. Romania is an enclave of Latin culture surrounded by Slavs and Hungarians. These cautions should offer guidance through the course of the following comparisons.

Spiritual Factors

Almost all respondents in the three countries agree that missions activity has begun because God is doing something in their countries. We must remember that they are missions leaders and so may have a different perspective than the normal person in the churches. These leaders see God as working in answer to prayers that they be able to send missionaries, or that he has sovereignly created the conditions for them to become senders. They see his hand in supervising the political processes that have brought freedom and provided places for them to serve. Many have felt a direct call from God to become involved – some to missions in general, others to specific locations. Most see calling as important. Whether through a literal vision, a feeling, internal pressure or some other mystical sense of discovering God's will, "call" is an important topic among those people in this study. This emphasis on God's call takes on even greater importance given the fact that everything to do with missions is new, and the people involved are more pioneer types. They are stepping out into the unknown, and believe that God is giving them extra assurances that they are moving in the right direction.

When we come to the question of whether the missions activity is a result of spiritual revival or renewal within the churches, the answers are varied. I heard quite varied descriptions of the general spiritual life of churches in Hungary, Poland, and Romania. Respondents in Hungary and Poland feel their churches are generally sleepy and need to be awakened, more concerned about internal matters than external, and slow to catch a vision for local outreach much less for cross-cultural missions. In Romania, churches may be relatively slow in gaining a vision for cross-cultural missions, but they are much more alive and growing, with a commitment to local outreach.

Several scholars speak of the growth of religiosity in ECE in the years before the revolutions, following several years of decline in interest in religion (Borowik 1997; Tomka 1997). This may be true according to the indices measuring religiosity, including affirmations of belief in God or increased religious practice. Most respondents, however, do not recognize this increase as the result of revival and do not see it as having an effect on the general spiritual condition of the churches.

This difference in the level of spiritual life between Hungary and Poland on the one hand, and Romania on the other does not surprise anyone who has been involved in ministry in ECE over the years. In comparison to other Eastern European countries, Romania has always had more lively, larger, and faster growing churches than the rest of the region. Now, that activity and life is being channeled towards missions.

Does revival lead to missions, or does missions lead to revival? Romanians would generally say the former. Their churches are alive and they are taking the next logical step of outreach. Poles and Hungarians hope the latter, praying that their activities outside the country will have an enlivening effect at home.

Social Factors

We will examine the role of key people as well as the political/legal, economic, and ecclesiastical sub-systems. In addition, we will compare approaches to organization.

Key People

The focus in this section is not on the key people discussed during the case descriptions, but rather on the function of these key people. We will not look at them as personalities, but as people who played a specific role in generating missions interest. Rogers (1995) refers to innovators and early adapters. Gladwell (2000) speaks of connectors (people specialists), mavens (information specialists) and salesmen (persuaders). We can also speak of outsiders and insiders, those who come to the situation from outside the normal social channels and relationships, and those who are embedded in the social system, who are "at home".

Outsiders

Most of the Western missionaries who have been studied here are outsiders, particularly those in Romania. They have been participants in their respective movements for a relatively short period of time. Many speak the national language more or less respectably, teach in training programs or Bible schools of various kinds, and are well accepted by the people around them. Nevertheless, they remain outsiders. Despite this status, they have an influence in their particular circles, usually with certain national leaders. They correspond to Rogers' innovators or Gladwell's mavens, somewhat marginal to the society, but critical for introducing new ideas.

In each country some nationals are innovators. They are sometimes seen by the local people as outsiders. Some are young people who do not have much standing in the church. Others are visionaries who are too far ahead of the majority of people, and consequently are seen as "strange", "divisive", or "rebels". These early adopters of the missions vision may eventually bear fruit, but they may raise opposition along the way.

9. A Thematic Comparison of the Cases

Insiders

In contrast to the innovators, who may be too far ahead of the crowd, the key people who have a true impact are usually well connected, respected people within their social system. These early adapters (Rogers 1995), connectors or salesmen (Gladwell 2000) may be influenced by the innovators, but they are better placed to bring about positive change. Their role is to take the message and communicate it in such a way that it can be understood and accepted by the group at large.

Most insiders are nationals of the respective countries, but a few outsiders have made themselves insiders (including Anne-Marie Kool in Hungary, Malcolm Clegg in Poland, and Tom Keppeler in Romania). They have been fully accepted into the national society, because of their mastery of the language and culture, their willingness to live like the people, their humility and willingness to learn, and usually, by their presence in the country before the revolution.

In summary, key persons are critical to get things started. They perform a catalytic role in helping people see the world in a new way and in opening opportunities for people to act on the basis of that new understanding. However, a variety of other motivating factors also need to be in place which allow people to catch the vision and actually go as missionaries.

Economic Factors

Participants in each case studied have dealt with the reality of a difficult economic situation. At the same time, they have also dealt with the question of the relationship between vision and generosity. The lines between social and cultural systems become very difficult to distinguish in such a case. Parsons, however, reminds us that distinguishing them is not as important as recognizing the interactions (Parsons 1971). Economics as such belongs to the social system; vision, attitude toward money and giving belong to the culture system. They overlap at the point where decisions to give are made in the midst of a weak economy.

Everyone involved recognizes that churches in ECE do not have a lot of money, although significant differences exist between the countries in terms of per capita income. Hungary and Poland are relatively wealthier than Romania. Nevertheless, in all three countries, churches struggle to pay their pastors, maintain their facilities, and provide social and financial assistance for church members who are unemployed, handicapped, widowed, or somehow otherwise left uncared for by the national social security system (cf. Tomka 1997). Many, especially in Romania, have taken on large building programs which have left them beggars for help from Christians in the West. Few wealthy businessmen belong to evangelical churches, and normal believers are often living on the edge of survival. In none of the cases studied do national Christians fully support their own missionaries.

Exacerbating the actual financial difficulties, Christians in these countries are used to thinking of themselves as poor. They do not think they have the resources to try things. Romanians say, "without money we can't do anything." Hungarians are convinced that without Western partners they will not be able to send missionaries. Polish young people are worried they will not be able to be sent without outside help. This attitude of poverty has caused them to expect help from the West, and has inhibited them from reaching into new areas of service unless they have guarantees of financial assistance.

Despite these handicaps, most leaders interviewed felt that the necessary financial resources could be found, if a compelling vision for missions can be communicated. Financial difficulties exist, but people will give sacrificially if they believe the cause is worth the sacrifice. Respondents in every case gave examples of how people had sacrificed to give to causes they deemed worthy. Christians in ECE have offered relief for flood victims, supplied food and clothing for Gypsy villages, published Bibles for people who had never had them, and sent missionaries to unreached areas. In addition to local donors, foreign supporters have been motivated to give when they saw that their gifts were going to a good cause. Personal relationships are one of the keys to developing a sufficient support base. Respondents regularly spoke of the importance of relationship in their region of the world. What is increasingly true in the West, that people give to those with whom they have a relationship, is even more true in ECE, whose societies in general are more relationally oriented than in the West. The personal relationship with a missionary on the field will generate both financial and prayer support that impersonal appeals never will. Several missionaries observed that, when they returned from their country of service, prayer and giving for missions decreased.

Believers in ECE tend to be spontaneous givers, sharing generously in practical and material ways if shown the need, and giving money if convinced of the need. Regular, monthly support is desired by the missions agencies and churches, but this habit has not yet been widely developed.

Political and Legal Factors

The political revolutions of 1989 form the historical context for all these cases. However, perhaps ironically, the revolutions themselves do not seem to be a significant factor in rising interest in the world, aside from bringing the freedom to attempt new things. Not only were Christians in ECE unable to actually go to other countries as missionaries, they were unable to conceive of the idea of going. Communism meant not just the restriction of movement (travel), but the restriction of mental movement (imagination). The revolutions brought not just freedom to act but freedom to think about acting. The primary effect of the changes was the creation of the conditions for missions activity to become a reality. Referring to other movements coming into the countries from outside, Borowik describes the situation, but what she says is true for missions ideas as well.

> The most obvious reason for spreading NRMs [New Religious Movements] is simply the possibility of the open borders and democratization of post-Communist societies ... . The collapse of Communism means, not only a free market of goods, but also a free market of ideas – political, economic, scientific, and religious. (Borowik 1997, 21).

Not only did freedom open the door for new ideas to come into the country from outside. Perhaps even more importantly, the freedom for people to travel outside their countries allowed them to gain a new perspective on the world and on their situations. They were able to see and hear about the needs of the world, they were able to see that they could be used to meet those needs, some of which could even be found in the countries of Western Europe or North America that they had often envied.

Here again one is confronted with the theoretical complications of the systems construct. Freedom to travel is a social/political issue, but the desire to travel and search for adventure is a cultural (or personal) issue, and deals with the questions of motivation.

Ecclesiastical Factors

The political and legal issues form part of the macro context, providing the freedom to consider and try new things. Ecclesiastical factors, on the other hand, are much more relevant to the four cases studied.

The larger religious context has not been considered to this point, but it seems appropriate to mention it here. In many ways, a hundred years or more of living as a minority church has been more decisive in shaping the evangelical church's identity than forty-five years of Communism. The difference between the Hungarian case and those in Poland and Romania may lie here as much as anywhere else, in the difference between being a movement within a state church and one which takes place in free churches. Evangelical churches in Hungary, Poland and Romania have experienced more opposition from the national churches than from the government, whether Communist, fascist, or liberal. Since the revolution, the large churches have attempted to regain the religious hegemony they lost with the advent of the Communists (Barker 1997; Borowik 1997; Richardson 1997; Tomka 1997). This has brought with it a suspicion of and opposition to the evangelical churches.

> All post-Communist countries experience pluralism, expressed by a growing number of NRMs and Protestant Churches of mainly Evangelical tradition. The reaction of traditional churches towards them is common in all countries under consideration, i.e., more or less open hostility. (Borowik 1997, 17).

This experience of opposition from the large churches has contributed to the sense of inferiority and defensiveness many respondents described. Persecution has caused them to build thick walls and made outreach psychologically difficult. These barriers carry over into their thinking about cross-cultural outreach as well. In this sense, the situation confronting the Poles and Romanians in these cases is more similar to that of new missions movements in Austria, Italy or Greece than that of the Hungarian case studied here.

Moving from the macro level to the local, in each of the countries it is clear that local church pastors play a critical role in the acceptance or rejection of missions vision or any new idea. Their advocacy can open the door for young people to accept a missions vision, find prayer and financial support and have a chance to encourage others. Their opposition can sideline potential missionary candidates, either silencing their enthusiasm or sending them away to look for a more welcoming environment.

The lines between structures and mindset are not easy to separate here. To separate the promoting or hindering role of the pastor in the social setting of the church, for instance, from his (or occasionally, her) personal commitment and/or resistance to missions (a cultural feature), is both difficult and unrealistic.

Approach to Organization

An interesting area of comparison is the approach the different groups take to organization and structure. MIR had to wrestle early on with the questions of how it should develop: whether as an organization or a network. They made the decision to seek formal government recognition, even before any activity was taking place. A lot of time was spent on the development of the organizational structure. To be registered, MIR had to develop structures, complete with a constitution, task forces, departments, and officers. As one participant described the situation, "We developed the forms, then tried to figure out what it should do." (DP). This approach is in great contrast to BMS in Poland, especially the MttE branch, where structure has been seen as a necessary evil, the less the better. Structures have been developed only to the extent that they are absolutely crucial. The other Romanian case and the Hungarian tend to lean in this direction as well, whose leaders see the need for structure which will enable ministry, but not restrict it.

Cultural factors

The way we understand our responsibility for the world will have an effect on how we act towards the world. We will examine how the leaders in these cases understand the biblical and theological mandate of missions. We will also look at the ways and reasons their understanding might have changed in the past ten years. Other areas to be explored include the extent to which missions interest

9. A Thematic Comparison of the Cases

existed before the revolution, the role of theological education, the impact of Western missionaries, and the way ECE Christians see themselves and those who are different, and how these views may have changed.

Biblical and Theological Understanding of Missions

In what way, if any, did theological factors play a part? In particular, how did missions leaders understand their church's missions responsibility before 1989 and how has it changed since then? How did and do people understand "missions"? How have any changes in understanding come about?

Across ECE, before the revolutions the common understanding of mission or missions was of some kind of ministry which took place somewhere other than in one's home church. For many people still today this is the common understanding. Very few people in ECE are wrestling with developing a biblical theology of mission. Most people are still at the initial stages of building interest and motivation. They have not yet done much reading in missiology, which is mostly available only in English or German. Any literature mentioned by respondents was of a more basic kind, involving resources like the *Perspectives* course, *Operation World*, or missionary biographies. When a biblical and theological understanding of missions is discussed here, it refers much more to the question of whether people understand missions as something which is only local outreach, or whether they have come to see it as including a cross-cultural component.

Missions is understood by most people first of all as something which is done locally. In the Hungarian mainline churches, missions became the totality of church ministry. In Romania and Poland, mission means ministry outside one's own local church. Sending the choir to another church to sing, sending a preacher to another church to hold an evangelistic meeting, handing out tracts on the street, helping poor people, and running a drug rehabilitation center or clinic were, and still are, seen as missions.

The notable exception to this conception of missions comes from Lutheran Mission Society of the Hungarian Lutheran Church, whose members had been involved in foreign missions as young people, and who kept that vision alive among themselves. A few people prayed for missionaries in other countries, but did not dream of missions for themselves. Otherwise, the overwhelming majority of people saw missions only as local ministry, in some ways synonymous with evangelism or simply ministry (everything the church did).

After the revolutions some people gradually came to understand that their missions responsibility was much larger than they had imagined. For the first time, when they read words such as "go into all the world and preach the gospel", or "you will be my witnesses ... to the ends of the earth", or "go, therefore, and make disciples of all nations", they could read them as though the texts were meant for them. Before, their political situation had so restricted their movement and their imagination that they could barely even see these verses. With the coming of freedom came the possibility for them to apply them, so they suddenly became real.

That new understanding did not occur to everyone. Many pastors and church members continue with their old understanding of mission. They still think of missionaries as those deacons in their church who go to visit the old people in the next village who do not have a pastor. So why did some people get the message while many others have not? At least two factors stand out: first, some people gained a new perspective through their experiences in other countries, where they were confronted with needs that they did not know existed. Second, some people, through their previous ministry experience were predisposed to see new possibilities. Malcolm Gladwell (2000) speaks of the "stickiness" of a message, that is, the chance that a message will be caught and owned. He, along with Rogers (1995), affirms that the likelihood that a new message will catch on is related to how similar it is to an already accepted idea. The implication is that missions will be more attractive, interesting, and will draw people more, if those people are already involved in evangelism or some kind of innovative ministry, or as one respondent repeatedly said, "new paradigm". Missions becomes the logical next step rather than something totally new. This is confirmed in interviews with a variety of people, in several countries (Horyza, Molodovan, Hoban); because they were already active in outreach ministry, it was easier for them to catch the idea of cross-cultural missions. This was a relatively small step. The converse of this is, naturally, that those people who are not active in evangelism locally will have a much more difficult time seeing the need for missions far away.

An interesting comparison can be made here between the Hungarian and Romanian cases. In Hungary, the church leaders are arguing whether mission means home or foreign, but not doing much of either. In Romania, they are doing mission at home, and then moving naturally to other countries when they get the vision and information. Those doing mission at home, especially church planting, find it pretty easy to expand outward.

The important role of the local church in missionary sending is a theme heard across the region. The local church, not a missions agency, should be the sending body and be ultimately responsible for sending. The agencies should support the churches, offering services that the churches themselves cannot handle. This emphasis seems stronger here in ECE that has traditionally been the case in Western Europe or the United States, although the central role of the church is being reemphasized in many circles also in the West.

The basic emphasis of missions from Poland and Romania is on evangelism and church planting. The missions leaders in these countries are concerned

9. A Thematic Comparison of the Cases 175

that people who have not had the chance of hear about Jesus hear the gospel and respond and be gathered into local churches. This can be contrasted with the missiology of the Hungarian respondents, which is far more academic and more ecumenical. One wonders to what extent sharing one's faith is part of the Hungarian historic church message and practice, at least as it would be defined by the evangelical groups. The emphasis is more on service, and on the living out of one's faith in daily life, rather than on evangelism per se, or on a public proclamation of the gospel. The comment that American evangelicals "can go 'Shine, Jesus, Shine' somewhere else" (DZ) illustrates this. It is not possible to determine at this time to what extent this evangelistic reserve is the effect of having the movement led by a missiologist rather than a pastor or evangelist, or to what extent it reflects theologically more liberal views present in the historic churches.

I wonder to what extent those who are involved in the historic churches in Hungary would be comfortable with the missionaries from Poland and Romania. The Hungarians from the mainline churches say that the evangelicals speak a different language, even when they speak Hungarian. "It hurts your ears" (AMK). They would very likely have a hard time understanding those from the other two countries. The mission theology and approach to missions is quite different. To what extent this difference will work itself out is a subject for further study. In Poland and Romania one does not hear the kind of questioning of truth or of the gospel that one does in Hungary. The movement is driven by a simplicity of message which would be seen as simplistic by those involved in the case in Hungary.

Interest before Revolution

Next we turn to the question of missions interest before the revolution. Here the question is, was missions interest something which was present in ECE churches but dammed up by the political conditions, waiting for the onset of freedom to be released like a flood, or is the current missions interest something which has developed new since the revolution?

Except for a very small number of people in ECE, primarily in Hungary, churches and individuals did not consider cross-cultural or foreign missions before the revolutions. A few people were praying for missionaries or for countries of the world which needed to hear the gospel. Even fewer people were starting to think about missions for themselves, or trying to find ways to leave the country to serve as missionaries. For most people, however, the idea of cross-cultural missions has developed since 1989.

Educational Factors

Theological education seems to have played a very limited role in the rise of missions interest, at least in any formal way. The curriculum of most seminaries and Bible schools includes missions in a very peripheral way, if at all. To ask the question is not to assume that educational institutions should have promoted missions interest. It only ask whether they have had an influence.

Several of the key people involved in the various cases teach in theological education programs. These institutions have therefore provided a platform for the presentation of missions information and motivation. This being the case, many of the missionaries have gained their visions and conviction for missions in the context of theological or missiological study.

We find a contrast of approach between MttE and the others regarding the need for training. Romanians are starting many missions schools to prepare people, even though few sending structures have been developed. PIMS in Hungary began before widespread missions interest existed. Wycliffe-Poland places a very high value on preparation, particularly because of its emphasis on linguistics, Bible translation, and literacy. MttE, on the other hand, has developed training programs and structures only as people have expressed the need for them. This approach to training corresponds to the difference in approaches to structures in general, noted above. It is too early to determine which approach will ultimately be more effective in equipping missionaries.

Role of Western Missionaries

The role of Western missionaries in the rise of missionary interest and engagement has been ambiguous. Mission leaders speak of both positive and negative influences. The ones who have interest or experience with missions have all had extensive contact with Westerners. Yet the impressions that Eastern Europeans have of Western missionaries is not always positive.

Many of those questioned spoke enthusiastically about the role that Western missionaries have played in encouraging missions from their countries.[32] Missionaries have demonstrated, simply by coming, the value of going to other countries. Some have been role models as servants. They came to learn the language and culture, and showed by their behavior that they wanted and needed to learn before they could teach. Some were very positive toward the possibilities of the national churches sending missionaries, often when the national believers themselves were not.

---

[32] Central and Eastern Europeans are very gracious and hospitable people. Therefore, it must always be kept in mind their tendency to say things which they think the interviewer (whom they know as a Western missionary) wants to hear, and to not say things which might make him or her feel bad. Comments about the positive value of Western missionaries should often, then, be treated a little bit less positively than recorded. Likewise, any negative comment about Western missionaries is liable to be stated more diplomatically and positively than is really felt.

On the negative side, numerous examples were given of missionaries who did not model such humility and willingness to learn. These missionaries refused to learn the language and the culture, and did not try to understand the religious and historical context of the country. Some were motivated by a simplistic view that, as a consequence of decades of Communism, Eastern Europe was a spiritual desert, and the Christians were waiting with parched mouths for someone to bring them the cold water of the gospel. Some foreign missionaries used money indiscriminately, and attracted people with less than pure motives, or pulled people from established churches.

Whether as positive or negative examples personally, missionaries have had a motivating effect in all three countries. Even the negative examples have motivated Central and Eastern European Christians both positively and negatively. Positively, they have shown nationals believers that they can be missionaries themselves. "If that is what it takes to be a missionary, we can do better than that." Negatively, those who have seen or experienced such negative examples have learned what they need to avoid in their own missionary ministries. They have experienced paternalism, favoritism, financial manipulation, and cultural insensitivity, and they are determined not to repeat those same mistakes. The examples of those missionaries, such as Kool and Clegg, who have identified well with the people they serve, give the new missionaries models to emulate.

Ethnocentrism and View of Self

To what extent did the way people view themselves and others affect whether they became interested in missionary sending? The question is not first of all whether ethnocentrism exists in ECE. Every people group has its own ethnocentrisms against which it must struggle. Stereotypically, Hungarians despise Romanians and Romanians despise Gypsies. Overcoming ethnocentrism is a normal part of adjustment to a new country and culture, and ECE missionaries interviewed expressed their surprise at discovering that they needed to deal with it.

The question here is rather to what extent ethnocentrism is a hindering factor in the rise of missions interest. Ethnocentrism can keep one from going to another people, because they are not worth the effort and their problems are their own fault. Ethnocentrism can motivate to go out of a superior attitude that says, "I've got something that they need, and I'm going to make sure they get it."

A further question is, does having something to offer necessarily carry with it seeds of superior attitudes? Missions only happens when people feel that what they have to give will be valuable to others. To what extent is it then "one beggar telling another beggar where to find bread", and to what extent is it a rich man offering a beggar scraps? Missionaries from ECE for the most part do not come with financial resources or with the potential to have a significantly higher standard of living than those they will serve. Therefore, it is rather the attitude that is important, more than the material resources.

Christians from ECE countries have a general attitude of inferiority vis-a-vis those from the West, based on the Westerner's greater access to a wide variety of resources that the Eastern churches did not have. Circumstances are now reversed, as these churches send missionaries of their own. They only begin to wrestle with the issues as they get to the field and discover in themselves unconscious attitudes of superiority regarding culture, society or church life. Those missionaries who have already been serving report experiencing such things, which they had not anticipated in advance. Perhaps Romanians, most of all, will have to deal with questions of form and function, many of them coming as they do from large and successful churches, who will want to replicate what has been successful at home.

One of the fascinating aspects of the missions movement of Central and Eastern Europeans is their growing awareness of cultural difference. This can be illustrated in two simple areas: hospitality and relationships. A Pole, in speaking about Ukrainian Gypsies, said, "The food was good, but they fixed way too much. We should tell them to cook for us the way they do for themselves." However, is this realistic or possible? The Poles themselves did not do this in the old days. They gave their best to guests. A Romanian spoke of Albanian hospitality, saying, "We are nothing in comparison to Albania in terms of hospitality! They give you everything there!" (CM). This comes from someone from a culture which practices, as Codrescu says:

> the Romanian art of aggressive hospitality. That's when your host offers you everything in the house and you must fight not to take it. The object, for the guest, is to leave the house with as few things as possible, while the host considers his victory great if he can succeed in standing naked on the frozen earth while waving good-bye to you, dressed in his clothes, bent to the ground with his possessions. (Codrescu 1991, 180).

Poles emphasize the family and group emphasis of the Central Asians with whom they work, and the importance of relationships. They also comment on the spontaneity of life that the people enjoy.

Hospitality and relationships are both areas of strength for people from ECE. These are the very points that Westerners emphasize about Polish and Romanian culture. Yet the Poles and Romanians notice how much more hospitable and how much more relational are people further east and south of them. This shows two things. One is how the Poles and others from the region, are able to relate more easily to Central Asians than are Westerners. Second is how certain cultural characteristics are on a continuum which moves as you travel further east.

Interaction between Factors

A variety of interactions between the spiritual, social and culture systems have been discussed in the various cases. Four important interactions seem to be common to all the cases. These include the role of spiritual factors, the impact of personal experience, the ways in which the economic system is affected by the others, and the role of Western missionaries in bringing about changes in other systems.

Spiritual Factors Influencing Social and Culture Systems

People involved in missions in ECE take God's work very seriously. While acknowledging and expounding human factors in the development of a movement towards missions, they see all these happening because God has chosen to act in a new way. Several areas of God's action come through clearly.

First, God was at work in changing the political situation. The revolutions of 1989 did not happen by accident; God ultimately controlled the process. People had been praying that God would act and he did, in ways far beyond what most people could have imagined. Second, in his sovereignty he had prepared people's hearts, so that when freedom came, they were ready to hear the message of responsibility towards the world. Third, in some cases God spoke directly, calling people to a specific involvement in missions. This work of God's Spirit into the human situation has had natural consequences on people's thinking and on the way they have developed structures for ministry. Finally, when God is at work and brings spiritual vitality, obstacles such as financial difficulties come to be seen as insignificant.

Personal Experience Influencing Cultural System

The role of personal experience in the development of missions vision was not addressed explicitly in the interview protocol. However, it rapidly emerged as a very central theme. Two kinds of personal experience were decisive: previous involvement in innovative or evangelistic ministry, and travels outside the country. Those who had been involved in mission, regardless of how it was defined, were more likely to be open to missions in new cultures. Their ministry activity predisposed them to look for new opportunities. Further, over and over respondents commented on how their eyes were opened by their travels outside the country. Some went to international conferences, others had specific missions experiences, others had prolonged contact with Western missionaries, and others studied in other countries. This has emerged as one of the most significant factors in the development of missionary interest and commitment, especially for the key people involved.

Spiritual and Culture Factors Influencing Economic System

Economic capability and commitment are clearly affected by both spiritual and cultural factors. People's willingness to give to missions-related causes is influenced first of all by the level to which a spiritual vitality empowers their lives and faith. Their degree of faith in God's provision will allow them to stretch beyond their own financial capabilities, because they know God will provide. When a church is spiritually thriving, its people will give. Likewise, a church that has a compelling vision (a cultural factor) will give, even out of poverty. A Romanian pastor told of a Nazarene church in București, made up of six families, each with at least five children, which fully supports a missionary family in Ethiopia, because they have the vision to see Ethiopia reached with the gospel (CS).

The converse of this vision-driven generosity is the effect that the offer of financial help can have on a church's or a leader's vision or theology. The offer (or the threat of the withdrawal of the offer) of financial assistance has caused numerous leaders to compromise their own vision or theological position.

Western Missionaries Influencing Culture and Social Systems

The fourth area of interaction which is common to all the cases is the social role of Western missionaries in helping change the thinking of people in the various countries. Westerners (and occasionally, Easterners) have provided models of what missionaries are and do. They have encouraged ECE Christians to see that they have a role to play in the world missions movement. They have helped people see that the Great Commission is meant also for them, and they have provided a variety of resources, including literature, finances and connections to international organizations. In all cases, even when individual missionaries were not considered role models, the fact that Western missionaries were involved was decisive for the development of missions vision and action.

Why Have New Missionary Sending Movements Begun in ECE?

In this section we will review the most important factors in each case. Following this we will attempt to summarize the most important factors which were found common to all the cases.

Key Factors in Each Case

What were the essential factors which led to the beginning of each of these movements? The most important factor in each case, by far, was a key person, or persons, who were able to influence others, through either their personality or their writings, to consider missions.

Case 1 – Book and Person

Anne-Marie Kool's research on Hungarian missions history was the spark that started many people thinking about missions. Further, as a foreign missionary, and a neutral outsider, she was able to gather people together and get them talking. Her skills as a motivator, intermediary, and networker were crucial in

9. A Thematic Comparison of the Cases 181

helping people see the place of the Hungarian historic churches in world mission.

Case 2 – Person and Vision

Marcel Hoban and his vision from God was the catalyst for missions thinking. Cornel Marincu was a visionary pastor who demonstrated a willingness to lead the church into a new kind of vision. He had the skills and ability to convince the church members that they should be involved, even though the church was small and young.

Case 3 – People

Malcolm Clegg, a foreign missionary who saw Polish potential for world missions, was able to influence a group of young theological students to consider missions. His contacts with other missionaries made possible a lot of short term trips, which then helped people see that they could be involved long term in missions outreach. Jurek Marcol, who developed a missions conviction over time, and whose vision was catalyzed through contact with a missions leader from outside the country, brought a particular missions emphasis into a particular group of churches.

Case 4 – Article and People

An article by an American missionary, outlining how Romania should and could be a major missionary sending force, started some people thinking in a new way. Several foreign missionaries, working in a variety of places with a variety of people and groups, early on saw the potential for Romanians to be missionaries and began planning and talking about it. Finally, several key Romanian pastors and ministry leaders caught the vision and began to spread it in their circles.

Factors Common to All The Cases

What then are those common factors which occurred, making possible the rise of the respective movements? The most important factors are:

- God at work in giving spiritual life and vision to a specific group,
- a key person,
- a particular set of personal experiences, which open the eyes of participants to see that missions is necessary and possible for their country,
- a prepared context which allows the acceptance of the missions challenge.

Perhaps the process can be summarized in the following way: God places a strong person, who has a vision and passion to see national missionaries, a position of influence, and good communication skills, into a context where some people are prepared to listen to the message.

Work of God

The spiritual conditions of the countries considered in this study are very different. Romania (and likewise Ukraine and Moldova) is very different from Hungary and Poland. What is the difference? Can we say that God is working in these countries in a different way than in the others? It definitely seems to be true that the level of spiritual activity and vitality is higher in the countries further east. However, it is very difficult to determine why this is so.

Nevertheless, certain common features emerge concerning the spiritual conditions necessary for a missions movement to begin. One common feature is the recognition, on the part of some people, that God is doing something. Even if there is no evident revival in the church as a whole, revival, or renewal, or openness to innovation must be present in certain circles of the church for new attitudes and actions to arise. A second common feature is a recognition of the importance of prayer. Both before and since the revolution, prayer has been instrumental in preparing people to think in new ways. God often used prayer to direct people's attention in new directions and to motivate them to meet needs that they have discovered and for which they have prayed.

The interaction between spiritual and human factors is difficult to describe or separate. It seems clear that where there is little or no spiritual life, missions will not appear, at least in an evangelical form (maybe humanitarian, out of a desire to help people.) Nevertheless, where there is openness for personal and church growth and renewal, and a willingness to pray and seek God's direction, new vision for outreach beyond the local ministry can develop.

Role of Key Person

In the cases studied, the key people always included missionaries from outside, who function, either to give the initial spark (Aletheia, W-P) or as a driving force (Hungary, MttE). It is safe to say that without contact with missionaries from outside the country, missions is unlikely to happen. At least contact with the outside world is necessary. However, even these contacts were often mediated by missionaries. The key person has a catalytic role in the initial movements, but not necessarily a decisive role in keeping the movement ongoing.

We can identify two kinds of key person. The first is the innovator, who brought the idea of missions to a group, but whose thinking may have been too advanced for the group to follow. The second was the person who could convince the group that the idea was a good one and help them to adopt the idea as their own. At times, the innovator and the "salesman" were the same person. The key person could be either an expatriate missionary or a national Christian.

What is that key person like? What characteristics do these people have in common? They are fired by passion for God and are gripped by the needs of

9. A Thematic Comparison of the Cases 183

the world. They have eyes open to see the potential of the country, and are full of faith that God can meet the needs. They are in positions of influence, and can communicate well the vision God has given.

Role of Personal Experience

Respondents were unanimous in stating that personal experience was crucial in developing vision and understanding about missions. Two kinds of experience were important: local ministry and international exposure.

Almost without exception, those who became leaders of missions movements were active in some kind of ministry outside of a local church. They were doing evangelism or other kinds of outreach, they were active in starting new churches, or they were engaged in developing innovative ministries of training or discipleship. They were not simply maintaining the status quo of the church.

All of those involved in these movements had some kind of international exposure beyond their local ministry commitments. This exposure had two aspects. First, most of the participants had contact with missionaries coming secretly from the outside before the revolution. Many of them studied with BEE or some other kind of outside ministry (notably Navigators) before the revolution, which opened their eyes to new ways of doing ministry and theological education. This is also a partial explanation why so many of them were involved in innovative kinds of ministry (see preceding point).

Second, all of them were able to travel outside the country, where they were confronted with a different world than they had known. For almost every one of them, this experience outside the country came only after the revolution. Some of that travel was to the West, where they attended international conferences, where they met people who encouraged them and where they heard about needs. Some of the travel was to the south or east, where they personally saw the needs for the gospel elsewhere in the world. There they began to see that they could offer something which would help spread the kingdom of God.

Because of these exposures to the outside world, they began to understand the task of their church in a different way than they had previously. Perhaps they understood the missions mandate in a theoretical, intellectual way, but saw it as something which was impossible for them to fulfill. Consequently, the Great Commission was interpreted as a command to baptize, or as a responsibility to evangelize, but a global component simply did not exist.

After international exposure, however, they came to see the Great Commission and related passages as having been written also for them. They could now see beyond the barriers that were erected and could envision becoming personally involved in obeying the command. Perhaps equally as importantly, they were now able to pray in ways that were previously impossible. Before, they imagined the world in a certain way, and, because their sources for missions knowledge and of the state of the world were so sketchy, they had a very limited picture of what the world was really like. The first hand experience widened their vision and allowed them to pray, and to encourage others to pray, in new ways.

Importance of a Prepared Context

A key person was critical as a catalyst. Equally important was a prepared context. A person could talk missions all they want, but if the ground is not ready, nothing will happen. (This is actually very similar to evangelism in hard places. Missionaries or national Christians may wait years before they see any visible fruit of their efforts, because the time is simply not yet ripe.) This also means that a person with vision may need to work a long time to prepare the ground.

What Constitutes a Prepared Context?

The first aspect of a prepared context is a setting where people have ongoing exposure to missions message and vision. This might be a local church, a student group at the university, or a theological institution.

The second aspect is the freedom to travel, both to gain exposure and to actually leave to serve in another country. We have seen international exposure as an essential component in the rise of missions interest. This factor may need to be tested and tempered by reports from other emerging missions movements, such as in China. There people are being called to missions and immediately, without cross-cultural exposure at all, leave to go to another people or even country. This despite the lack of freedom, or legal possibility, to cross international borders.

The third aspect is a pool of people with interest and willingness to go. This normally means young people who are not already tied down with families, careers, and houses. They need to have the desire to do something new, with an openness to learn and change.

The final aspect of a prepared context is a church which is willing to pray and give and release people. They need to have a vision and passion to see people meet Jesus and a clear understanding of the biblical mandate for missions. They must be willing to sacrifice their own interests for the wider interests of a world in need of the gospel.

Notably missing from this list is the ability to give. Considering the importance of finances, is this a critical factor? Should an ability to give significant amounts of money be considered necessary for missions movements to begin? Participants in these cases say economics should not be the decisive factor.

9. A Thematic Comparison of the Cases 185

Other elements are more important. Nevertheless, financial ability (or the perception of ability) does play a role. The question is simply how important a role.

Does poverty (or the perception of poverty) have an absolute inhibiting effect? While recognizing that their countries are not rich, no missions leader in ECE claims that they are poverty-stricken. One of the surprises that they experienced after the revolutions was that other people were poorer than they were. The attitude is the crucial question.

We could fruitfully compare these countries with truly poor countries to see to what extent lack of money inhibits missions vision. One thinks of the Friends Missionary Prayer Band, in India, which is supported in part by homemakers who set aside a handful of rice each day. We could also look at the situation in Romania, where villagers often help pastors with products from their farms. I have traveled with a number of Romanian pastors who come home to the city after a Sunday serving village churches, with the car trunk full of eggs, milk, meat, potatoes and other food items. The church people did not have enough cash to pay the pastor much, but cared for him and his family in ways that did not show up on his paycheck. A similar example came from the women involved with the Lutheran Missionary Society in Hungary. During the 1950s, when no missions activity was possible and no money could leave the country, the women created handcrafts and sent them to the West where they were sold and the money sent to missionaries. The same mentality could be encouraged in the area of support for missionaries.

Issue of Foreign Investment, Partnership, Paternalism, Control

Just as the ECE countries have needed foreign investment to get their national economies moving (Stojaspal 2000), so also the emerging missions movements will probably need foreign investment to keep their momentum. Everyone says that economic difficulties are real and will be difficult to overcome. Moreover, regardless of the desire on the part of mission leaders to gain financial support for missionaries from their home countries, most recognize the need for help, especially as missions sending has become more expensive. The possibilities for Romanian churches, for example, to send missionaries to countries which are several times as expensive (which just about any country they go to will be), are very small.[33] The need for outside funding is obvious.

This need raises a whole set of issues which will have to be resolved. MIR has a department which, as part of its assignment, is supposed to find and build

---

[33] As a point of comparison, I calculate that American missionaries would need to raise between $500,000 to $1,000,000 per year in order to serve in some countries. One imagines how difficult it would be for American missionaries to raise support from American churches with those numbers!

relationships with outside donors. BSM and Aletheia have several people and churches from the West who support their mission efforts, but nothing has been developed specifically to promote fund-raising from the West. Western donors give primarily because of relationships with the missionaries themselves, not because a church or mission has sought them out. The Hungarians have developed official partnerships with the Reformed Church of America to provide partial funding for the project in India.

Missionaries from ECE will also face issues of partnership, paternalism and control. For the most part, they will participate on international teams. Already I heard of both positive and negative experiences. They will be minorities, probably will be a lot poorer than the others, probably will not be as self-confident or assertive, and therefore have a better chance of feeling misused or unappreciated. Repeatedly, possibilities for jealousy, envy and competition will occur in working with those colleagues from richer countries.

At the same time, the new missionaries will have to overcome their own ethnocentrism and cultural blindness in relation to the people they want to reach. They will need training in contextualization, sensitivity, and such issues if they want to avoid the mistakes they themselves experienced from missionaries from other countries.

Implications for Theory

The purpose of this study has not been hypothesis confirmation or theory advancement, but simply to discover what is happening right now. However, the study does have some theory implications.

Systems of systems theory has been very useful as an analytical tool. For simplicity and clarity of design, only three systems were used. However the limitations of the design became apparent in the course of the study. In particular, the exclusion of the personal system became a weakness, because it was not possible to deal clearly with the question of personal motivations. I explored the reasons some people became involved in missions, but unfortunately, rather peripherally. Particularly since the groups studied here are so young, the personal motivations of those who are involved and leading the movements play a large part. A repeat of the study should include the personality system as an integral part.

Another observation on systems theory concerns the overlap of systems. We made the point in the theoretical discussion of systems that the overlap between systems is often very difficult to determine. This was very clearly confirmed in practice. The systems were examined separately, followed by the interaction between the systems. However, this is clearly only a heuristic device, which breaks down if we push it too far.

9. A Thematic Comparison of the Cases 187

As we saw earlier, in nearly every subsystem the point was made how difficult it is to separate systems. As examples, in the realm of economic capability to support missions, the overlap between finances and motivations became obvious. Considering the role of Western missionaries, the distinction between their social role and the openness of the people to have contact with them was fuzzy. Concerning ecclesiastical factors, the interaction between church structures, especially the social role of the pastor as gatekeeper, and his promoting or hindering cultural role made it difficult to distinguish the boundaries between systems. The question of the effect of freedom to travel as a result of political changes is intrinsically tied to the desire to travel, the desire for adventure, and the wish to escape difficult social and economic conditions. The boundaries between the spiritual and cultural systems can be very difficult to distinguish. This is made more difficult since religion is a subsystem of the cultural system. We have separated religion and spiritual here so as not to diminish the possibility of recognizing a true work of God, or to avoid simply subsuming it under the religious system. Nevertheless, their overlap is obvious and undeniable.

Equally difficult is determining how the systems affect each other. As we saw above, the influences are never simple or one way. The spiritual affects both social and cultural systems at the same time. With all three systems it is the same. The diagrams that I drew to aid analysis sometimes looked like spaghetti. At the same time, the very complexity of systems theory is what allows non-simplistic analysis, because it does not imagine simple unidirectional cause-and-effect description. Affects are multidirectional and reciprocal.

The particular missions movements have been placed into the center of the systems diagrams for analysis. We could profitably study other elements in the same way: individual missionaries, training programs, churches, teams on the field that missionaries from ECE are joining, and so on. The possibility of examining different aspects of the systems at different levels of complexity gives great opportunities for deep analysis.

Where does the role of personal experience fit into theory? Do we need to add person to the theoretical construct? Person would be considered in the social role, and key person fits fine here. However, personal experience is an essential factor in all the cases, and it is not clear whether it fits under either social or culture. Perhaps the easiest way to demonstrate the relationship is through metaphor. Different metaphors illustrate how the different systems can function. For instance, an orchestra shows three or four systems in interaction. The orchestra is the social system, the music they play is the culture system, and the communication or inspiration that powers the musicians and the hearers could be the spiritual system. We must also ask the question about the composer. As a person he probably fits into both social and cultural systems, but it is difficult to classify the personal experience that makes him what he is. In this view, MIR might be seen as an orchestra, but nobody has written the music yet.

Finally, we might ask the question, why use systems theory at all. Why not simply treat the movements as history? In this study, systems theory has been a heuristic devise, a tool to guard against reductionism. Any historical study used a theoretical grid, whether explicit or implicit. Systems theory makes the grid explicit, and allows us to ask questions that we might miss otherwise. The categories of analysis suggested by Parsons pointed to specific areas of questioning. The emphasis on interactions between systems guarded against simplistic answers. Interpretations of the revolutions of 1989 have suffered from simplistic thinking. However, no single answer explains the dramatic events of those days. Neither prayer by Christians, Reagan's military buildup and tough political stance against the USSR, economic chaos, nor the spiritual bankruptcy of Marxism are sufficient causes of the fall of Communism. They are all partially true.

The same is true with the rise of missionary sending movements. Neither the role of Western missionaries, the advent of political freedom, nor any of the other factors explored here is sufficient explanation for new developments. They are all partially true. Any single answer would be unsatisfactory. Systems theory does not ensure that we will find all the right answers or that we will not leave some important factors unexplored. It does help us to explore areas that might be missed with a less complex model.

10. Conclusions

An understanding of the various factors involved in the development of new missionary sending movements should allow church leaders to anticipate when conditions are favorable for new movements to arise. Further, a study of the factors relating to the rise of these movements will, incidentally, lead to a better understanding of these movements themselves. This knowledge can facilitate the development of programs of recruitment, fund-raising, missionary training and other aspects necessary for growth in missionary sending.

In this chapter, we will address the following topics: the research process, with reflections with some of the lessons learned, missiological implications of this study, possible practical applications, some tentative recommendations, and suggestions for further research.

To What Extent Are These Cases Movements?

In many ways it is still too early to really talk of movements. All these groups began to send missionaries less than ten years ago. They are still only in the beginning stages. People with missions vision are beginning to "infect", to "contaminate" others with a missions passion. Only time will show how strongly this develops.

Gladwell (2000, 192) says the paradox of the epidemic is "that in order to create one contagious movement, you often have to create many small movements first." In this regard, Romania has a better chance than Poland to develop a missionary sending movement, because many small initiatives are starting. Among the mainline churches of Hungary, it will be difficult to find many small movements, but if we count initiatives among evangelicals maybe there is greater potential.

MIR seems to be on the way to truly becoming a movement. It is broad-based, with a wide acceptance across a variety of churches. The others may be moving in that direction, but it is difficult to perceive a movement yet, at least at a national level. Part of the nature of movements is that they must be somehow self-sustaining. Would Hungarian missions interest continue in the mainline churches if Anne-Marie Kool left? Would MttE continue if Malcolm Clegg left? He is trying to pass leadership along, but has been largely unsuccessful to this point. Romania seems to be far enough advanced that if any one of the key players stepped aside, things would continue.

We have treated MIR and Aletheia as separate cases here. However, the two are swimming in the same contextual waters, and are not isolated from each other. It is possible that Aletheia would one day join MIR, especially to the extent that MIR remains a network rather than a closely defined independent missions agency. Like Aletheia, MIR is committed to the primacy of the local church in sending. Aletheia, then, would not have to give up any autonomy or responsibility if it joined MIR.

At some time, MIR could become a "national mission movement" in the WEF Missions Commission sense: that is, a body designed to network, support, encourage and resource a variety of churches, agencies, and training programs.

Many questions remain to be answered before we can really speak of missions movements. No answers will be attempted here, but the questions will need to be asked at some point. Some of the most important are:

- ❏ What will it take to overcome the financial difficulties, imagined or real?
- ❏ What will it take to win pastors over to the idea that they should support missions?
- ❏ What is the critical mass needed for the movement to become self-sustaining?
- ❏ Can the movements become really grounded in the churches without the support of top denominational leadership?

Projections

Although to this point probably more Poles have participated personally in some kind of missions experience, the likelihood is that Romanian churches will soon take and hold the lead in missionary sending. The Hungarian Reformed Church is the largest of all the churches surveyed here, but its active population is smaller than the evangelical churches of Romania. Poland's population is nearly twice as large as Romania's, but the evangelical population of Romania is dramatically larger. The evangelical churches of Poland and Hungary are minuscule, whereas in Romania they number around half a million (6%). Unless there is a significant awakening in Poland and Hungary, leading to dramatic church growth, the Polish and Hungarian churches will soon reach their saturation point with missionaries[34]. Romania is much poorer than the other two, with an average income of only around a third of that of Poland

---

[34] The Czech Republic, which, though in the ECE region was not included in this study, fits the same profile as Poland and Hungary. It has a very small evangelical church which has sent a few missionaries. Ronald Davies reports, "A few students from the Evangelical Seminary in Prague are already serving in Asia. With encouragement, the trickle could develop into a flood" (2000a, 259). But given the small size of the evangelical churches, it is difficult to see that this "flood" could become very large.

or Hungary,[35] which will retard the growth somewhat. However, in terms of human and spiritual resources they show more potential for growth.

In addition, the theological position of the Hungarian mainline churches is liable to hinder their growth. The concerns over proselytism expressed by some Reformed leaders leaves the unspoken implication that they are not too happy with the idea of conversion in general. They are angry because evangelicals are "fishing in their neighbor's pond" (Volf 1996) among those who are already "Christian" (even though they may be completely inactive). Therefore, they themselves are more likely to be reluctant to fish in anyone else's pond, even if those people are *not* already Christian.

Practical Applications

What must happen if a new movement is to start? Here again the cautions about differing social and historical settings apply. However, what about other countries which have similar demographics, such as Southern Europe or perhaps parts of Africa or Asia? What steps will be necessary? From the lessons learned from this study, at least some of the following steps will be necessary.

- ❏ Missionaries from outside will need to start talking about missions.
- ❏ A key national leader of vision and stature will need to be won.
- ❏ People will need to start teaching and preaching about missions and a literature will need to be spread. A vocabulary will need to be developed which will make discourse about missions possible. The Great Commission will need to be made alive. For example, Romanians learned the strategic language of E-1, E-2, and E-3. The *Perspectives* course gave them a common language to use when referring to missions.
- ❏ Opportunities are needed for nationals to get exposure and experience outside the country, or at least in a cross-cultural situation within the country. Because freedom was new for ECE Christians after the revolution, any kind of travel was novel and eye opening. In a situation where the freedom to travel is normal, and perhaps travel itself, as tourists, is normal, the experiences will need to be more intentionally missionary in nature. Specific short-term missions trips can be used to open people's eyes to the needs and opportunities of the world.

Points three and four recognize again the reciprocal nature of motivations. Experience can lead to a new understanding. In ECE this was the primary path traveled. Equally possible, though perhaps less common, is that new understanding can lead to new action and commitments.

---

[35] However, they are not as poor as Ukraine and Moldova, the other two large missionary senders in the region.

Recommendations

How might it look if things really changed at a cultural and social level? Those who are actively promoting missions interest in the ECE countries can answer this question better than I can. They are the ones who have an insight into their countries and churches, which will allow them to reflect carefully on the shape of the missions picture in their countries. Nevertheless, a very sketchy and impressionistic overview will be attempted, which is intended more to promote further thought than to give answers.

ECE Church

We might be tempted to imagine structures and programs which replicate the best features of missions in the home churches. However, this would ignore two critical realities. First, the cultural and social context of ECE is different than in the West, and second, structures and programs in the USA are being fundamentally rethought. Missions agencies are wrestling with the issues of relations between missions agencies and churches, the resourcing of missionary personnel, international partnerships, mobilizing short-termers, and many other topics. So to prescribe a certain solution to a problem, or a certain pattern to a vision, based on historic developments and successes at home would be to short-circuit the development process of the emerging movements.

To the extent that the ECE situation resembles that of the days of missionary beginnings in the USA, attempts at imitation of Western solutions might not be too bad. Missions leaders from ECE are open and eager to learn all they can from their more experienced colleagues in other parts of the world (not just the West), but they have to discover the authentically Polish or Hungarian or Romanian way to do missions. ECE is being rapidly integrated into Europe, and it is probable that Western European models will prove more useful, despite the fact that the Easterners have been more influenced by American missionaries than by ones from Europe.

How, then, might things look? How would an outsider become aware of the fact that missions is a high priority in a church or denomination?

Cultural Level

As we have repeatedly noted, culture functions at a number of levels, from the public and obvious to the hidden and unconscious. What might it look like if missions vision and commitment became embedded in the cultural system of ECE churches?

Symbols

▶ Missions magazines published, then displayed in places where they are easily seen.

10. Conclusions

- ▶ World maps with pictures of missionaries and their place of service.
- ▶ Missionaries are prominent when they are home.

Rituals
- ▶ Regular commissioning services as missionaries are sent.
- ▶ Missionaries preach in churches, not just give reports.
- ▶ Missions conferences, both in local churches and as the association of churches level.

Attitudes
- ▶ "Missions belong to us".
- ▶ "Missions is what we do".
- ▶ Missions is talked about.
- ▶ These are "our" missionaries.
- ▶ Strategy for recruiting, training, sending, and caring for missionaries.

Values
- ▶ "Missions is who we are".
- ▶ Regular, spontaneous prayer for missions.

Worldview

Worldview is notoriously difficult to identify and change. It is more or less unconscious. Maybe this means something like a deep awareness that we are part of the world and have a responsibility for the world, which infuses the actions and attitudes of church members.

Social Level

At a social level, we might imagine suggestions for structures, relationship, and economics.

Structures
- ❑ Missions committees/missions pastors.
- ❑ People who are responsible for the missionaries.
- ❑ Denominational missions programs with a budget and profile. We can contrast the current situation in one Romanian church, where a denominational program exists, but even denominational officers do not realize that it belongs to the denomination.

Relationships
- ❑ People visit the missionaries on their field of service.

Economics

The commitment of money is probably the single biggest indicator that a church places a priority on something. Therefore, a large percentage of the budget designated for missions would be a strong statement of commitment.

Missionary Training

When the proposal for this research was written, very little was being done in missionary training. In the past three years many missionary training programs have sprung up. The issues is no longer the need for training programs. Nevertheless, it is important to consider the important issues that training should address.

Presently the situation regarding missionary training is very uneven. Some new missionaries are graduates of a Bible college or seminary, while others have no theological or ministry training whatsoever. However, regardless of the amount of training they have received, few have much specific training for intercultural *missionary* ministry. Therefore, a real need exists for programs which will better equip them for life in their new cultural and social settings.

Some current programs are very academic, with little practical emphasis. Some programs are Bible schools with a couple of missions courses. Very few of the teachers or trainers have a background in intercultural studies or education. Many of the Western missionaries are still in their first term of service. In many cases, people are teaching whose own cross-cultural experience is minimal. This means training stays either intellectual/academic or experientially limited.

Missionaries in ECE typically receive a lot less training than pastors receive. It is not yet widely accepted or recognized that cross-cultural missionary service is more complicated than that at home, and that missionaries need correspondingly *more* training, not less.

What implications might all this have for training programs? Only a couple of suggestions are possible here. A system of systems approach to training can help, assuring that all the basic areas of cross-cultural live and ministry are covered.

- ❑ The spiritual component should be emphasized.
- ❑ Issues arising from the social, cultural, interpersonal, spiritual, and personal systems should be introduced. Practical experience cross-culturally should be integrated with classroom study.
- ❑ Reflection should be integrated with practice. Experience without reflection stays at the level of experience, but does not offer opportunity for learning and personal growth.

10. Conclusions

- Care should be taken that the training itself if appropriate to the home culture and not simply something imported from outside. Certain cross-cultural issues have to be faced in any training, but the way they are treated will probably vary greatly from one country to the next.

Western Church

On the basis of this study, two recommendations to the Western church could be made. One is in relation to Western involvement in ECE and the other regards the Western church at home.

The importance of the role of key people and of Western missionaries might lead the Western church to a false conclusion. The way to promote missionary sending in ECE is not simply to send more missionaries, in the hope that they will model missionary life and thus encourage new missionaries. More important is to send better missionaries, not simply more missionaries. In fact, most churches in ECE are not looking for more missionaries from the West. They are looking for special kinds of missionaries, people who can partner with them and offer expertise in areas they have not developed yet and who can model servanthood and sensitivity.

The role that experience outside the country played for ECE missions leaders and short-term missionary experience leads to a second possible false conclusion. Short-term missions is a rapidly growing trend in Western churches. Missions leaders hope that these experiences will encourage participants to gain a vision for long term missions for themselves. In ECE this is happening, because all missions experience is new. In the West, it is questionable whether simply sending thousands of young people on short-term missions trips is or will significantly advance the cause of Christ around the world.

Areas for Further Research

The missions situation in the Ukraine should be explored in more depth. It has some features which distinguish is somewhat from the ECE countries farther west. It was not a major missionary-receiving country, due to isolation during Communism, although there are a large number of missionaries there now. It has now become a major missionary-sending country. The mission Light of the Gospel itself is probably worth a full-scale study. In addition, the Czech Republic needs to be studied.

Further, this study is a snapshot, taken at a specific point in the historical development of the groups. It would be good to come back and see how things develop. Perhaps movement theory could be applied to determine to what extent events in ECE confirm expectations. Ten years is too short a time to evaluate the development of the movements. In fact, these groups have been sending missionaries for eight years or less. The groups / movements are just at the beginning, and are experiencing all kinds of growing pains, direction questions, issues of vision and structure, and many other issues. It will be interesting to see whether, since the Hungarian case has a quite different ecclesiastical setting, it develops further or significantly differently than the others.

Other countries which are just starting to develop a missions vision could be studied to see if the same kind of factors are operating. Especially countries which are not emerging from Communism or totalitarianism could be compared, to see whether, from a different perspective, Communism in fact had a greater impact than has been discerned here.

It would be interesting to trace the path of diffusion of missions contacts. From whom did key national leaders learn about missions, or receive their impetus or vision. In a couple of cases this is very clear, even without a formal instrument (Hungary and MttE, for example). In other cases (MIR in particular, as it represents a more national movement), it would be fascinating to discover the flow of communication which spread the vision.

Soon researchers will be able to evaluate ECE missionaries' effectiveness. ECE missionaries can begin to participate in attrition and effectiveness studies. A few "long-termers" are already returning to their home countries. We need to learn why they are returning. Is this simply the fulfillment of their commitment? Have or did they never consider service longer than three to five years? Are there other reasons they are returning home? Are there things that would have helped them stay longer? On the other hand, does staying longer hinder the growth of the churches they are starting?

Research has focused on those involved in missions movements. Further research could be done with those not involved in the movements, particularly church leaders, to determine how widespread is the acceptance of the movement or to what extent it is marginal to church life.

To what extent does the fact that evangelicals are marginalized in their own societies make them more (or less) open to leaving as missionaries?

Evaluation of the Research

If this study were to be done again, one significant change in the design should be made. The place of personal stories needs to be taken much more seriously. They need to be intentionally built into the design. The respondents were asked to relate the story of the movement in which they are involved. Often times their own story came out, but in an incidental way. Often the roots of the movement came in the personal encounter of the person with the message or experience of missions.

Westerners in particular were not asked where their missions vision or call came from, coming as they do out of an evangelical milieu where missions is a normal part of church life. This may not be critical. However, for national leaders it is an important question, as it represents something new.

Conclusion

In East-Central Europe in the years since the revolutions of 1989, God placed strong persons with a vision and passion to see national missionaries, and with good communication skills, into a context where some people are prepared to listen to the message.

God is raising up a group of young missionaries from the countries of East-Central Europe. They can go where Western missionaries cannot and they can bridge cultures between East and West. They have been uniquely prepared, through a certain kind of political system, educational background, and experiences with God, to carry the gospel to new areas in new ways. The way has just begun, but it looks like it will continue and grow.

Reference List

Aslund, Anders, Peter Boone, et al. 1996. How to stabilize: lessons from post-communist countries. *Brookings Papers on Economic Activity* 1: 217-91, 309-13.

Babinski, Grzegorz. 1995. Nationalism and religion in east central Europe: An outline of the problem. In *The future of religion: East and west*, ed. Irena Borowik and Przemyslaw Jablonski, 135-146. Krakow: NOMOS.

Balders, Günter. 1978. *Theurer Bruder Oncken: Das Leben Johann Gerhard Onckens in Bildern und Dokumenten*. Wuppertal und Kassel: Oncken Verlag.

Barker, Eileen. 1997. But who's going to win? National and minority religions in post-communist society. In *New religious phenomena in central and eastern Europe*, ed. Irena Borowik and Grzegorz Babinski, 25-62. Krakow: NOMOS.

Barnes, Jim and Laurie. 1998. The Czech spiritual landscape in the post-communist era. *East-West Church & Ministry Report* 6 (2, Spring 1998): 6-8.

Beeson, Trevor. 1982. *Discretion and Valour: Religious conditions in Russia and Eastern Europe*. London: Fount Paperbacks.

Bertalanffy, Ludwig von. 1968. *General system theory: Foundations, development, applications*. New York: George Braziller.

Bookman, Milica Z. 1995. The transformation of East Central Europe. *Orbis* 39: 604-22.

Borowik, Irena. 1995. Religion and religious conflicts in contemporary eastern Europe. In *The future of religion: East and west*, ed. Irena Borowik and Przemyslaw Jablonski, 147-152. Krakow: NOMOS.

Borowik, Irena. 1997. Introduction. Religion in post-communist societies – confronting the frozen past and the peculiarities of the transformation. In *New religious phenomena in central and eastern Europe*, ed. Irena Borowik and Grzegorz Babinski, 7-23. Krakow: NOMOS.

Bosch, David J. 1991. *Transforming mission: Paradigm shifts in theology of mission*. Maryknoll, NY: Orbis.

Bourdeaux, Michael. 1992. *The role of religion in the fall of Soviet communism*. London: Centre for Policy Studies.

Brachmann, G. 1991. "Die Brüder- und Baptistengemeinden in Ostdeutschland (DDR) nach 1945 und ihr Verhältnis zur Außenmission." *Evangelikale Missiologie* 1991(2): 18-22.

Bultman, Bud. 1991. *Revolution by candlelight: The real story behind the changes in Eastern Europe*. Portland, OR: Multnomah Press.

Byrnes, Timothy A. 1996. The Catholic Church and Poland's return to Europe. *East European Quarterly* 30 (Winter '96): 433-48.

Centeno, Miguel Angel and Tania Rands. 1996. The world they have lost: An assessment of change in Eastern Europe. *Social Research* 63: 369-402.

Church and Stasi. *The Wilson Quarterly* 19 (Spring 1995): 150.

Clark, Jere W. 1972. General ecology of knowledge in curriculums of the future. In *The relevance of general systems theory*, ed. Ervin Laszlo, 65-180. New York: George Braziller.

Codrescu, Andrei. 1991. *The hole in the flag: A Romanian exile's story of return and revolution.* New York: William Morrow.

Conner, Patrick. 1980. *The word in the world: Poland and the missions.* Techny, Ill.: Society for the Divine Word.

Conway, John S. 1994. The *Stasi* and the churches: Between coercion and compromise in East German Protestantism, 1949-89. *Journal of Church and State* 36.

Davies, Ronald. 2000a. Czech Republic and Slovakia. In *Evangelical dictionary of world missions*, ed. A. Scott Moreau, 259. Grand Rapids, Mich.: Baker.

Davies, Ronald. 2000b. Poland. In *Evangelical dictionary of world missions*. A. Scott Moreau. Grand Rapids, Mich.: Baker.

Dries, Angelyn. 1991. The foreign mission impulse of the American Catholic Church, 1893-1925. *International Bulletin of Missionary Research* 15: 61-66.

Elliot, Mark. 1996. East European missions, perestroika, and Orthodox-Evangelical tensions. *Journal of Ecumenical Studies* 33: 9-20.

Fiedler, Klaus. 1994. *The story of faith missions: From Hudson Taylor to present day Africa.* Oxford: Regnum Books.

Fiedler, Klaus. 1989. Wo sind die 20,000? Eine kritische Analyse von Lawrence E. Keyes' Konzept der 'transkulturellen Drittweltmissionare' und der ihm zugrundeliegenden Daten. *Evangelikale Missiologie* 3/89.

Gall, Meredith D., Walter R. Borg, et al. 1996. *Educational research: An introduction.* White Plains, NY: Longman Publishers.

Gautier, Mary L. 1997. Church attendance and religious belief in postcommunist societies. *Journal for the Scientific Study of Religion* 36: 289-96.

Gladwell, Malcolm. 2000. *The tipping point: How little things can make a big difference.* Boston, Little, Brown.

Gray, William. 1972. Bertalanffian principles as a basis for humanistic psychiatry. In *The relevance of general systems theory*, ed. Ervin Laszlo, 125-133. New York: Braziller.

Healey, Nigel M. 1996. Economic transformation in Central and Eastern Europe and the Commonwealth of Independent States: An interim report. *Contemporary Review* 268: 229-35.

Hiebert, Paul G. 1998. *Class Notes, Urban Evangelism*, Trinity International University.

Hiebert, Paul G., R. Daniel Shaw, et al. 1999. *Understanding folk religion: A Christian response to popular beliefs and practices*. Grand Rapids, Mich., Baker.

Hogan, Edmund M. 1979. The motivation of the modern Irish missionary movement 1912-1939. *Journal of Religion in Africa* 10: 157-173.

Iliesu, Mitika 2001. *Aletheia Mission of Timisoara Romania*. Report given at the Eastern European Evangelical Missions Consultation, Budapest, Hungary, 28-29 August 2001.

Isaac, Jeffrey C. 1996. The meanings of 1989. *Social Research* 63: 291-344.

Johnstone, Patrick. 1993. *Operation world: The day-to-day guide to praying for the world*. Grand Rapids, Mich: Zondervan.

Johnstone, Patrick and Jason Mandryk. 2001. *Operation world: When we pray God works*. Carlisle: Paternoster Lifestyle.

Kaplan, Robert D. 1993. *Balkan ghosts: A journey through history*. New York: St. Martin's Press.

Keyes, Lawrence E. 1982. Third world missionaries: More and better. *Evangelical Missions Quarterly* Oct.

Keyes, Lawrence E. 1983. *The last age of missions: A study of third world mission societies*. Pasadena: William Carey Library.

Keyes, Larry E. and Larry D. Pate. 1993. Two-thirds world missions: The next 100 years. *Missiology* 21: 187-206.

Klammt, Thomas. 1994. *„Ist die Heidenmission zu empfehlen?" Die deutschen Baptisten und die Mission in der Ferne (1848-1913)*. Bonn: Verlag für Kultur und Wissenschaft.

Kool, Anne-Marie. 2000. A Protestant perspective on mission in Eastern and Central Europe. *Religion in Eastern Europe: Christians Associated for Relations with Eastern Europe* XX (6, Dec. 2000): 1-21.

Kool, Anne-Marie. 2001a. Report from Hungary. Report given at the Eastern European Evangelical Missions Consultation, Budapest, Hungary, 28-29 August 2001.

Kool, Anne-Marie. 2001b. Signs of life from Hungary: Monthly prayer update on the ministry of the Protest Institute for Mission Studies VIII (68). May 2001

Kool, Anne-Marie. 2002. Signs of life from Hungary: Monthly prayer update on the ministry of the Protest Institute for Mission Studies IX (74) Jan. 2002

Kool, Anne-Marie. n.d. 5 years Protestant Institute for Missions Studies (1995-2000). Unpublished report.

Kool, Anne-Marie. 1993. *God moves in a mysterious way: The Hungarian Protestant Foreign Mission Movement (1756-1951)*. Zoetermeer: Uitgeverij Boekencentrum.

Kvale, Steinar. 1996. *InterViews: An introduction to qualitative research interviewing*. Thousand Oaks, Calif, Sage.

Lash, Scott. 2002. Forward by Scott Lash: Individualization in a non-linear mode. In *Individualization*. Ulrich Beck and Elisabeth Beck-Gernsheim. London: Sage.

Laszlo, Ervin, ed. 1972. *The relevance of general systems theory*. International Library of Systems Theory and Philosophy. New York, George Braziller.

Laszlo, Ervin. 1996. *The systems view of the world: A holistic vision for our time*. Cresskill, N.J.: Hampton Press.

Latourette, Kenneth Scott. 1970. *Three Centuries of Advance, A.D. 1500-A.D. 1800*. Grand Rapids, Mich.: Zondervan.

Linzey, Sharon. 1994. Indigenous Christian Missions in the Former Soviet Union. *East-West Church & Ministry Report* 2 (Winter 1994): 6.

Luckey, Hans. 1958. *Johann Gerhard Oncken und die Anfänge des deutschen Baptismus*. Kassel: J. G. Oncken Verlag.

Luthans, Fred, Richard R Patrick, et al. 1995. Doing business in Central and Eastern Europe: Political, economic, and cultural diversity. Business Horizons 38 (Sept./Oct.): 9-16.

Mach, Zdislaw. 2000. Polish national culture and its shifting centres. *Website of the Centre for European Studies, Jagiellonian University, Krakow, Poland* 2002 (March 7).

Manualul bisericii "Aletheia" 1998. Unpublished document.

Marcol, Jerzy. 1998. Was sich in Polen so alles tut ... *Übersetzung heute* 2: 10.

Meroff, Debbie 2001. A first for Hungary: Missions Expo 2001. *World Pulse*. 36: 4.

MIR 2000. Statutul de organizare, MIR. Unpublished document.

Mitchell, Russ. 1998. Now is the time to mobilize Romanians for missions! Unpublished paper.

Moldovan, Gavi 2001. Report – MMU Romania. Report given at the Eastern European Evangelical Missions Consultation, Budapest, Hungary, 28-29 August 2001.

Monshipouri, Mahmood and John W. Arnold. 1996. The Christians in socialism – and after: The church in East Germany. *Journal of Church and State* 38: 751-773.

Moreau, A. Scott, ed. 2000. *Evangelical dictionary of world missions*. Grand Rapids, Mich.: Baker.

Nelson, Daniel N. 1996. Civil society endangered. *Social Research* 63: 345-368.

Nelson, Marlin L., ed. 1976. *Reading in third world missions: A collection of essential documents*. Pasadena, Calif: William Carey Library.

OC International and Misiunea Mondiala Unita. 2001. *Inima lui dumnezeu bate pentru Romania: Implinirea Marii Insarchinari in intreaga tara*. Raport privind situatia bisericilor evanghelice din Romania 2001. București.

Palmer, Parker J. 1998. The courage to teach: Exploring the inner landscape of a teacher's life. San Francisco: Jossey-Bass Publishers.

Park, Jong Koo 1994. An analytical study of the contemporary movement of the world mission of the Korean Church and a projection to AD 2000: --With an illustration of the Mission Tight-Way campaign of the Inter-Mission International--. D.Miss. diss. Western Conservative Baptist Seminary.

Parsons, Talcott. 1951. *The social system*. New York: The Free Press.

Parsons, Talcott. 1968. Systems analysis: Social systems. In *International Encyclopedia of the Social Sciences*, ed. David L. Sills. New York: Macmillan.

Parsons, Talcott. 1971. *The system of modern societies*. Englewood Cliffs, N.J.: Prentice-Hall.

Parsons, Talcott and Edward A. Shils. 1952. *Toward a general theory of action*. Cambridge, Mass.: Harvard University Press.

Pate, Larry D. 1991. The changing balance in global mission. *International Bulletin of Missionary Research* 15: 56-61.

Patton, Michael Q. 1990. *Qualitative evaluation and research methods*. Thousand Oaks, Calif.: Sage.

Piaget, Jean. 1970. *Structuralism*. New York: Basic Books.

Piper, John. 1993. *Let the nations be glad: The supremacy of God in missions*. Grand Rapids, Mich.: Baker.

Plesu, Andrei. 1996. Post-totalitarian pathology: Notes on Romania six years after December 1989. *Social Research* 63: 559-571.

Ramet, Sabrina Petra. 1994. A Checklist of Issues to Track. *East-West Church & Ministry Report* 2 (Winter 1994): 2-3.

Richardson, James T. 1997. New religions and religious freedom in eastern and central Europe: A sociological analysis. In *New religious phenomena in central and eastern Europe*, ed. Irena Borowik and Grzegorz Babinski, 257-282. Krakow: NOMOS.

Rogers, Everett M. 1995. *Diffusion of innovations*. New York: Free Press.

Rosenberg, Tina. 1995. The haunted land: Facing Europe's ghosts after communism. New York, NY, Vintage Books.

Rubin, Herbert H. and Irene S. Rubin. 1995. *Qualitative interviewing: The art of hearing data*. Thousand Oaks, Calif.: Sage.

Schattschneider, David A. 1998. William Carey, modern missions, and the Moravian influence. *International Bulletin of Missionary Research* 22: 8-10.

Schöttelndreyer, Burkhard. 1998. Bibelübersetzer aus Osteuropa? *Übersetzung heute* 2: 8,9.

Schreiter, Robert J. 1997. The new catholicity: Theology between the global and the local. Maryknoll, N.Y.: Orbis.

Seidman, Irving. 1998. Interviewing as qualitative research: A guide for researchers in education and the social sciences. New York: Teachers College Press.

Siklova, Jirina. 1996. What did we lose after 1989? *Social Research* 63: 531-541.

Siklova, Jirina. 1997. Feminism and the roots of apathy in the Czech Republic. *Social Research* 64: 258-80.

Silverman, David. 1993. Interpreting qualitative data: Methods for analyzing talk, text and interactions. Thousand Oaks, Calif.: Sage.

Spradley, James P. 1979. *The ethnographic interview*. New York: Holt, Rinehart and Winston.

Stake, Robert E. 1994. Case Studies. In *Handbook of qualitative research*, ed. Norman K. Denzin and Yvonna S. Lincoln. Thousand Oaks, Calif.: Sage.

Standing, Guy. 1997. The folly of social safety nets: Why basic income is needed in Eastern Europe. *Social Research* 64: 339-1379.

Stewart, Charles J., Craig Allen Smith, et al. 1994. *Persuasion and Social Movements*. Prospect Heights, Ill.: Waveland Press.

Stojaspal, Jan. 2000. Back in the driver's seat. *Time*, Special Edition: Fast Foward Europe (Winter 2000/01): 138-9.

Swoboda, Jörg, ed. 1990. *Die Revolution der Kerzen: Christen in den Umwälzungen der DDR*. Wuppertal: Onckenverlag.

Swoboda, Jörg and Richard V. Pierard, eds. 1996. The revolution of the candles: Christians in the Revolution of the German Democratic Republic. Macon, Ga.: Mercer University Press.

Tomes, Igor. 1997. Overview of the social income reform approaches of the countries of Central and Eastern Europe. *Social Research* 64: 1471-1498.

Tomka, Miklós. 1991. Secularization or anomy? Interpreting religious change in communist societies. *Social Compass* 38: 93-102.

Tomka, Miklós. 1995. The changing social role of religion in Eastern and Central Europe: Religion's revival and its contradictions. *Social Compass* 42: 17-26.

Tomka, Miklós. 1997. Hungarian post-world war II religious development and the present challenge of new churches and new religious movements. In *New religious phenomena in central and eastern Europe*, ed. Irena Borowik and Grzegorz Babinski, 203-233. Krakow: NOMOS.

Trojan, Jakub. 1994. Theology and economics in the postcommunist era. *The Christian Century* 111 (Mar. 16): 278-80.

Volf, Miroslav. 1996. Fishing in the neighbor's pond: Mission and proselytism in Eastern Europe. *International Bulletin of Missionary Research* 20: 26-33.

Steven Paas
Johannes Rebmann

A Servant of God in Africa before the Rise of Western Colonialism

Johannes Rebmann was a 19th-century German Christian, deeply influenced by the Movement of Württemberg Pietism. He was trained to be a missionary in Basel, Switzerland, and he joined the English Church Missionary Society (CMS) which sent him to the Muslim-ruled and slavery-ridden Mombasa area of present-day Kenya. There he stayed for 29 years before returning home to Gerlingen near Stuttgart, blind and sick, soon to die. As a witness of Christ and an expert in languages he paved the way for Christianity to deploy in East and Central Africa. One of his outstanding lexicographical achievements is the first ever Dictionary of the main language of Nyasaland, now Malawi, a country situated at a distance of more than 2000 km of which he scarcely knew the location. He compiled his collection of vocabulary of Chichewa with the help of a slave, Salimini, who like many others was cruelly captured West of Lake Malawi, and through the Swahili-Arab slave market of Zanzibar was sold to a slave-owner in Mombasa. Much in Rebmann's biography is a paradigm of experiences of today's transcultural workers in Africa.

Pb. • 274 pp • € 19.80 • £ 18.45 • $ 29.95
ISBN 978-3-941750-48-7

VTR Publications • Gogolstr. 33 • 90475 Nürnberg • Germany
info@vtr-online.com • http://www.vtr-online.com

Deborah Meroff
Europe: Restoring Hope

The continent known for over 1000 years as the heartland of Christianity has gone into spiritual arrest. Drawing from the experience of many individuals and organisations, this book takes a hard look at four population groups at the centre of Europe's heart trouble: marginalised people, Muslims, youth and nominal and secular Europeans. Here is proof that it is possible to restore hope to this great continent when God's people work together. This practical resource supplies all the motivation and information we need to get started.

"Europe is very likely a battleground for the future of global Christianity ... I hope that whoever reads these pages will be encouraged and inspired to prayer and action." Jirí Unger, President of the European Evangelical Alliance

"My wife Drena and I have now been based in Europe for 50 years. Debbie Meroff's book True Grit was one of the most important books in our lives, and her new book on Europe is another cutting edge, must-read!" George Verwer, Founder and International Co-ordinator Emeritus, OM International

"This book shows that God is still at work in Europe. He is building his church despite many challenges. And he wants to see each one of us playing an active part in restoring hope to Europe!" Frank Hinkelmann, European Director, OM International

Pb. • VIII, 295 pp • € 14.95 • £ 14.95 • $ 29.95
ISBN 978-3-941750-06-7

VTR Publications • Gogolstr. 33 • 90475 Nürnberg • Germany
info@vtr-online.com • http://www.vtr-online.com

www.ingramcontent.com/pod-product-compliance
Lightning Source LLC
Chambersburg PA
CBHW060340170426
43202CB00014B/2834